STANDING UP TO COLONIAL POWER

**New Visions in Native American
and Indigenous Studies**

SERIES EDITORS

Margaret D. Jacobs
Robert Miller

Standing Up to Colonial Power

The Lives of Henry Roe and
Elizabeth Bender Cloud

Renya K. Ramirez

CO-PUBLISHED BY THE UNIVERSITY OF NEBRASKA PRESS

AND THE AMERICAN PHILOSOPHICAL SOCIETY

Portions of this book previously appeared as: "From Henry Roe Cloud to Henry Cloud," *Settler Colonial Studies* 2, not. 2 (2012): 117–37; "Ho-Chunk Warrior, Intellecutal, and Activist: Henry Roe Cloud Fights for the Apaches," *American Indian Quarterly* 37, no. 3 (Summer 2013): 290–309; and "Henry Roe Cloud: A Granddaughter's Native Feminist Biographical Account," *Wicazo Sa Review* 24, no. 2 (Fall 2009): 77–103.

♾

Library of Congress Cataloging-in-Publication Data
Names: Ramirez, Renya K., 1959–, author.
Title: Standing up to colonial power: the lives of Henry Roe and Elizabeth Bender Cloud / Renya K. Ramirez.
Other titles: New visions in Native American and indigenous studies.
Description: Lincoln: Co-published by the University of Nebraska Press and the American Philosophical Society, 2018. | Series: New visions in Native American and indigenous studies | Includes bibliographical references and index.
Identifiers: LCCN 2018028389
ISBN 9781496211729 (cloth: alk. paper)
ISBN 9781496212689 (epub)
ISBN 9781496212696 (mobi)
ISBN 9781496212702 (pdf)
Subjects: LCSH: Cloud, Henry Roe, 1885–1950. | Cloud, Elizabeth Bender, 1887–1965 | Indian activists—United States—Biography. | LCGFT: Biographies.
Classification: LCC E89.R34 2018 | DDC 371.829/97526073—dc23 LC record available at https://lccn.loc.gov/2018028389

Set in Charis by Mikala R. Kolander.

*For my grandparents, Henry and Elizabeth Cloud;
my mother, Woesha Cloud North; and all our
relatives, both living and in the spirit world*

CONTENTS

ILLUSTRATIONS

ACKNOWLEDGMENTS

Without the continual support of my family, including my ancestors in the spirit world, this book would have never been written. Because this book is a family-tribal history, I am forever grateful to my siblings, Woesha Hampson, Mary McNeil, Robert Cloud North, and Trynka Adachi, who has passed away; my parents, Robert North and Woesha Cloud North; and all my cousins, nieces, nephews, and Ho-Chunk and Ojibwe relatives, whose love and support helped me with every aspect of writing this book, including research and each successive draft. My family supported me with phone calls when I traveled to visit archives and help with airfare so my son, Gilbert, could accompany me to read colonial letters together in the Yale Sterling Library. My sister Woesha Hampson and her husband, Tom Hampson, hosted me as I visited archives. They listened to me, and we discussed our various thoughts and insights. My cousin Robin Butterfield welcomed me into her home when I visited archives in Washington DC. She and I had great conversations about our grandparents, and she offered me wonderful perceptions and understandings. My cousin Mark Butterfield hosted me and my two sons, Lucio and Gilbert, as we worked on the film about our grandfather and great-grandfather, Henry Roe Cloud, and conducted interviews of Ho-Chunk cultural and political leaders. Our conversations with Mark Butterfield were incredibly helpful and insightful. I want to thank my sons, Lucio and Gilbert, who traveled with me and my daughter, Mirasol, and were of tremendous support, while making the film. My sister Mary McNeil, brother-in-law Chris McNeil, and niece Tasha Adams were amazingly supportive, reading through the entire book manuscript and giving me both editorial and substantive feedback. Both Mary and Chris McNeil were wonderful supporters of the film about Henry Roe Cloud. My children, Lucio, Gilbert, and Mirasol, helped me by listening to me talk about this family-tribal history, reading drafts, and encouraging me every step of the way. My granddaughters, Raquel and Mahaya, gave me frequent hugs and words of encouragement. My husband, Gilbert, and nephew, Colin Cloud Hampson, read drafts and listened to me discuss the ups and downs of writing, researching, and juggling my many professorial duties.

I must also thank my Ho-Chunk colleague, Amy Lonetree, who encouraged me to write this book and patiently listened to me discuss my experiences doing archival research. I also appreciate our Indigenous Studies Writing Group here at UCSC, which included Amy Lonetree, Beth Haas, Mattie Harper, Megan Moodie, Jon Daehkne, and Tsim Schneider, all of whom read drafts and encouraged me through the long process of writing this book. I must thank my colleagues Ned Blackhawk, Chadwick Allen, Cathleen Cahill, Cristina Stanciu, Kristina Ackley, Steve Crum, Scott Morgenson, Alyssa Mt. Pleasant, Jim Clifford, Deborah Miranda, Gloria Chacon, and Margaret Jacobs, all of whom who read drafts and encouraged me. I especially appreciated being invited to a Society of American Indian conference held at Ohio University and participating on a panel with Kristina Ackley and Christina Stanciu. The result was an amazing special issue regarding the SAI organization, coedited by Chadwick Allen and Beth Piatote. I met many wonderful scholars and colleagues, who are also writing about SAI intellectuals.

I want to thank all the members of my UCSC American studies program, especially Eric Porter, Catherine Ramirez, Kimberly Lau, and Amy Lonetree, and my Anthropology Department, including Danilyn Rutherford, Nancy Chen, Olga Najera-Ramirez, Mark Anderson, Andrew Matthews, Anna Tsing, Don Brenneis, Melissa Caldwell, Lisa Rofel, Tsim Schneider, Jon Daekhe, Triloki Pandy, Mayanthi Fernando, Jerry Zee, Megan Moodie, Guerillmo Delgado, Judith Habicht Mauche, and Chelsea Blackmore, who have been amazing colleagues, encouraging me to undertake an archival project that included visiting archives, conducting interviews, and painstakingly collecting lots of archival material. I need to express thanks to those I see in my local coffee shop, especially Melissa West and Sarah-Hope Marmeter, who encouraged me while I was writing to follow my instincts. I am also grateful to Anna Montgomery, who edited the book manuscript draft before I sent it off to the press for review, and to my Gender and Cultural Citizenship Working Group, including Kia Caldwell, Kathleen Coll, Tracy Fisher, and Lok Siu, who have nourished me as a Native feminist scholar. I especially thank Kia Caldwell, who was my writing coach and provided me with encouragement throughout the long writing process.

I could not have written this book without receiving a Newberry Fellowship to conduct research in the Society of American Indian archives in Chicago and Yale's Walter McClintock Fellowship so I could conduct archival research in Yale's Sterling Library. I also received support from UCLA's Institute of American Cultures, American Indian Postdoctoral Fellowship, and Jessica Catellino was a great supporter and mentor, while Native studies colleagues Mishauna Goeman, Maylei Blackwell, Angela Riley, Rebecca Tsotsie Hernandez, and others were very encouraging and supportive. During my UCLA fellowship, I lived with my sister Mary McNeil and enjoyed seeing her family, including my brother-in-law Chris McNeil; my niece Tasha Adams; her husband, Nick Adams; and their children, Paloma and Coltrane, who was in utero. After a long day of writing in a nearby coffee shop, it was a wonderful to share my thoughts and reflections with my Los Angeles family. I also received support from UCSC's CORE grant, travel grants, and the Institute of Humanities Research fellowship, which supported travel to various archives.

Furthermore, this book is based on some of my already published articles (see the bibliography). The introduction and chapters 1 and 3 are based on "Henry Roe Cloud: A Granddaughter's Native Feminist Biographical Approach." The introduction and chapter 1 is greatly influenced by "From Henry Roe Cloud to Henry Cloud: Ho-Chunk Strategies and Colonialism," and chapter 2 is informed by "Ho-Chunk Warrior, Intellectual, and Activist: Henry Roe Cloud Fights for the Apaches." I also want to thank the various journals, editors, and reviewers who gave me great feedback on my writing.

Working on this family-tribal history has brought me closer to many family members, colleagues, Ho-Chunk and Ojibwe relatives, and my ancestors, who have passed away. When my mother started traveling to archives to collect family letters and documents, and she would call me, I was proud of her working on a book dedicated to her parents, Henry and Elizabeth Cloud. I hope that my mother, Woesha, is proud of the book that I wrote to finish the book project she began. I truly love my family and my relatives, both living and in the spirit world. This book is for all of you.

STANDING UP TO COLONIAL POWER

Introduction

When my mother, Woesha Cloud North, a Ho-Chunk–Ojibwe, passed away, I inherited a couple of cardboard boxes filled with her archival research regarding her parents, Henry Roe Cloud, a Ho-Chunk, and Elizabeth Bender Cloud, an Ojibwe. Sadly, my mother died when I was in graduate school. I deeply mourned her loss, as she was my best friend. She was by my side during the first years of my marriage and helped raise my three children. I finally opened one of the boxes gathering dust underneath my desk and peeked inside. The first thing I saw was my precious mother's handwriting, and I shoved the flap of the cardboard box down and sobbed uncontrollably. It was much too soon to look through these important boxes. My grief was still too fresh and tender. I didn't examine the contents of the boxes until more than ten years later, when my painful emotions had mostly subsided and healed. Thus began this journey to write the book that my mother envisioned about her parents but died before she completed her goal. I begin this introduction writing about her, because her amazing spirit and my memory of her provided me the strength, determination, and resolve to complete an incredibly daunting task.

The idea for this family-tribal history, however, did not begin with my mother. It started with her sister Marion Cloud Hughes and their mother, Elizabeth Bender Cloud. They were the first ones in our Cloud family to start gathering materials with the goal of publishing a book about Henry, their beloved husband and father. Marion and Elizabeth collected and saved family letters, newspaper articles, government reports, and documents. Marion, unfortunately, was unable to write the book, because her career as a social worker kept her too busy. After the deaths of Marion and Elizabeth, my mother, Woesha, decided to start working on her own book about her parents. She traveled to many archives, including Yale's Sterling Library and the Hampton Institute, collecting additional archival documents. Her cherished collection of family material became the basis for this book manuscript about her mother and father. The idea for this book and the job of gathering together family archival materials, therefore, was passed from one female relative to another. My mom's old cardboard boxes sitting in my office were a continual reminder of my Ho-Chunk and Ojibwe ancestors wanting a family-tribal history written. With my career as an anthropology and Native studies professor at UC Santa Cruz, I had the time and resources to finish this undertaking my female ancestors started. Indeed, I traveled to many archives, the Winnebago Reservation in Nebraska, and Ho-Chunk tribal territory in Wisconsin, following a similar route to the one my mom had taken. I felt her spirit with me every step of the way. Over the course of seven years, I traveled to the home of my sister Woesha Hampson; to the residences of my cousins Robin and Mark Butterfield; and to numerous archives, to conduct interviews and collect family letters, government documents, newspaper articles, pictures, and family memoirs. I wrote this family-tribal history as a tribute to my ancestors Elizabeth and Henry Cloud and to my female relatives Elizabeth, Marion, and Woesha, who ultimately started this book-making process.

This book involves the lives, activism, policy, and intellectual contributions of Henry Roe Cloud (1884–1950) and Elizabeth Bender Cloud (1887–1965). Their political activism and intellectual work spans the first half of the twentieth century, including participation in the Society of American Indians (SAI), General Federation of Women's Clubs (GFWC), and National Congress of American Indians (NCAI). Even though Elizabeth Bender Cloud was the Indian Welfare chair of the GFWC and fought against tribal termination, only one article has been written about her.[1] Surprisingly, while Henry Roe Cloud has been hailed as a very important

Native policy maker of the early twentieth century, only two books and four articles have been published about him.[2] Henry co-wrote the pivotal Meriam Report of 1928, which laid the foundation for the Indian Reorganization Act of 1934—an act, according to available evidence, he also coauthored.[3] Indeed, this is the first book-length analysis of Henry and Elizabeth that uniquely relies on Cloud family-tribal knowledge and perspectives.

Belonging, Native and Modern

Standing Up to Colonial Power is a family-tribal history that argues that the Clouds were intellectuals who combined Native warrior and modern identities as a creative strategy to challenge settler colonialism, to become full members of the U.S. nation-state, and to fight for tribal sovereignty. I use my definition of Native cultural citizenship, which is the right to be different and belong fully in the home, community, tribal nation, and nation-state to discuss the Clouds' struggles to belong.[4] I rely on Renato Rosaldo's definition of cultural citizenship, which is to discover subordinated groups' own notions of citizenship and belonging.[5] Indeed, Natives' senses of citizenship and belonging often revolve around dual citizenship—struggling to belong fully to the U.S. nation-state and their own tribal nations.

Scholars have written about Henry and Elizabeth Cloud, but there is no examination of how the Clouds indigenized modernity from a family-tribal perspective. The Clouds and many Natives of my grandparents' generation were viewed as assimilationists struggling to become U.S. citizens, as opposed to traditionalists maintaining a close connection to reservations and Native tradition, culture, and identity and fighting back against the U.S. settler-colonial state. The Clouds represented the modern, who were assumed to have lost a close connection to their reservations, tradition, culture, and identity. From this perspective the Clouds—and other members of their generation who co-founded the Society of American Indians in 1911, the first pantribal Native organization—have been maligned as "sell-outs" and "apples" (red on the outside and white on the inside).[6] Lucy Maddox, however, astutely argues that members of SAI were intellectuals who valiantly fought against racism and for U.S.

citizenship.[7] Joel Pfister, unfortunately, seems to assume that Henry Cloud's identities as Native and modern meant he became a cog in the wheel of modernity, while integrating into the U.S. nation-state.[8] The Clouds and other SAI intellectuals, however, combined their Native and modern identities, which gave them the potential to challenge the state.[9] The Clouds were "good" Indians who could act like whites but were not really whites—and in this slippage was the possibility of subversion.[10]

Challenging Static Culture and Identity

I use my family-tribal history to explore broader historical and anthropological concerns and to add to Ho-Chunk and Ojibwe studies.[11] Classic anthropologists, including Paul Radin and Ruth Densmore, use static notions of culture, thus supporting the "incarceration" of culture within Ho-Chunk and Ojibwe lands and the idea that Natives who move off the reservation lose their tribal culture and identity.[12] Similarly, literary scholar Joel Pfister, educational scholar David Messer, and historians Jason and Lisa Tetzloff seem to assume that the move of Henry and Elizabeth away from their reservations to urban areas meant a distinct break from their tribal communities and culture.[13] Some could consider the Clouds as "inauthentic," because they were "progressive" Natives who encouraged Native Americans to become modern and Christian. But these labels are based on static notions of identity in which one cannot be modern, Christian, and Native all at the same time. These categories are stuck in binaries between progressive and traditional Indians in which progressives are defined as wanting to assimilate into American society and traditional Natives are described as maintaining a strong connection to their tribal communities and traditions. Frederick Hoxie, Peter Iverson, Cathleen Cahill, Kristina Ackley, Cristina Stanciu, Joy Porter, and David Martinez, among others, have rescued progressives from this binary that defined them as Native Americans with little relationship to their tribal communities.[14] Similarly, my goal is to show how my grandparents' life and contributions defied these binary oppositions. Indeed, this book emphasizes how the Clouds' identity was incredibly complicated, filled with contradictions and fluidity—both modern *and* traditional.[15]

In contrast, I use the flexible and fluid notion of the hub, theorized by Laverne Roberts, a Paiute woman activist, which shows how Natives maintain their tribal culture, community, identity, gender, and belonging in urban areas both in geographic space, such as through meetings and powwows, and virtually, not based in space, such as through phone calling, writing letters, reading tribal newspapers, and storytelling. I utilize this diasporic concept to examine how the Clouds maintained connections to their tribes, tribal identity, community, and gender as well as developed Native-oriented strategies to challenge the U.S. and settler colonialism, away from their tribal homelands in Native hubs.[16]

Native Hubs, Storytelling, and Colonial Resistance

Storytelling is a powerful form of Native hub making because of its portability. Nowadays stories are shared in cars, classrooms, homes, and everywhere we travel. Storytelling is an ancient intellectual tradition that occurred in the winter when families lived in lodges, sharing food and resources.[17] Stories are vital to the transmission of Ho-Chunk and Ojibwe knowledge, in the past and in the present. Some stories are told only in ceremonial contexts, and others are told daily. Stories tell us our place in the universe, how we move from one location to another, and how we are connected to one another in tribal communities. They can have morals, suggesting right action and keeping us connected to our tribal homes.[18] Stories are the heartbeat of tribal communities.[19]

A major portion of Ojibwe and Ho-Chunk narratives are called "trickster stories."[20] Paul Radin, a classic anthropologist, wrote about Wakdjunkaga, or a Ho-Chunk trickster, as translated into English.[21] According to Niigonwedom James Sinclair, an Anishinaabe (Ojibwe) scholar, Radin's book, *The Trickster*, provides evidence of Indigenous peoples resisting colonialism by telling trickster stories.[22] Radin, unfortunately, assumes that Ho-Chunk and other tribal trickster stories represent a stage of undeveloped human thought, placing Natives' intellectual ideas low on a continuum between primitive and civilized and, therefore, linked to settler colonialism. Sam Blowsnake, a Ho-Chunk intellectual, recounted a "cycle" of Wakdjunkaga stories to Radin in 1912. Sinclair argues that Blowsnake sharing Wakdjunkaga stories is colonial resistance. During this time the Ho-Chunk suffered destructive attacks on tribal sovereignty, including reservation policies and federal boarding-school officials who kidnapped Native children, forcing them into an abusive process of assimilation, often hundreds or thousands of miles away from their homes.

When contemplated within this colonial context, stories can take on multiple meanings. How might Blowsnake's Wakdjunkaga stories—the trickster's wandering and building a community with other exiled creatures because the world is becoming a difficult place to live in, his finding a home where red oaks grow, his settling where the Mississippi meets the Missouri Rivers, and his transformation of parts of his penis into potatoes, turnips, artichokes, and ground beans for humans to eat—be considered within the history of migration and Ho-Chunk removals?[23] The federal government forcibly removed the Ho-Chunk multiple times away from our homelands in Wisconsin (a story told more fully in chapter 1). Blowsnake's telling of the trickster's wandering could point to how federal officials forced Ho-Chunks to move from place to place. Therefore, Blowsnake's retelling of Wakdjnkaga stories in 1912 points to a doubleness in his narrative, and its underlying meaning could allude to the colonial context. Rather than representing a "lower" mentality than whites, as Radin argues, I assert that trickster stories were foundational to Ho-Chunk and Ojibwe education, teaching children, young people, and adults how to resist and subvert colonialism.[24]

Elizabeth and Henry Cloud must have learned doubleness speech while living in a colonial environment and listening to Ho-Chunk and Ojibwe stories. This traditional tribal educational process would have taught them how to tell and understand stories with multiple meanings.[25] The Clouds grew up dealing with oppressive colonial policies where doubleness of speech was absolutely essential to speak the unspeakable without the colonizer's awareness. Thus, they must have learned how to tell stories embedded with criticism. On the surface the colonizer most likely would not notice anything subversive. Underneath the surface, however, the oppressed could communicate a critique of the colonizer. Doubleness speech generates two meanings: one appears dispassionate and agreeable; the other could express possibly subversive material or ideas.[26]

Places and moments where colonizers and Natives interacted were saturated with power and domination; the contact zones included federal boarding schools, Christian missions, and Bureau of Indian Affairs (BIA) agencies.[27] Mary Louise Pratt, a literary theorist, asserts, "I use this term [the contact zone] to refer to social spaces where cultures meet, clash and grapple with each other, often in contexts of highly asymmetrical relationships of power, such as colonialism, slavery, or their aftermaths as they lived out in many parts of the world today."[28] In these contact zones the colonizer could not truly see or understand Henry or Elizabeth Cloud and other Natives of their generation but instead racialized them, made them an "other," and saw them as "savages," "primitives," and, for Elizabeth, as "Pocahontas" or "savage drudge"— not full human beings.[29] To deal with this racist and oppressive context, our Indigenous ancestors had to learn to juggle two realities, their own Native perspective and the colonizer's. The Clouds had to master various ways of behaving and speaking in different social settings and to divergent audiences, including other Natives, white missionaries, and BIA officials, both in the private and public sphere. Their ability to speak and write in various cultural registers, including mixing dominant and Native discourses to diverse audiences, could explain how their behavior and speech could seem contradictory. In other words, the Clouds, for example, could speak using mostly dominant rhetoric with white reformers and Native-centric discourses when conversing with other Indigenous peoples. Their ability to speak, write, and act using differing cultural registers was absolutely necessary during the racist and oppressive context at the end of the nineteenth century and the first half of the twentieth century.[30]

To not only survive but also gain power among whites, the Clouds could learn other subversive strategies from listening to tribal trickster stories. Ho-Chunk and Ojibwe trickster abilities embrace adaptability; changing shapes and forms, including male to female; and being humorous and creative.[31] Hearing trickster stories, Elizabeth and Henry could learn shape-shifting and the performance of various identities, such as a "good" Indian and a "bad" Indian, playing with multiple meanings that could hide one's true thoughts or feelings.[32] A good Indian is one who appears to be a helper of whites and assimilated, and a bad Indian challenges whites and resists assimilation.[33] But underneath Elizabeth and Henry could preserve and protect their warrior identities. Indeed, Henry and Elizabeth could be simultaneously good and bad Indians.[34]

Shape-shifting, a trickster strategy, therefore, includes both verbal as well as nonverbal performance.[35] Being oppressed must have encouraged Henry and Elizabeth Cloud to use many subversive strategies to not only survive but also excel, including masking and camouflage to protect their innermost thoughts and feelings.[36] They quickly must have discovered that criticism, complaints, and unhappiness, or asserting themselves, could bring immediate punishment from the colonizer. In this dangerous colonial environment, they soon learned that tactical and careful manipulation of appearance was essential for survival.[37]

This book, therefore, contributes to the reclamation of Ho-Chunk and Ojibwe history.[38] By incorporating tribally specific kinship, stories, writing, culture, and gender into my analysis, I bring new insight into archival letters and writings often pitched to a colonial audience.[39] While new imperial histories present nuanced gendered analyses of colonialism, they fail to show how Natives rework colonialism for their own purposes. To this end, Native histories emphasize Indigenous peoples as active agents rather than passive victims of colonialism at the expense of complex treatments of colonialism.[40] Thus, I combine new imperial and Native histories to discuss how the Clouds were complicit in, challenged, and reworked colonialism for their own purposes.[41] But to recognize the importance of the Clouds' intellectual work and activism, an understanding of settler colonialism is needed.

Settler Colonialism

Indigenous scholars and activists challenge the eradication of Native peoples and the settler-colonial aspects of land. There are more and more scholarly efforts—called "settler colonial studies," defined by Patrick Wolfe's 1999 book, *Settler Colonialism and the Transformation of Anthropology*; his 2006 article, "Settler Colonialism and the Elimination of the Native"; and, more recently, articles in *Settler Colonial Studies*—which focus on Native feminisms, queer and sexuality studies, and Indigenous studies.[42] Settler colonialism is theoretically divergent from other colonialisms in that it concentrates on the elimination of Indigenous peoples and relationships from and with the land.[43] Wolfe argues that settler colonialism is a structure rather than an event, and it involves land as the primary motive of eliminating the Native; settlers come to stay: they take up residence, including building homes, creating businesses, and farming the land.

Not only is settler colonialism about taking over the land, but it is also linked to modernity and to the development of the modern nation-state. It is about the nation-state eliminating the Native physically, spiritually, and culturally, through federal policies of boarding schools and the Dawes Allotment Act, among others. It is related to the early development of classic anthropology, including Lewis Henry Morgan's evaluation of Natives as at the bottom of a continuum between the primitive and the civilized.[44] As part of classic anthropology, settler colonialism contributed to the dominant discourse of the vanishing Indian that was replayed over and over in Edward Curtis's photos of Natives and Henry Hamilton Bennett's photographs of the Ho-Chunk.[45] Settler colonialism was also reenacted in celebrations of white settlers' victories over Natives in Wild West shows and other public displays. Classic anthropology supports static notions of culture that create a binary between the traditional and the modern and roots Native culture in the land.[46] Accordingly, Richard Pratt, creator of the Native federal boarding schools, likely believed kidnapping Indigenous children—and separating them from their families and Native lands—forced them to lose their culture and identity and thus to assimilate into U.S. society.

Settler colonialism not only involves an insatiable hunger for land and a continual dispossession of Indigenous peoples from our land but also is linked to Christianity and capitalism. Colonizers view the land as a menacing and scary wilderness, a place of available and untapped resources, a location to accomplish God's work, and a site of natural, untouched magnificence. Christianity influences colonizers' relationship and connection to land, justifying their dominion over "pagans" and encouraging their exploitation of all creatures and land for enjoyment and profit. Christianity ultimately places humans' needs above those of nonhumans. Colonizers see Indigenous peoples as inferior beings, wild and potentially dangerous (like the land), roving without purpose, and not influenced by the power and habit of civilization. Colonizers view the world in binaries: European civilization as good, and nature, dangerous forests, wild beasts, and Natives as bad and inferior.[47] Colonizers perceive the land as empty of full human presence, a commodity to be owned and farmed, meadows to be parceled and fenced. From a settler-colonial mindset, waterways must be controlled and mountains must be dug up and exploited for gold and other precious and valuable metals.[48]

Capitalism and colonizers' insatiable desire for control drive tragic dam-building projects, which harness the power of water for agriculture, electricity, profit, and other human needs in exchange for the life of the land, plants, fish, and animals. Settlers work to colonize not only Indigenous peoples but all living things. They import new, domesticated animals, plants, insects, birds, and other species to colonize the land for their own profit and use.[49] Settler colonialism, therefore, disrupts Natives' long-standing relationships with the land and all life forms and interrupts our supply of food and traditional medicines, thus contributing to poverty, diseases, and other problems. Integral to dispossessing us from our land, it interferes with Natives' relationship to the spiritual realm and our access to sacred and ceremonial sites.

Margaret Jacobs in *White Mother to a Dark Race* discusses how settler colonialism is used to describe how people of European descent gained dominance in nation-states, including the United States and Australia. Indeed, settler colonialism is a colonial process that can be studied worldwide, including in Palestine.[50] Settlers, according to Jacobs, are often imagined in relatively innocent terms as *immigrants* and *emigrants* peacefully spreading across the land, building homes and clearing fields that they assumed were empty lands for the taking. Therefore, the purpose of settler colonialism is to challenge the ways that dominant narratives are told to keep Native perspectives of history and effects of colonialism hidden and not faced. Indeed, settler colonialism supports a consciousness that anyone can be blinded by, regardless of racial or ethnic background, and therefore is not only a problem for European descendants. *Standing Up to Colonial Power* is my effort to decolonize my own Native family history and be honest and face moments when my grandparents were implicated in colonialism, demonstrating that colonialism can be supported by Natives as well as non-Natives.[51]

Furthermore, settler colonialism includes a powerful gendered dimension. It infiltrates the most intimate places, even Indigenous peoples' personal relationships. Through these "intimacies of empire," Ann Stoler argues, racial classifications were created and challenged, and relations between colonizer and colonized powerfully defied or strengthened colonial power.[52] Gendered settler colonialism works to destroy Indigenous kinship systems, trying to supplant them with the heteronormative and patriarchal Eurocentric kinship model of the nuclear family. It attacks Native masculinity, treating Indigenous men as nonmen, indeed as children. And it attempts to force Native women to follow white ideas of gender and submit to men's wants and needs.

Scholars of settler-colonial studies work to transform the relationship between settlers and Indigenous peoples to decolonize and create a better world for Natives, human beings overall, and all living things.[53] Indigenous intellectuals, including Henry and Elizabeth Cloud, labored to reframe the conversation in support of Native sovereignty and to argue for a transformation of settler society through non-Natives learning, listening, and being changed from their involvement with Indigenous peoples.[54]

Native Intellectuals

Understanding the settler-colonial pressures that motivated the speeches, writings, and stories of Henry and Elizabeth Cloud as Native intellectuals requires a broader discussion of the dominant discourses and federal policies they confronted, including the rhetoric of civilizing and assimilating.[55] The principal assumption of the dominant discourses was the inferiority of Native American cultures, including our philosophies, languages, cultural practices, and spirituality.[56] By the late nineteenth century, colonizers assumed Native peoples' cultures were a vanishing, primitive past. And for our Indigenous ancestors to progress into the future, they were expected to replace their cultural traditions with Western civilization. The federal government enacted awful policies to attempt to force Natives to erase our tribal identities, spirituality, and cultures. These policies greatly traumatized our Native ancestors. The legacies of these policies continue today with tremendous Native language loss, increased teenage suicide, and many other issues.

In the 1880s, near the conclusion of Natives' armed opposition, the federal government passed the Allotment Act of 1887, an act that appealed to assimilation rather than violence to fulfill settler colonialism. The act worked to abrogate Native treaty rights and other special statuses, so the U.S. state could absorb Native Americans. The government divided Indigenous land into individual allotments. Heads of household, meaning Native men, were given 160 acres, single individuals were entitled to 80 acres, and those under eighteen years old were given 40 acres. Married women were not eligible for land under the original act. As a result, the Allotment Act supported the formation of heteropatriarchal households. Four years later each adult could receive 80 acres of land, regardless of family status.[57] Supporters of the Allotment Act assumed Native men would assimilate, learning white norms, becoming farmers, and submitting to whites, and Native women would assimilate, becoming farmwives and submitting to men. Then the millions of acres of "surplus" land were made available for white settlers and railroad development. In 1887 Natives owned 138 million acres, and by 1934, when the Allotment Act ended, Natives owned 54 million acres.[58]

Working in tandem with the Allotment Act's new program of assimilation, whites began to educate Native children in an attempt to prepare our Native ancestors for productive roles in white society and break our attachment to our Indigenous land. If Native children assimilated and no longer wanted their Indigenous lands, then more land would become available for the colonizers' use. Breaking Native children's sense of attachment to Indigenous land is, therefore, an act of settler colonialism. Starting in the 1880s white reformers' goals included child removal and placement in boarding schools. Government officials favored compulsory removal to reduce the influence of Native mothers, who were assumed to be "unfit." Estelle Reel, a longtime superintendent of Indian schools, explained, "The Indian child must be placed in school before the habits of barbarous life become fixed and there he must be kept until contact with our life has taught him to abandon his savage ways and walk in the path of Christian civilization."[59] From 1879 to 1902 the federal government created more than 150 boarding schools, 25 of which were off-reservation. The government hired police officers to convince parents to enroll their children, promising their children would be fed, housed, and educated. Native parents were often "convinced" under great duress.[60]

Upon Native children's arrival at boarding schools, government employees immediately cut our ancestors' hair and provided settler clothing, including military-style uniforms. The children were punished for speaking Native languages or practicing their Indigenous religions and rituals. Government employees taught boys to follow white notions of gender, including sexism, and to become heads of household, instructing them to be submissive to whites and teaching them farming and the trades. Girls were taught white female-gender norms and how to become wives, be submissive to males and whites, and perform domestic duties. The purpose of whites' education of Natives was a "social death." Col. Richard H. Pratt, the founder and head of the Carlisle federal boarding school, gave a famous speech in 1892: "A great general has said that the only good Indian is a dead one, and that high sanction of his destruction has been an enormous factor in promoting Indian massacres. In a sense, I agree with the sentiment, but only in this: that all the Indian there is in the race should be dead. Kill the Indian in him, and save the man."[61]

These settler-colonial worldviews of civilization and assimilation influenced the Bureau of Indian Affairs, a U.S. governmental apparatus created to control and colonize Native people, our land, and natural resources.[62] The BIA, initially known as the Office of Indian Affairs, was founded in 1824 as a settler-colonial tool to both assimilate and civilize Indigenous populations by executing federal Indian policy, starting with the huge land clearances in the U.S. South.[63] First the BIA was part of the War Department, then in 1849 it shifted to the recently established Department of the Interior (DOI). Since the very start the BIA worked hard to assimilate and colonize Native Americans, our land, and natural resources by making bureaucratic maps and inventories centrally positioned in Washington DC and relying on a huge network of military forts, Native agencies, and Christian missionaries throughout Indian Country. Since at least 1870, when the federal government allocated money to private corporations for railroad construction rather than to Natives, the BIA worked with white corporations.[64] The railroad also had timber interests, and with the assistance of a ruthless military campaign and federal Indian policy, Natives were dispossessed of their lands and natural resources.

Colonizers assumed the discourse of civilization and assimilation was the answer to the so-called Indian problem, and this excruciating rhetoric must have been at the forefront of the minds of Elizabeth and Henry Cloud. Native intellectuals at the time also felt the need to establish that we as Native peoples were fully human. Debates about the humanity of Indigenous peoples include the famous argument between the Spaniards Bartolomé de Las Casas, who argued in support of Native virtues, and Juan Ginés de Sepúlveda, who argued that in the Americas one could barely see traces of humanity in Indigenous peoples. Even by the start of the twentieth century, U.S. policies assumed Natives were human enough to be assimilated but still argued they were an underdeveloped people.[65] Furthermore, racist discourses transformed Natives into an "other," differentiated from whites of European racial stock. Thus, the Clouds and other Native intellectuals endeavored to prove Native humanity equal to white humanity. Indeed, at this historical juncture, Native intellectuals even worked to create a common humanity with whites who saw them as inferior, subhuman "savages."

Many Society of American Indians members, including the Clouds, argued for Native Americans' U.S. citizenship. Hazel Hertzberg and other scholars called these thinkers assimilationists, but this portrayal is inaccurate.[66] The Clouds and other procitizenship Native intellectuals were not in favor of following Richard Pratt and erasing tribal identities. Instead, following Maddox's argument, they used rhetorical strategies to be heard in the public sphere during an incredibly racist time. By mixing progressive notions, dominant discourses of racial uplift, and Native points of view, posits Maddox, these intellectuals established a speaking position that a mainstream audience could understand. Natives' struggle for U.S. citizenship was a fight to attain the recognition, rights, and protections afforded to white citizens.[67] At the same time, this battle for incorporation into the U.S. nation-state had its limitations; it could weaken the fight for tribal sovereignty.[68]

Despite Maddox's argument that Native members of the SAI were intellectuals, Henry and Elizabeth Cloud have not been recognized as Ho-Chunk and Ojibwe intellectuals who used speeches, writing, and advocacy to fight for Native peoples.[69] As I began working on this family-tribal history, I read notes written by my mother, Woesha Cloud North. She describes her parents' writing as a "thicket of white ideas," and this points to how her parents had to negotiate an extremely racist, settler-colonial context. To be heard in the public sphere, their speeches and writing had to incorporate both white and Native ideas. Woesha's idea of a "thicket" suggests how much her parents had to cover themselves in a white-centric camouflage while working toward positive social change for Native Americans. Both Henry and Elizabeth Cloud, as well as other Native intellectuals of this period, used white reform groups to gain access to political power, support, and resources. In this context using white-centric rhetoric was certainly necessary to work for Native goals and objectives. The Clouds have likely been understudied, because they were criticized for being assimilationists despite their tribal-centric agendas, which contradicted their support of acculturation. Another possible reason is that the Clouds' use of dominant Christian rhetoric might be challenging for contemporary audiences to the point that subversive actions and words could be missed. Furthermore, as a granddaughter of the Clouds, I grew up listening to family stories about them that are often not present in their published writing, giving me a family-tribal perspective to understand them. Along with the literatures of settler colonialism and Ho-Chunk and Ojibwe studies, this book builds on the scholarship of the Progressive Era, including the work of Philip Deloria, Frederick Hoxie, Kristina Ackley, Cristina Stanciu, Cathleen Cahill, and many others.[70] The book builds on the work of Native American literary critics, such as Robert Warrior and Mishauna Goeman, who highlight the subversive potential of Native peoples' writing.[71] It relies on the emerging field of Native feminisms.[72] And the book builds on these literatures by discussing a Native feminist approach, filling a gap in history, and honoring the Clouds as intellectuals who challenged and subverted colonialism.

A Native Feminist Approach to Family-Tribal History

My experience researching and writing about my grandparents has taught me some important methodological lessons about family-tribal history from an Indigenous and gendered lens.[73] The first lesson I learned was archival material related to Native families can include information that's not appropriate for public consumption. Indeed, individuals can choose to place archive material that Native family members wish were not in the public domain. For example, upon a person's death, families can donate letters to archives without discussing their decision with other family members. Because archival information can contain sensitive material, it is essential to consult the family to determine what information can be written about. Respecting a Native family's wishes is fundamental to protecting our right to privacy. It is a crucial ethical principle to follow and, consequently, a Native methodological concern. Indeed, rather than viewing Native peoples' lives as data for outside researchers to use to produce theory, we as Indigenous peoples demand the incorporation of our own needs, insights, and research agendas into the development and publication of any study, including family-tribal history.[74] Classic anthropologists' ethnographic observations of Indigenous peoples allowed imperial power to scrutinize us without consent and without taking Native peoples' analyses seriously. Likewise, archival researchers who use an imperial gaze to analyze Indigenous peoples' letters—without consent and without taking Native analyses seriously—are using a colonial methodology. I occupy a complicated position as both an outsider and an insider, since I am an academic and the granddaughter of Elizabeth and Henry Cloud. My dual social position encourages me to weave my reflections throughout the text from both of these distinct points of view. In this way I bring ethnography and family-tribal history together.[75]

Anther methodological lesson I learned was the value of using intersectional analysis when analyzing primary and secondary documents. Discussing the linkage between various oppressions, such as race, class, gender, and settler colonialism, encourages us not to make the mistake of emphasizing one kind of exclusion over another. Placing these intersecting oppressions and tribal sovereignty both at the center of one's analysis is a move toward developing a Native feminist awareness. Certainly, the first step toward decolonizing our ancestral histories is naming experiences as colonial. Because the Clouds confronted dominant discourses, I analyze the narratives they employed to be heard in the public sphere, mixing both Native and white rhetoric, which is a further Native feminist approach.

Finally, I learned the significance of highlighting our Native ancestors' agency, perspectives, and positions. I use long quotes from the Clouds' writings and speeches to highlight their intellectual prowess and points of view. Their Indigenous perspectives of the past can help us reconstruct a Native-centric history as well as empower us as a people. Together all of these methodological concerns explain why I choose to categorize this family-tribal history of my grandparents as a Native feminist approach.

As part of my effort to decolonize, I choose to call my grandparents the Clouds and not the Roe Clouds. Henry dropped his middle name "Clarence," which was given to him in the federal boarding school Genoa, and replaced it with the name "Roe," because the Roes, a white missionary couple, informally adopted him as a young Ho-Chunk man in his twenties. Henry relied on this relationship with Walter and Mary Roe to help him with educational loans, support him while he was attending Yale, and provide him with white upper-middle-class resources. The resources he gained through his relationship with the Roes helped Henry found the American Indian Institute (AII), a college-preparatory Christian high school for Native boys (the Clouds wished the school could include girls, but it wasn't possible at the time). But, as chapter 1 discusses, this informal adoption was ultimately a colonial relationship. Thus, I generally choose to drop "Roe" when referring to my grandparents, Henry and Elizabeth.

The Clouds fought stereotypes against Native people to create a world where we, as Native Americans, could become full members of U.S. society and Native communities. Their recent public acknowledgment can be attributed to a new trend in historical and Native studies literature (see for example, Deloria's *Indians in Unexpected Places* and Scott Lyon's *X-Marks*) that places Natives as central to discussions of modernity, rather than outside of modernity, and even outside of history itself.[76]

This book is my attempt to contribute to this new trend by discussing Henry and Elizabeth Cloud's intellectual work and activism, using a Ho-Chunk and Ojibwe family point of view, and relying on the notions of the hub, settler colonialism, and Native feminisms.

Chapter by Chapter

Chapter 1 argues that Henry Cloud, in his autobiographical narrative, relied on doubleness to assert a Native position, while writing for a missionary journal. As a Native and a Christian, he mixed white and Native rhetoric in his writing and speeches. As a modern Ho-Chunk man and warrior, he appropriated the white notion of the self-made man to increase his power in white society. Cloud's use of Ho-Chunk trickster strategies, including doubleness, shape-shifting, storytelling, humor, and creativity, helped him thrive in white schools. He argued for Natives to attend college, challenging racist ideas that Natives were not smart enough. He created a modern Ho-Chunk warrior identity by adding white concepts to his Ho-Chunk self. He created Ho-Chunk–centric hubs to help him survive, excel, and maintain his Ho-Chunk identity while a Yale University student and become the first "full-blood" Native to graduate with a bachelor's and a master's degree.

Chapter 2 investigates Henry Cloud's involvement in the SAI and his successful activist and intellectual work to free Geronimo, an Apache, and assist the Apaches, who chose to remain in Oklahoma and struggle against the federal government. It argues Henry Cloud, as a Ho-Chunk intellectual, combined his Yale education and his warrior training to fight for the Apaches. It also discusses Elizabeth Cloud's childhood on the White Earth Reservation, her white schooling, her involvement in the SAI, her marriage to Henry, and her partnership with him to run the American Indian Institute. In this chapter I assert that Elizabeth and Henry ran the AII, a Native hub, following complementary gender roles, and the school encouraged young men to become educated warriors for their tribes while challenging settler colonialism. It argues Elizabeth used doubleness, using both Native and white rhetoric, while combining Ojibwe and white notions of gender in her writing.

Chapter 3 examines Henry Cloud's coauthorship of the Meriam Report of 1928 and Indian Reorganization Act of 1934, arguing he was more centrally involved than is usually understood. He critiqued the colonial aspect of IRA's tribal constitution-writing process and the deleterious effects of the Allotment Act, thus challenging settler colonialism. It asserts that his involvement in writing reports that exposed the abuse rampant in federal boarding schools contested settler colonialism and reveal his potency as a modern Ho-Chunk warrior, intellectual, and activist. It argues that racism prevented Cloud from being taken seriously as a candidate for the commissioner of Indian Affairs. As a Ho-Chunk intellectual and activist, he used his settler-colonial position as superintendent of Haskell, a federal boarding school, to close the jail. All the while he supported Native history, culture, and cultural citizenship, and, as a member of his tribal council, he worked on Ho-Chunk land issues and other concerns.

Chapter 4 investigates the work of Henry and Elizabeth Cloud on the Umatilla Reservation in Oregon. It argues that the Indian Service transferred Henry to be an Indian agent as a punishment for his criticism of the Indian Service. His new position meant a big drop in pay and an attempt to get him to quit. He transformed his settler-colonial position from an Indigenous lens, supporting tribal sovereignty by arguing for Native hunting and fishing rights, challenging racism, and trying to change the settler-colonial Happy Canyon and Wild West Show performances, while being more flexible and open to listening to Natives' concerns in comparison to the prior white Indian agent Omar L. Babcock. Cloud's Ho-Chunk intellectual work was pathbreaking and foundational to Ho-Chunk and Native studies. He used treaties to support his argument regarding tribes' hunting and fishing rights, and he discussed Native notions of conservation, Indigenous history, and settler colonialism. Elizabeth founded the Oregon Trail Women's Club, a Native hub for Indigenous women on the Umatilla Reservation, which supported women's empowerment and leadership while developing their tribal and modern identities.

Chapter 5 examines Elizabeth Cloud's efforts as a member of NCAI and her intellectual work on the national stage—she was named American Mother of the Year and Indian Welfare chair of the GFWC. While initially she seemed to view termination as inevitable, later, as the field secretary of NCAI and Indian welfare chair of GFWC, she fought against tribal termination. With her title as Mother of the Year, she relied on storytelling, doubleness, and shape-shifting in her struggle for tribal sovereignty and Native cultural citizenship. And as the assistant director of the American Indian Development (AID) project for NCAI, she organized community workshops and pantribal hubs while supporting the development of tribal self-determination and sovereignty. This chapter argues that Cloud, even in her capacity as a "good" Christian woman, was subversive. She wore professional dresses and great hats as camouflage, while underneath she was a powerful Ojibwe warrior woman, fighting in support of tribal sovereignty and struggling for Native cultural citizenship. She was complicated, a shape-shifter, citizen, warrior, and Christian. She was simultaneously a "good" and "bad" Indian. Elizabeth Cloud, as an Ojibwe intellectual, warrior woman, and member of NCAI, backed women's right to be on tribal councils and supported gender and tribal sovereignty and even later discussions of Native feminisms.

CHAPTER 1

Henry Cloud's Childhood and Young Adulthood

In this chapter I discuss Henry Cloud's early years, his youth on the Winnebago Reservation with his beloved family, his Ho-Chunk education, and his training in white schools, including Yale University. In his published autobiographical narrative for a missionary journal, a doubleness is present that revolves around his Christian conversion. Even while writing for a white Christian audience, he remains true to his Native position. As a child, he refused to forget his Ho-Chunk language and identity, resisting the federal government's settler-colonial attempt to assimilate him in the federal boarding schools and challenging the conservative Christian doctrine that pagan identities must be forgotten. As a Native *and* Christian, he had access to white ideas, which he strategically used for Native goals and objectives. As an orator and writer, he was able to perform in various cultural registers, using both Eurocentric and Indigenous concepts to sway his audience. As a Ho-Chunk modern man and warrior, he appropriated the popular rhetoric of white masculinity of the "self-made man" to increase his power in white society, ultimately challenging attempts of settler-colonial forces to take away his masculine power and turn him into a "non-man."

Later in his life, during a speech to a graduating class of Alaska Native students, Cloud articulated a strong Ho-Chunk position. Indeed, Cloud had a tremendous sense of humor and was a great teller of tales. He

attributed his storytelling ability to his precious Ho-Chunk grandmother, who would tell him stories only in the winter.[1] Cloud used Ho-Chunk trickster strategies to help him survive and excel in the midst of colonialism, including doubleness, shape-shifting, humor, and creativity. Cloud was a Ho-Chunk intellectual, who argued that Natives should attend college, thus challenging settler-colonial and racist assumptions that Natives were not smart enough. He developed a modern Ho-Chunk warrior identity by adding white concepts to his core Ho-Chunk philosophy and educational training. His additive, flexible, and fluid cultural and intellectual methodology disputes the subtractive and static approach of federal boarding schools and classic anthropology—both of which are linked to settler colonialism. He created Ho-Chunk–centric hubs to support his Ho-Chunk identity and culture while living away from his tribe.

Ho-Chunk, "People of the Big Voice," and Removals

Some historical background regarding the Ho-Chunk will help to set the scene for Cloud's childhood and his later life. The Ho-Chunk, or the "People of the Big Voice," lived for centuries in our homelands in present-day Wisconsin. In 1634 the Ho-Chunks encountered the French settler Jean Nicolet when he landed at Red Banks, Wisconsin. The French called our Ho-Chunk people the Winnebago. (Even though I am an enrolled member of the Winnebago Tribe of Nebraska, I will be using the name Ho-Chunk: an act of decolonization, as this is the name we gave ourselves.) Due to colonization Ho-Chunks are now divided into two distinct tribal nations. These two tribal nations are the Ho-Chunk Nation, whose members live on our traditional homelands in Wisconsin, and the Winnebago Tribe of Nebraska, whose members live on the reservation in Nebraska created by the federal government. The Ho-Chunk Nation reclaimed their original tribal name in 1994.[2]

As soon as the colonizer arrived, our people began experiencing settler colonialism. Colonizers made treaties with our Ho-Chunk ancestors to dispossess us of our precious and cherished land. As part of the Treaty

Fig. 1. Cloud as a young Ho-Chunk man, probably in his early twenties, at the Winnebago Reservation in Nebraska. Photograph courtesy of the Cloud family.

of 1825, our tribal territory extended from Green Bay, beyond Lake Winnebago, to the Wisconsin River and the Rock River in Illinois, including 8.5 million acres. Once colonization started, our story as Ho-Chunks is one of much suffering and incredible hardships. Much of our misery began in the late 1820s, when miners began to pour into southwestern Wisconsin. Treaty commissioners promised they would punish whites who entered Ho-Chunk lands. But the lure of mineral-rich, lush farmlands proved too strong, and the colonizer sincerely believed that Indigenous lands were available for the taking. Within ten years the federal government reversed its position and forced the Ho-Chunk to sell our land at a meager percentage of its value. Federal officials then forcibly removed our Ho-Chunk ancestors from Wisconsin.

After the signing of the 1832 treaty, the Ho-Chunk were first removed to land in Iowa, called the "Neutral Ground"; it was supposed to act as a buffer between the Sac and Fox and Dakota Nations. We were then removed to a wooded region of northeastern Minnesota in 1846, to act as a barrier between the Ojibwe and the Lakota. Consequently, the Ho-Chunk suffered from the raids of both tribes. After the signing of the 1855 treaty, the federal officials removed the Ho-Chunk to land near the Blue Earth River in southern Minnesota. As soon as we arrived, white settlers demanded our removal yet again. In 1863 our people were forcibly removed to the Crow Creek Reservation in South Dakota, and more than 550 people died on our horrific journey. The Ho-Chunk requested that the federal government exchange their South Dakota reservation for lands near the friendly Omahas in 1865. The Omahas' reservation was situated in northeastern Nebraska, next to the Missouri River and close to present-day South Sioux City, Iowa.[3]

The memories of our Ho-Chunk ancestors include stories about being rounded up at gunpoint, loaded into boxcars, and shipped to our reservation in Nebraska. My mother told me that there were many Ho-Chunk casualties as a result of these multiple removals. Being forcibly removed away from our homelands is a psychic wound that we, as the descendants, carry within our hearts, spirits, and minds. My grandfather's parents were likely born in the 1860s, suffered through this very difficult history, and lived on our newly created reservation in Nebraska next to the Missouri River. After these removals many Ho-Chunks returned to their ancestral homelands in Wisconsin and eventually created the Ho-Chunk Nation in Wisconsin.

Cloud and Ho-Chunk Naming

Henry Cloud's Ho-Chunk name was Wo-Na-Xi-Lay-Hunka, meaning "War Chief." Cloud describes it in a letter in a metaphorical rather than literal way as the "Chief of the Place of Fear."[4] Ho-Chunk naming provides the clan and the family a mechanism to emphasize the child's place in a support system, and this network, or Ho-Chunk hub, serves the child throughout life. Remembering the circumstances of naming and the crucial role it plays is fundamental to Ho-Chunk education. Naming ceremonies are tribal educational structures that introduce one's place in the tribe and the universe. Children were often named at tribal feasts.[5]

Cloud was a member of the Thunderbird Clan—the clan, he explained, that "obstructed and permitted war."[6] Cloud's father, Chayskagah (White Buffalo), told a significant prophecy about his son. During a winter when food became very scarce, his son did not eat for ten days. Then his father found a frozen beaver hut, killed the animals, traded some of their skins for corn, boiled the beaver meat, and prepared a feast. During the feast his father discussed his prophecy. He told his son, "Eat, War Chief, for I am hungry but will not eat until you have tasted food. I am old and it makes no difference if I starve, but you are young. The future of the Winnebagos [Ho-Chunks] lies within you."[7] White Buffalo told War Chief this important prophecy, which, according to my mother, encouraged her dad throughout his life to fight as a Ho-Chunk warrior for the survival and in defense of his people. This story also shares a core value of a Ho-Chunk warrior identity: put the survival of the young before one's own continued existence. Cloud's telling and retelling this powerful story created a Ho-Chunk–centric, gendered hub—not based in geographic space but carried in his heart and mind even as he lived away from his Ho-Chunk people.

Cloud's name and clan membership were central to his identities as a Ho-Chunk man, leader, and modern-day warrior. From a Ho-Chunk perspective a warrior not only fought in war for the survival of his people but also was a servant to his people, placing the needs of others first. My mother, Woesha, taught me that learning strength and self-discipline is central to a Ho-Chunk warrior identity. The traditional practice of fasting taught this value at an early age. Going without food and water for four days is not an easy task but rather a practice that helped Ho-Chunk boys and girls become strong, self-disciplined, and close to Ma-un-a (Ho-Chunk for Earth Maker or Creator). Indeed, fasting is a crucial Ho-Chunk educational experience. It is through fasting that a child learns self-control, beginning with short-lived fasting experiences that gradually become of longer duration, while connecting to the spiritual world.[8]

Cloud was born in a traditional Ho-Chunk bark home next to the Missouri River on the Winnebago Reservation, surrounded by his family and tribe. Cloud and his family felt closely connected to the seasons and natural surroundings, including the powerful Missouri River. His father, Chayskagah (White Buffalo) and his mother, Hard to See, picked wild plants to eat and reeds from the water to craft mats for sleeping.[9] His beloved grandmother's name was Mashunpeewingah (or Good Feather Woman), the same name I was given as a child at our Ho-Chunk naming ceremony in Winnebago, Nebraska.[10] Ho-Chunk names incorporate the "-gah" suffix when one is talking about the person and in direct address drop the suffix.

Our family story is that Hard to See married often because flu epidemics and diseases caused the deaths of many Ho-Chunks, including Hard to See's husbands. My Ho-Chunk relatives Francis Cassiman and Alice Mallory Porter, with the assistance of our cousin Robin Butterfield, prepared our genealogy. Hard to See was married to James Noble and together had their daughter, Hahmpgoomahnee'inga, or Susan Noble Ewing; to another Ho-Chunk whose name is no longer remembered and birthed a son, Anson Brown; to Charlie Rice and had a son, Fred Rice (whom I gratefully met, as he was present at our family's Ho-Chunk naming); to Yellow Cloud; and to Chayskagah (White Buffalo). Many years later, when Cloud's children wanted to celebrate his birthday, he chose December 28, 1884, but the actual date could have been one year earlier.[11]

Cloud's autobiography, "From Wigwam to Pulpit: A Red Man's Own Story of His Progress from Darkness to Light," is a tale of his conversion to Christianity.[12] He describes stark contrasts within his traditional Ho-Chunk upbringing. He discusses the inviting smells of meat roasting over the fire in his one-room, circular wigwam, where he, his brother, mother, father, and sometimes his grandmother lived. He describes the lean times he experienced when he went to bed without supper, and he recalls the kindness of being woken up and fed first when food was brought home in the middle of the night. (As already discussed, feeding the young first is central to a Ho-Chunk warrior identity.) He recounts the harshness of his uncle's disciplinary measures, which were generally a result of Cloud disobeying his grandmother, refusing fasting, fighting other Indian boys, or crying without sufficient reason. This fear of discipline usually kept him and his brother from disobedience.

Even though his life story is a Christian conversion tale, there are many suggestive details about his upbringing. His Ho-Chunk education regarding culture and tradition particularly signal the importance of his Ho-Chunk identity, thus creating a Ho-Chunk–centric virtual hub and showing the doubleness of the narrative. He describes how his grandfather taught him to dodge the arrows of his enemies, and his uncle showed him to worship and pray. He recounts how his father took him to the nearby Missouri River, built a fire, and taught him songs to sing to the fire and river while throwing offerings of tobacco, red feathers, and oak twigs. He tells how his family trapped beaver and otter for their skins, teaching him their use for ceremony and trade. Early on he learned to shoot bows and arrows, and his mother taught him traditional Ho-Chunk stories. For example, when he lost an arrow, his mother told him, that Wakdjunkaga (Jester) one of the sons of Ma-un-a had hidden it, and he must cry aloud to Wakdjunkaga to bring the arrow back. During winter he especially enjoyed hearing his grandmother's stories. Her stories were of mighty deeds of heroes, war, spirits, nature, and her childhood. His grandmother's stories, including those of Wakdjunkaga (the Don Quixote of Ho-Chunk lore), he explains, made the winter "one long laugh" for him. Later in life he told these traditional Ho-Chunk stories to his children.

In 1949, during the speech he gave to Alaska Natives graduating from Mount Edgecumbe federal boarding school, he recalled his grandmother telling him Ho-Chunk stories, creating a Ho-Chunk–centric hub:

In winter times, our grandmother . . . would say, "If you grandchildren want any stories, you must first get the wood." And so we went into the woods and gathered all the dry wood and sticks that we could find because we lived in the woods. . . . And grandmother was very wise indeed to reserve her stories for the winter season when fifty degrees below zero was experienced and the ice-coated limbs were creaking above our heads above the wigwam. So we carried in the wood and we supplied all that she needed and we were warm in the wigwam as we listened to the stories. She used to tell us about these four great spirits. We called it cosmology and the world became a world full of spirits to me. . . . She often said that no child should eat the marrow of the bone because if he did he would loose his teeth. I later discovered that she had no teeth and could eat nothing but the marrow of the bone. She used to say that no child should eat a long ear of corn for . . . the long ear would be too long for the width of his stomach here. The long-eared corn would stick too far out and give him a pain in the side. . . . So we had nothing but short ears and grandmother and all the old people got all the long ears of corn.[13]

Cloud's narrative portrays a sense of warmth and comfort, sitting together with his cherished and much-loved grandmother and family in their wigwam, protected from the frigid Nebraska winters, challenging the colonial representations of traditional Indigenous homes as primitive, dirty, and disorganized.[14] Cloud emphasizes his grandmother's wisdom and how she taught him about Ho-Chunk spirituality, cosmology, and important values, including contributing to the well-being of the community by bringing firewood. His grandmother also taught Ho-Chunk children to put the needs of elders first so they would have enough nutritious food to eat. By telling these stories, he shows the significance of Ho-Chunk humor, encouraging his audience of young Alaska Natives to laugh about his grandmother outwitting him while she protected the elders' food supply. He also accentuates how central his grandmother and her storytelling were to his spiritual and intellectual development as a Ho-Chunk person.

Ho-Chunk storytelling is foundational to Ho-Chunk education. Waikun stories are about Ma-un-a, creations overall, or realms of the sacred. These

Waikun tales can be shared only in winter, when snakes are below the ground and when Ho-Chunk children are focusing their minds. Although there is no sharp distinction between one kind of story or the other, Worak stories are about daily life. Waikun and Worak stories share elements, but the tales end differently. The Worak stories end tragically in death or a comparison of the incompleteness of the characters to life's negative experiences.[15]

The aspects of the sacred and everyday life in Waikun and Worak tales can relate to cultural heroes who have both divine and human characteristics. The "clown" cultural heroes (that Paul Radin and others call tricksters) have both Waikun and Worak importance, and their stories are not to be told during the summer. According to Minnie Littlebear, a Ho-Chunk intellectual and elder, children could be told "clown stories." Littlebear gives examples of Keh-chung-geh-ga (Turtle) and Wax-chung-gay-ga (Hare) stories.[16] These clown stories could be humorous, and in fact humor is central to our Ho-Chunk culture.

Various kinds of stories, according to Felix White Sr., Ho-Chunk elder and intellectual, were told at various stages of a Ho-Chunk child's development, depending on the child's maturity. White emphasizes that Ho-Chunk children heard stories, and that stories were a sort of developmental psychology. Stories taught children suitable behavior from aunts, uncles, elders, and other family members.[17] Thus, Cloud's grandmother and parents were pivotal and powerful Ho-Chunk educators for him as a young boy.

When Cloud discusses his traditional Ho-Chunk spiritual knowledge in a missionary journal, he shows his uncertainty of specific aspects by using quotation marks. He thus proves himself to be a good Christian, telling a story the colonizer would find appropriate and showing the doubleness of the narrative. He learned how to fast, seek visions, and ask for spiritual guidance from Ma-un-a. The purpose of these fasts is to receive compassion and blessing from the spirits. While giving these gifts, the spirits reveal themselves. These mighty spirits impart powers and secrets to Natives that can be used for war, the hunt, and medicine. Fasting helps prepare Indians for hard times in war and during sickness. When Cloud discusses the importance of fasting, he places quotation marks around certain words to show his skepticism of these spiritual practices. He writes, "Any one who has such a 'dream' is considered blessed beyond his fellows." Later he told his children that fasting was a helpful practice, which taught self-discipline and inner strength, a central component of a Ho-Chunk warrior identity. Showing a change in perspective later in life, he even said he believed people could receive blessings from the Creator through this practice. He also writes, "I have heard many Indians call upon the 'Spirit' whom they claim to have seen and heard." By inserting the word "claim" and placing quotation marks around the word "Spirit," he questions whether the Indian actually sees the Spirit. Indeed, he emphasizes that he never had a dream himself.[18]

In the same speech to graduating Alaska Native students in 1949, Cloud carves out another Ho-Chunk–centric hub and describes the crucial role of fasting, connecting to Ho-Chunk spirituality, and including one's guardian spirit, the Great Spirit, and the four Great Spirits from the four directions. In this venue Cloud could be open. He appears not to cover himself in as much camouflage in comparison to his writing in the missionary journal. Cloud's examination of Ho-Chunk spirituality underscores the significance of fasting as a regimen and an institution that acts as a conduit to communicate to the spiritual world. His use of the words "institution" and "regime" underscores Ho-Chunk spirituality as a philosophy to be taken seriously rather than automatically discounted as pagan, and thus lower on the socioevolutionary scale between civilized and primitive. He explains,

I was taught there were four great spirits in [the] universe, commanding the four corners of the universe and under them there were a hierarchy of spirits innumerable and certain definite authorities and responsibilities were given these spirits to govern their section of the universe, and under these spirits there were other spirits who could communicate with human beings on the face of this earth and to those the Great Spirit intended that the Red men of America should approach and become acquainted with and have fellowship with in due time. And the institution that was set up for this communion and fellowship was fasting periods, eating nothing four days and nights. So

I passed through that regime and after the fourth day hunger seized my brother and me and thirst. And father and mother promised that we would have something to eat at the end of the fourth day's fasting. In the meantime, we went into the deep woods on the banks of the Missouri River to pray to these spirits that some (one) of them might take pity and speak out of the eternal heavens and to our souls. . . . We were encouraged not to be common men but to become uncommon men that the common man of this world, without supernatural assistance, did not amount to anything and success is prohibited at this time. . . . There must be in your soul a guardian spirit to assist you and that was what we were seeking and trying to achieve.[19]

Cloud's arduous Ho-Chunk warrior training, which included fasting and learning to rely on spirituality, enabled him to weather many difficult challenges during this time, including going without food, as it was often scarce. Cloud alludes to how his parents used fasting and connection to one's Creator and guardian spirit as a training for him to become an "uncommon" man. Ho-Chunk boys and girls were expected to fast, and adults were not considered a fully grown man or woman unless they tried fasting.[20] However, since as a teenager Cloud converted to Christianity, it is surprising that Cloud emphasizes that his Ho-Chunk training encouraged him to become an uncommon man. His discussion of fasting at sixty-five years old is much more Ho-Chunk–centric than his writing in a missionary journal in 1915, which highlights, in a skeptical tone, that he never did have a fasting vision.[21]

These differing viewpoints point to his Ho-Chunk trickster ability of doubleness. He wrote in a way that the colonizer would not find objectionable in a missionary journal. These divergent perspectives could also allude to a relaxing of his strict Christian position one year before his death as compared to his younger days or not feeling comfortable to be totally honest when writing in a missionary journal. His sharing of Ho-Chunk knowledge also reflects his respect for his tribal philosophy, encouraging young Alaska Natives to value their Indigenous knowledge. Furthermore, his discussion points to his development of a strong Ho-Chunk spiritual foundation, on which he later added his Christian training.

In other words, rather than totally reject his Ho-Chunk educational and spiritual training, he greatly relied on various aspects.

When Cloud discusses his brother being forcibly taken to Genoa, a federal Indian boarding school, he switches the tone of his speech from humorous to somber. The purpose of these federal boarding schools was to assimilate Natives into American society, punishing Native students for speaking our Indigenous languages and teaching subservience to whites, not leadership of our own people.[22] In 1879 Richard H. Pratt, a military man, founded Carlisle, the first federal boarding school (see introduction). At Carlisle and other boarding schools, policemen kidnapped Native children and forced our ancestors to attend these horrific settler-colonial environments far away from our loving families. They were unsafe, unhealthy, and abusive places, so our people suffered tremendously.[23] Cloud discusses the schools:

> One day a policeman came to our lodge in the wigwam in the deep woods and seized my older brother. They were taking him to [a federal boarding] school. . . . I was only five years of age. He was my only playmate. I cried a great deal in losing him so my mother agreed that I would go along with him. He [the policeman] took me to a government institution called Genoa, Nebraska and I stayed there for awhile and then came back to the reservation boarding school where we played all manner of games and learned to speak English and [later] they took me to Santee Mission School in Northeastern Nebraska and there I was taught to learn a trade.[24]

Cloud's emphasis of his tremendous suffering and grief, regarding losing his brother, is an example of the sorrow Native children and our families experienced because of the federal-government schools that separated small children from their parents. Because a policeman forcibly took Cloud's brother, and his mother allowed Cloud to accompany him, their parents became separated from two sons rather than only one. This separation must have caused enormous sadness for the entire family. Cloud recounts his brother being taken by force, using the word "seized," to a federal boarding school, Genoa. And he speaks more positively about attending a school on the Winnebago Reservation, probably because he was close to his extended family and tribe, saying, "we played all manner of games." The words "taken" and "seized" speak volumes regarding the lack of control, distress, and anguish Cloud experienced. Indeed, his difficult and painful federal boarding-school experience encouraged him to struggle to end this policy and coauthor the Meriam Report of 1928, which documented the abuses of the federal boarding schools. The fact that Cloud's discussion of federal boarding-school policy was more open with Alaska Natives than in a missionary journal shows that he took off his mask when he wasn't speaking to the colonizer.

In contrast, while discussing his boarding-school experiences in his autobiography published in white missionary journal, he holds back. To satisfy his white Christian audience, he does not openly discuss his traumatic experiences. At the same time, he remains true to his own Native position by mentioning that a Native classmate died there, showing the doubleness of the narrative. When he was a little boy, a policeman came to his home to take his brother "to see some writing," in other words, to attend a government boarding school. Here Cloud discusses the dubious and nefarious tactics policemen used to trick Native children to accompany them to a federal boarding school. This instance represents another moment of subversion and critique of this settler-colonial policy, thus emphasizing his Native position. He remembers crying because he wished to be with his brother. He writes about how after two years he had forgotten his own Ho-Chunk language. He was there with Sioux, Omahas, Apaches, Potawatomis, Otoes, Arapahos, and Cheyennes. He forgot his language, he explains, because many Native children from other tribes surrounded him. He fails to mention that he was punished for speaking his tribal language, which was a very common practice in the boarding schools. His desire to not upset his white Christian audience, who would likely cringe when hearing boarding-school abuses, may explain this omission.

Cloud recounts other everyday events, such as fighting his classmate John Hunter (another Ho-Chunk and a very close friend), herding sheep, stealing grapes and cherries in the summer, going to the hospital with a splinter in his foot, and Fred Hensley dying at that school. His recounting the death of his Native classmate greatly shocked and disturbed me, as his granddaughter. It rings out as a moment in his Christian conversion narrative that is subversive, encouraging me to imagine the many Native children who suffered death and countless abuses in government boarding schools. In contrast, decades later, speaking to a Native audience, he was much more honest and open about his boarding-school experiences. While he was superintendent of the Umatilla Agency in 1941, during his address to other Bureau of Indian Affairs officials, he said, "Everything Indian was to be destroyed [in the boarding schools]. How well do I remember marching with a dozen other Indian lads half a day round and round in a room in the government school because we were talking our Native language."[25]

After two years in this school, his family came to take him home. He rode on the back of a horse behind his dad, without saying a word. He could not understand his dad, and his dad could not understand him, since he could not longer speak in Ho-Chunk. He emphasizes in his Christian-conversion story that in three weeks' time he remembered his Ho-Chunk language, and he never lost it for the rest of his life. By highlighting this very important fact in his story, he demonstrates his resistance to the federal government's goal to assimilate him. He also shows his opposition to the aspect of Christian doctrine that teaches Indian converts that their Native identity is pagan and thus not commensurate with a civilized, Christian standard. Soon after this, he went to the Winnebago Industrial School in Macy, Nebraska.[26]

Conversion to Christianity

While attending the Winnebago Industrial School, he converted to Christianity. Every Cross Day or Sunday, he would march with others to a white building with a cross on it. He liked marching there because he was a member of the school band. He even got to march at the head of the procession, playing his cornet. At these meetings (Sunday school), the teachers gave them cards with pictures on them and would tell them about God, the Great Spirit. One dark night, when he was thirteen, long after midnight, an officer of the school woke him up and told him to go downstairs, because a man wanted to see him. The man waiting for him was Rev. William T. Findley, a Presbyterian minister. The same man led the Sunday school meetings and used to visit his family at their log cabin and wigwam in the woods near the river. The previous Cross Day, he explains, the lesson had been about "Christ before Pilate," when Pilate was asked what he would do with Jesus. His teacher, Mrs. Findley, asked each of the Indian boys what they would do with Jesus. Cloud's answer was that he would like to be his friend, and this response encouraged Mr. Findley to call for him that memorable night. I find it odd that Cloud describes his Christian conversion as occurring in the middle of the night. Maybe he decided to set his conversion tale to occur late at night to add a dramatic flair. Otherwise, it seems suspicious and strange for Mr. Findley to call a small Native boy out of bed. Indigenous children most likely would have felt scared, wondering if something dreadful was going to happen to them, especially in the context of an Indian mission school where children were routinely physically punished.

Findley and my grandfather sat together. Findley told him that Jesus Christ had a "real claim" on his friendship. My grandfather reveals that a Native idea of friendship encouraged him to accept Christianity. Friendship making, explains my grandfather, is a "meaningful and very formal act among Indians." He learned that night that he would stand by Jesus, and Jesus would stand by him for the rest of his life. Thus, he accepted Christianity while relying on a Native belief about friendship. In other words, rather than rejecting Native ideas to accept Christianity, Ho-Chunk ideas were integral to his Christian conversion. This suggests that he accommodated Christianity while maintaining his Ho-Chunk core identity intact.[27] By the end of the night, he became what the others Indians at the school called a "preaching listener," a Native who accepted Christianity. In this way he combined an element of modernity, Christianity, with his Native identity.

His conversion to Christianity was not without challenges, however. He discusses how his family teased him and how his friends questioned his decision. Because of this conversion, he no longer played marbles for keeps. He joined a short-lived society called the Band of Mercy, which urged its members not to kill animals, causing more ridicule from the other Native children. His grandmother even warned him about the difficulties of becoming a Christian. She told him a story about a Christian

Native who found out after his death that he was not accepted in either the white or Indian afterlife. Even though Cloud faced many challenges to his Christian beliefs, he kept his faith strong.[28]

Shortly before my grandfather's conversion to Christianity, his mother, father, and grandmother all died in less than twelve months. I can only imagine how horribly difficult and traumatizing it must have been to become an orphan and lose three members of his very close family, one right after the other. My mother always told me that his family died from a flu epidemic that swept through the reservation during that time. Hearing how so many of my ancestors died around the same time shocked me as a young child. I remember picturing in my mind a horrific sight of my relatives getting ill and eventually dying after much suffering. It certainly makes sense that my grandfather would decide to convert to Christianity after the loss of so many members of his family. The notion of connecting to another friend, Jesus, must have felt comforting to a lonely, grief-stricken Ho-Chunk boy. After he lost his parents and grandparents, his beloved aunt, Alice Mallory, looked after him, and the local agency superintendent appointed John Nunn to be his guardian. The Mallory family, including the LaRose family, are our closest relatives, whom we always visit when we travel to Winnebago. And the "Mallory Song" is sung when we participate in honoring ceremonies on our reservation.

Santee Indian Mission School

Around 1898 or 1899 Cloud, along with seven other Winnebago boys, went to Santee Indian Mission School, a Presbyterian Indian boarding school, in northeastern Nebraska among the Sioux, one hundred miles away from home. After one week six of the Ho-Chunk boys ran way, and a week later the seventh boy told him that he was so homesick he could no longer stand being there. My grandfather struggled within himself about whether he should stay or go. Something greater than human power was at work in him, and he decided to stay.[29] At the same time, Cloud's discussion of how the other boys defied settler colonization and ran away is another place in his narrative that reflects his Native position.

In 1870 two Presbyterian missionaries, Thomas Williamson and Stephen Riggs, founded the Santee Indian Mission School. Their goal was to convert the Santee Sioux. By 1885 the school had eighteen buildings and more than 150 students. The school was unusual, since it differed from government boarding schools. Rather than teaching only vocational education, the school provided a general high-school curriculum. It offered courses in literature, history, music, and drawing.[30] Also, teachers at the school taught in Dakota, not just in English. This was a radical departure from government boarding schools where Indigenous children were punished for speaking their Native language. Riggs ignored government regulations requiring classroom instruction in English. Cloud credited the school for teaching him in Dakota, a Native language, which he learned quickly as a student there. The school newspaper, *Word Carrier*, or *Iapi Oave*, was published in English and Dakota. Cloud, who worked in the print shop, argued that he could set type faster in Dakota than in English.[31] As soon as he started school, he always dressed in a suit and a clean shirt unless he was working. He also read constantly. His white guardian, Nellie Nunn, used to say that he would lose his mind because he studied and read too much, and that he was five years ahead of his time.[32]

Santee Indian Mission School was in session from November through May. Back home in Winnebago, during the summers, there was work to be done for white farmers who had leased reservation land. Whites leasing Ho-Chunk land made it difficult for our people to survive, since it meant that most of the profits went to the white farmers. Cloud dug potatoes, threshed wheat, and shucked corn. Many years later he would tell his children that he was the best corn-husker in Nebraska. He also played baseball.[33]

Self-Help and Self-Support

The Santee mission school, according to Cloud, was where he read Samuel Smiles's book *Self-Help*, which, he wrote, changed his life. Samuel Smiles filled his book with biographies, not of the great heroes of the rich but of achievers who worked hard and never gave up on their ambitions. Smiles hoped to encourage the ordinary man to better himself. The book sold around twenty thousand copies in the first year of publication, fifty-five thousand copies after five years, and about one quarter million by the end of the century.³⁴ It is very likely that the vast majority of readers were men rather than women, especially since the biographies are all about men. It is, therefore, to men that Smiles delivers his message of hard work, self-denial, self-reliance, perseverance in the face of adversity, and a will to excel in business, industry, engineering, and the arts. Indeed, the primary purpose of the self-help ideal was to help the ordinary man become a self-made man. Smiles discusses the spirit of self-help as the root of all genuine growth in the individual. He also argues that the value placed on legislation as an agent for human advancement was overestimated and that, instead, the function of government is negative and restrictive rather than positive and active. After reading the book, Cloud discusses his resolution never to attend a government institution, to be self-supporting, and to earn his way through school.

In 1907 John M. Oskison, a Cherokee novelist and journalist who was an active member of the Society of American Indians, wrote that the public needed to recognize the emergence of a new Indian. This new Indian, he wrote, was capable of being self-supporting and could live off the reservation. Oskison emphasizes that there is a difference between the "modern Indian" and the "dirty beggar" who was formed by old conditions, such as the reservation system.³⁵ Cloud's use of the popular rhetoric of self-help was a creative strategy to align his Native identity with a positive image, the new Indian, who was not a dirty beggar but who was self-supporting, demonstrating his engagement with popular narratives of progress and modernity.

At Santee Indian Mission School, E. Jean Kennedy, a matron at the school, told Cloud about Mount Herman, a college-preparatory school for teenage boys. Kennedy had met Rev. Dwight L. Moody, who founded Mount Herman. It was a work-study school. Its mission was to help disadvantaged youth get ready for college. It had a strong Christian focus. Kennedy urged him to go, because Mount Herman could offer him a better education than Santee ever could. At this time sons of wealthy families, along with disadvantaged youth, who needed extra preparation to attend college, also attended the school.³⁶

Northfield Mount Herman School

On May 28, 1901, Henry Clarence Cloud filled out his application to the college-preparatory Northfield Mount Herman School. He answered questions about his goal in life ("Gospel missionary") and kind of education (under "Geography," he jotted down, "very little"). His medical certificate in his application packet said he was nineteen years old, five feet eight and one-quarter inches tall, 142 pounds, with no medical problems.[37]

Riggs from Santee wrote in support of his application, but in a condescending tone, commenting on his race. "Henry C. Cloud is an exceptionally bright and reliable Indian boy. He is an earnest and consistent Christian. He has made good progress in his studies and in the industrial classes. You would not expect in him the grade of advancement of a white boy of the best advantages, but I can say that he is much better than the average Indian."[38]

Findley also wrote in support of his application. "We have never seen anything amiss in him—he has stood the test of home life among his people, and that is a big thing to say. He is an intelligent young Christian of fine comprehension and splendid spirit. He is an Indian, but it is my opinion that few white boys of eighteen years surpass him in traits of character such as we most esteem. His ability is good as far as he has had opportunity to show development. Presumably everyone has a limit to ability and Indians sometimes show a limit sooner than the white race, but Dr. Riggs's judgment in that line is much better than mine as the lad has been under his instruction for three years."[39]

These two letters signal the racial and settler-colonial climate Cloud was living in. Native Americans were assumed to be inherently inferior to whites, lower on the social evolutionary ladder. Lewis Henry Morgan discusses notions of racial difference extensively in his 1877 influential book, *Ancient Society*. Morgan argues that all groups moved through two stages, savagery and barbarism, on their progress toward civilization, but they proceeded at very different rates. Relying on his universal theory of human evolution, Morgan argues that studying Native Americans could help one understand all of human history, because Indians' relatively slow rate of progress as compared to whites made them a living museum of human development.[40] Findley and Riggs seemed to share a racist assumption influenced by Morgan's social evolutionary theory, which Findley expresses directly. Indians show a limit to their ability sooner than whites. Whites surrounded Cloud. Whites believed in these racist discourses, which are linked to settler colonialism. Placing Natives lower on a social-evolutionary scale provided white settlers an excuse to take over Indigenous land, forcibly place us in Native boarding schools, and eliminate us culturally.[41] Cloud had to use his Ho-Chunk trickster strategies of camouflage and doubleness to not only survive but thrive.

Cloud left for Mount Hermon in 1902 before graduating from Santee Indian Mission School, with one hundred dollars sewn in his undershirt to guard against the dangers of traveling among white people. He feared that white people would steal his money.[42] Here is another place in his autobiographical narrative where he asserts his Native perspective and position, again showing the doubleness of his writing in a missionary journal.

Cloud's entrance examination demonstrated that he had some weaknesses. He passed the sections of the exam on the Bible, geography, penmanship, and spelling but failed English, grammar, arithmetic, and history. These difficulties were an indication of his schooling at Santee rather than his own personal lacking. His grade reports in his first year showed he had challenges, but his grades quickly improved, and he performed very well at this college-preparatory school. Math was always a tough field of study for him, but he did well in his Bible, history, and English classes. He took Greek, Latin, German, ancient history, European history, and physics. These kinds of classes were not taught at any school for Natives during this time.[43]

While at Mount Herman, Cloud could not return home for the holidays. He must have felt terribly lonely. During his first Christmas vacation, he was put to work. Mount Herman required all students to perform daily manual labor. He was told to dig a ditch fifteen feet deep for a water pipe. Cloud recounts,

> I was digging that ditch with pickaxe and shovel, and I felt sorry for myself. They put me in here to dig this ditch because I had no home to go to and I had to stay there. I had that spirit in my heart when one day

a young lad was placed beside me by the name of James McConaughy. [In 1946 McConaughy would became governor of Connecticut.] He lived on the campus; he did not need to go away to school; his father was one of the great teachers of the institution and they set him with me to dig the ditch. He didn't have to work in that ditch, and I began to revise my feeling. Perhaps they put this young fellow in with me to dig this ditch because there is a water pipe that we are laying here that will be a source of great joy to the whole community. It'll bring about contentment, health, and satisfaction to thousands of people in this neighborhood. . . . I wasn't placed in that ditch because I was an orphan lad, but because of the great blessing my job would result for an entire community. . . . He and I discovered the great secret of life in that ditch, the dignity of labor and its quality to bless all mankind, even though the job itself may be despised by the uncritical.[44]

Cloud told this story to those graduating Alaska Native students in 1949. His words give us an insight into how he saw the world. One lesson he taught these Native students was that one should view the world as half-full rather than half-empty. In other words, it is important to see the positives in one's experience rather than the difficulties. He also taught them the dignity of labor and its ability to teach people, whatever one's class status. In this story, however, his discussions of labor were not so much about individual self-improvement, a white idea, but rather about contributing to the overall community, which is a Native-oriented concept. Thus, he refashioned a Eurocentric notion about the importance of individual labor into a Native idea about the significance of work to contribute to the group as a whole. Indeed, contributing to Native community well-being is fundamental to a Ho-Chunk warrior identity. Thus, my grandfather combined a white concept about individual labor with his Ho-Chunk warrior identity, supporting the creation of a Native male modern identity.

This self-supporting theme continues. He discusses how he had to leave Mount Herman for one year to make enough money to pay his way. So far he had paid for his school with lease money from his reservation allotment; some assistance from his guardian, John Nunn; and some gifts from alumni from Mount Herman whom he had impressed.[45] He worked for an entire year on a farm in New Jersey to earn money. He learned to pay for what he received and came to understand the value of the dollar, the meaning of hard work, and the worth of time. These are all values that he discusses to prove he was closer to the "modern" Indian ideal than the "dirty beggar." They were a good camouflage for portraying himself as a "good" Indian, not a "bad," "dirty," "primitive," "lazy" Indian. As my grandfather followed a mule team all day long on this Jersey farm, he practiced his Greek conjugations. He wrote them on cards that he attached to his plow.

Self-Support and Self-Made Man

Being self-supporting is also inextricably linked to Cloud's assertion of his masculine power—a self-made man who rose from humble beginnings. In the middle of the market revolution of the early to mid-nineteenth century, the "self-made" man embodied economic success and personal achievement and was a new type of heroic, white American man. Benjamin Franklin and Horatio Alger Jr. were self-made men. This new archetype incorporated an individualistic spirit of self-interest. During the late nineteenth and early twentieth centuries, African American male leaders were also considered as examples of heroic masculinity. Frederick Douglass, Booker T. Washington, and W. E. B. Du Bois were viewed as heroic fighters for racial equality. Their heroism originated not only from their ability to rise above an impoverished childhood, but, even more important, from their public commitment to their racially defined communities.[46]

Similarly, by emphasizing his humble beginnings and hardworking nature, Cloud appropriated the rhetoric of the self-made man. Cloud's use of the self-made man could possibly act as another Ho-Chunk trickster strategy—a protective mask and a modern identity that could make him acceptable for the colonizer, a good Indian, despite his dealing with horrible racism. At the same time, he could hide any Ho-Chunk warrior subversive thoughts or actions. He was also incorporating aspects of a modern identity that could give him power in the public sphere. In this way he asserted a Native heroic masculinity during a time when the U.S.

Western novel had greatly reduced Native male power. This masculine power was encapsulated by two extremes: those who remain standing and those who fall down. The prone were portrayed as nonmen, a category that included generally Natives, Mexicans, small children, and women. Even though Natives defeated George Armstrong Custer, for example, he is always portrayed as dying on his feet, emphasizing his white male masculinity.[47] Cloud's assertion of his self-made masculine character was a creative and smart strategy to increase his masculine power so that he would not be viewed as a Native nonman.

Cloud lived during a time when the white idea of masculinity was changing. Industrialization had transformed the labor force from a mostly agricultural and domestic industry to an economy where men departed their households daily to work jobs created by others. New masculine qualities, such as strength of character and competitiveness, were needed together with more old-fashioned personal characteristics, such as sobriety, honesty, politeness, industry, and diligence. As white-collar, corporate labor entailed less and less of the old-fashioned qualities, men spent time in the gym to build muscles, turned to sports, and joined fraternal organizations, all of which encouraged more physical, adventurous notions of masculinity than those needed by their workplace.[48]

Cloud's story of finishing his education against great odds and his transformation from "savage" to "civilized" meant that he was a self-made man. His "exotic" past as a member of a tribe and a warrior pointed to his inherently masculine character. White men during this time romanticized the frontier and wanted to be physically strong outdoorsmen. Theodore Roosevelt, for example, changed his rather effeminate appearance to look more like an adventurous frontiersman. Thus, Cloud could fit within these popular notions of masculinity better than most. His Native American features could remind whites that even though he dressed in white man's clothing, he was also a "savage" and a "warrior" with physical and spiritual capacities.[49]

At Mount Herman Cloud excelled not only in academics but also in sports. He was on the football team in 1905. Unfortunately, he became injured. He hurt his shoulder and broke his arm and nose. Even so, he was also on the baseball team in 1905 and 1906. He finished second

in the hundred-yard dash during Mount Herman's track-and-field day on August 7, 1905.[50] Cloud's involvement in athletics in an all-white college-preparatory school was another strategy to be viewed as a *real* man instead of a Native nonman. At the turn of the century, white masculinity relied not only on the image of the frontiersman but also on stereotypical notions of Native masculinity. White men embraced an ideal that stressed physical prowess, including stereotypical notions of Native warrior identity, while creating a linkage between white supremacy and male dominance. Custer, for example, embodied masculine notions of a warrior and a masculine drive to conquer and succeed.[51] Cloud's involvement in sports could fit into the popular Native male stereotype of a man with innate physical prowess. At the same time, his athleticism could be viewed as his attempt to reappropriate the male prowess imagery stolen from stereotypical Native notions of masculinity—and in the process increase his own masculine power.

Cloud's participation in sports was also a way for him to create a Ho-Chunk–centric hub and connect to his Ho-Chunk identity while being away from his tribe in Winnebago, Nebraska. Even though he lived away from our people, every time he played sports it could stimulate memories of playing baseball back home on the Winnebago Reservation. Cloud's involvement in athletics at a white school was in fact a continuation of his reservation athletic activities and therefore a strategy for him to feel a connection to his Ho-Chunk tribe and his people. Being involved in sports was also a traditional Ho-Chunk activity. Native Americans have been involved in physical activity and games since before colonization. Lacrosse, for example, is a game that the Haudenosaunee (Iroquois) and other northeast tribes, as well as the Ho-Chunk, played. The Ho-Chunk also used bows and arrows to compete against one another, a game now named archery. They played the game "Chunkey," in which a circular "chunkey stone" was rolled over the ground or ice. Many players flung spears to try to establish where the stone would stop. The nearest player, whose spear did not strike the stone, won the game. These games were

Fig. 2. Cloud, possibly in his late twenties, having his picture taken holding a camera, with a beaming smile on his face. Photograph courtesy of the Cloud family.

important for the Ho-Chunk because they improved dexterity, hand-eye coordination, and perseverance, all talents that were essential for hunting and battle.[52]

While at Mount Herman, Cloud occupied the dormitory officer position of Crossley Hall in 1904. He had to ensure that his fellow students completed their studies. He performed well as a leader of his dorm, and his peers respected him. His position as a leader of his white peers points to his unusual ability as a Native young man to assert his masculine power in a white environment. Cloud also participated in the Young Men's Christian Association Orchestra and served as YMCA district worker for three years. He was interested in politics, joining the Good Government Club and many service organizations.[53] His involvement in sports, studious nature, outgoing personality, excellent Ho-Chunk oratory skills, and identities as a Christian and Ho-Chunk warrior—which taught him to contribute to the well-being of the community—were all aspects of his character that might have contributed to his development as a leader in an all-male, white school. Cloud's sense of identity was complicated and complex—Christian, athlete, Ho-Chunk, warrior, self-made man, and a good student.

When he graduated from Mount Herman in 1906, he was the president of his class and gave the commencement address. In this speech he discusses the importance of work "as essential to the development of character, whether that work is digging in the ditch, working in the field or in the shop." He ends his address, "We believe that the purpose for which this school was founded was that every young man who comes within its walls should learn to make education and culture, however important they may be in themselves, subservient to the one purpose of uplifting our fellow man."[54] In this way Cloud engages in popular white rhetoric about work and uplift, emphasizing the importance of labor to build character and showing his use of dominant discourses to increase his power as a Native young man. Cloud's position as president of his graduating class is remarkable in itself, especially since during this time the public was not certain whether Native Americans were smart enough to be college material. As already mentioned, whites viewed Indians as childlike, less intelligent, and lower on the social evolutionary ladder than whites. Cloud's statement as graduating class president weighed in on an important debate of his day. He too, as a member of the Native race and alongside his white classmates, deserved to be fully educated and to be involved in the United States' changing civic culture. He was also asserting Natives' right to be educated and belong in the public sphere, his right to cultural citizenship.

Yale University

After Cloud graduated from Northfield Mount Herman School, Yale University accepted him, and he entered as a freshman in 1906. He studied English, German, Greek, history, and mathematics. When he first arrived on campus, he was invited to the Yale president's house for a freshmen reception. Even though he had attended Mount Herman, he had never attended a white-oriented activity at an elite university in the home of the president. Because he wanted to show his respect, he rented a tuxedo, but to his dismay he was the only one so dressed up. When he met the president, he bowed very low to show his respect to such an important person. The president, seeing that my grandfather felt awkward, told a group of freshmen that they too should have worn a tuxedo. During another dinner at the president's house, his fellow freshmen did wear tuxedos, while he wore a suit. It was very difficult for him, explained my aunt Marion Hughes, because even though he had gone to Mount Herman, he was not accustomed to Yale's white upper-middle-class social customs.[55]

Cloud told our family other stories about his Yale experiences. He was a great teller of tales and had a wonderful sense of humor. Indeed, his children were not always certain whether he was telling the truth, because he loved to mix fact and fiction. He attributed his storytelling ability to his grandmother, because in the winter she told them all of the traditional Ho-Chunk stories, as already mentioned. His children used to ask him to tell these Ho-Chunk stories, and he would never tell them until after they told him a story first. This was perfect training for them, according to my Aunt Marion, so they could develop their ability to remember the stories, understand underlying meanings, and tell them to others. He learned this approach from his grandmother and passed it

Fig. 3. Henry Cloud at Yale University. Photograph courtesy of the Cloud family.

down to them.[56] His telling Ho-Chunk tales to his children demonstrates that he maintained his Ho-Chunk identity. Even though he worked hard to learn white culture, he, according to the Cloud family, never forgot his Ho-Chunk culture and its values. Every time he told Ho-Chunk stories to his children, he created a Ho-Chunk–centric virtual hub—not one based in a geographic location but a hub that could be transported anywhere Cloud traveled. And, ultimately, this transportability challenged settler colonialism's attempts to root Native culture and identity to a distinct geographic location.

Another story he told was set in the woods in New Haven, where Yale University is located. While he was walking, he heard a faint voice, so he kept trying to get nearer to it. He finally came upon a fallen log. It was open at the ends, and the voice was coming out from that log. He spoke up and said, "What seems to be the matter?" The voice responded, "Well, I crawled into this log, and I got stuck, and I can't get out." It continued, "This is no place for a Harvard man." And Cloud said, "Well, it's too bad. I'm not a Harvard man, but I'm a Yale man, and I'd be glad to try to help you." And the voice responded, "You don't have to help me." When he heard I was a Yale man, he somehow shrank [his body] and crawled out [from the log]."[57] There was a sense of rivalry between Yale and Harvard men, and Cloud's story pokes fun at Harvard men. His story also shows his ability to place his Yale experiences into a Ho-Chunk storytelling tradition, emphasizing how the Harvard student shrank his body, an example of shape-shifting. Thus, rather than erasing his Ho-Chunk identity while he learned Eurocentric culture, he accommodated Eurocentric experiences into a Ho-Chunk framework. Further, his Ho-Chunk humorous, trickster storytelling abilities helped him survive and be successful. Cloud could share funny stories with others and get them to laugh and connect with him in Yale's alien competitive, white environment.

Cloud recounted yet another story that included his train trip to New York City with his Yale roommate, Duncan [surname unknown]. On their way back, they were in the smoking car, because Duncan smoked a pipe. This woman was in the same car and reached over and grabbed Duncan's pipe out of his mouth and proceeded to throw it out the window. She had a little dog, so Duncan grabbed her dog and threw it out the window.

They stopped at the next station, got out, looked back down the railroad track, and there was the dog, running toward them with Duncan's pipe in his mouth![58] Cloud's traditional Ho-Chunk upbringing taught him how to tell humorous stories and jokes, mixing fact and fiction.

In the speech to graduating Alaska Native Mount Edgecumbe students in 1949, Cloud discussed his experience at Yale University, where he became the first "full-blood" Native American to graduate with a bachelor's degree in 1910 and a master's degree in 1914. He recounted,

> As I entered [Yale] I began to work my way through the institution. I didn't have any money. I entered it with only 60 dollars in my pocket and they required in those days something over 1000 dollars a year. I had the confidence that laboring with my hands, doing all sorts of jobs, waiting on tables, doing jobs for the rich people, selling Navajo rugs, selling all kinds of articles to the student body, [and] selling tickets at the great university games that I could somehow make ends meet. When I graduated I was still 60 dollars in debt, but having paid all the other expenses from my own labors . . . I went into all kinds of athletics. . . . I gained confidence because I could compete in athletics. I gained confidence because I could compete in oratory and debate. And one of my competitors was the president William Taft's son [Robert]. . . . When I stood up against him, debated against him and won prizes on the same platform with a man whose father had been President of the United States before, I began to feel a welling up of confidence in myself. Why I began to realize that I can do things just as this man can and somehow my spirit became ready for the battle or any sort of a battle that might come my way.[59]

Cloud describes himself as a hard worker and self-supporting, challenging dominant ideas that Natives were lazy. He discusses selling Native cultural objects to support himself financially. Native Americans selling cherished cultural objects, unfortunately, was a common practice, especially when they were poor.[60] He quickly learned how precious Native artifacts were to curious whites, and he used it to help support himself.[61] Even so, it was difficult for me, as his granddaughter, to learn that he decided to sell these precious Ho-Chunk cultural objects to pay for his expenses as a college student. This self-supporting theme is inextricably linked to Cloud's proclamation of his masculine influence as a self-made man of importance who came from humble beginnings.[62]

Similarly, Cloud indigenized the idea of the self-made man, becoming a heroic fighter for Natives and helping him increase his power in the public sphere during a time when white society viewed Native men as nonmen.[63] The passage quoted earlier also emphasizes Cloud's prowess as an orator and a debater, which was grounded in his Ho-Chunk grandmother's storytelling and oratory training. He carried his Ho-Chunk oratory skills from his grandmother's training all the way to Yale. And he honed them by rehearsing speeches and creating arguments. His public-speaking competition with the president's son improved his confidence and prepared him for "battle," highlighting his Native masculinity and warrior identity. He used the word *battle* to defeat his rich, white male adversaries, demonstrating his verbal and intellectual abilities and defying dominant racist notions that Natives were inarticulate, stupid, and slow. He emphasized his poverty as compared to Yale's rich white community, while asserting that his lower economic status did not interfere with his attendance or success at an elite, white college. In this way he attempts to motivate Alaska Native students, who were likely poor, to attend college, even when college must have seemed out of reach.

Mary Roe, a Colonial Mother

During his freshman year he met Mary Roe, a white missionary who addressed the Yale student body regarding the subject of American Indians. She spoke of thousands of Native Christians in Oklahoma. This excited Cloud, because he had not met many Native Christians in his life. She invited him to travel to Oklahoma so he could see these Christian Indians for himself. There he met her husband, Walter. Because this couple had a son who died in infancy and, had he lived, would have been about Cloud's age, they decided informally to adopt him. He took on their last name as his middle name.[64] Dr. Roe had a goal to establish an interdenominational Christian school for the purpose of training Christian Native leaders from the different tribes, but he died before realizing this goal. Cloud decided to work to complete his objective and proceeded to found an early college-preparatory Christian high school for Native young men and boys.

Mary Roe, unfortunately, used settler-colonial tactics to begin her relationship with him during his first year at Yale University. These maneuvers involved flattery and sympathy to attempt to cause a psychological barrier between him and the memory of his Ho-Chunk grandmother. She also took advantage of his loneliness and intense sadness caused by living among whites and away from his extended Ho-Chunk family and tribe.[65] In this way Mary Roe, as a representative of settler colonialism, attempted to extinguish Cloud's sense of his Ho-Chunk kinship system.

Mary Roe illustrates her maternal role in a 1909 letter to Cloud. Colonialism is apparent:

> Oh, Henry, if I had you here this very minute I believe I could make you see the strength and power of that marvelous other love which has been born in my soul and is gathering up all the repressed motherhood and instinct which have always been part of my nature but have never been given outlet. . . . I know I am a changed woman with a love for *all* little children, a yearning that is almost pain over unmothered boys, all because the picture of *my* beloved little son [Cloud] running barefoot ragged and neglected possibly around and around a stump crying with natural fright as the arrows whizzed by that dear little head amidst the laughter of drunken revelry. Darling, I will make up to you and for your sake to every unhappy child for all those children's sorrows.[66]

Mary Roe details all the repressed "mother-love" within her, which, she argues, requires an outlet. She then discusses her role as a mother to Cloud, a Ho-Chunk and an orphan. She describes Cloud as "ragged and neglected." She presumes Ho-Chunks are "drunken," violent, and careless. She assumes that Cloud was "neglected" by his people. In this way she privileges her own competence as a white woman to protect and nurture Native children over the Ho-Chunk peoples' ability. Indeed, she assumes that Ho-Chunks are not only neglectful but also indifferent of our children's welfare. Her depiction arises from her white imagination, since Cloud had a deeply loving and affectionate Ho-Chunk family. This colonial, "maternal" assumption must have been trying and agonizing for Cloud, who cherished and valued his Ho-Chunk people. According to Margaret Jacobs, white women used these kinds of gendered settler-colonial assumptions when they forcibly removed Native children and put them in federal boarding schools.[67] These kinds of colonial assumptions are also inextricably linked to the white adoption of Native children.

As I sat next to my son, Gilbert, in Yale's archive, reading Mary Roe's letters to my grandfather, I felt that I was witnessing the negative impact of a very intimate, gendered aspect of settler colonialism on a close family member. The impact occurred not in the past but in the present, and I had no power to stop it. Even though I knew that I could not change what had happened in my family's history, I hoped that writing about it could help my family and others understand the challenges our ancestor faced. I also remembered that my beloved mother, Woesha, sat in the very same archive and read through hundreds of distressing colonial letters. She would call me after spending a long day in the archive, crying and telling me how horribly difficult it was to read the letters. While listening to her, I had no idea that I would follow in her footsteps and travel to the same archives she visited. As I sat in the hard wooden chair in the Sterling Library, I felt my mom's spiritual presence. It was helpful to have frequent phone calls with my Ho-Chunk colleague, Amy Lonetree, who understood my pain, and with my sister, Mary, who supported my son traveling with me.

Furthermore, Mary Roe shared romantic advice with Cloud related to race, class, and gender—adding another layer of settler colonialism for Cloud to deal with. She treated him as an exotic Native man. She wrote that Bessie, his white "cousin," Mary Roe's niece, was angry with him because he had answered her correspondence by wrongly dispatching a telegram rather than a letter.[68] In contrast, "well-taught" white girls, she explained, knew how men should relate to them, while the girls he was used to, "Indian girls" and "half-educated [white] girls," did not comprehend how to act properly. Mary Roe put Cloud higher on the social evolutionary ladder than both "Indian girls" and "half-educated [white] girls." She pushed him to locate "appropriate" companions who appreciated proper social graces. By inspiring him to find a suitable white, upper-class woman for friendship and possibly marriage, she again tried to cut his ties to a Ho-Chunk sense of kinship. She cautioned that Vassar girls were attracted to him only because of his race, not recognizing his intelligence, good-looking features, and captivating nature. Instead, she emphasized only his "exotism" as an Indigenous young man. She urged him to rely on his "exotic" characteristics to further his Christian mission. Rather than deciding to abide by Mary's romantic recommendations, which did not acknowledge the possibility of a well-educated Native woman, in 1916 Cloud married my Ojibwe grandmother, Elizabeth Bender Cloud, reinforcing his Native kinship ties.[69]

While Cloud became friends with the Roes, he also confronted power dynamics in his relationship with them. The Roes were upper-middle-class, white, Christian missionaries. He was a Ho-Chunk man born in poverty on the Winnebago Reservation. His decision to become an "adopted" member of a white missionary family put him immediately into a position of subservience. Mary Roe, for example, treated him as a boy, not as a man, even though he was in his midtwenties. She wrote to Cloud, "My own, my very own, dear boy—a man but to Mother still a boy."[70] She felt it was her role to train him to be a proper Christian man, including telling him to control his inherent "animal nature" to master his sex drive—a nature that was distinctly Native and lower on the social evolutionary scale as compared to whites. Using guilt and continual discussions of her love in her letters, she interfered with his relationships with other women and encouraged him to be emotionally dependent on her.[71] For example, when Cloud discussed his affection for Ethel Hyde, a white woman, and her liking of him, Mary wrote him, saying she "would give much to take your black head right [in] my arms and talk it all over." Her racial comment places Cloud in a subservient role and asserts her power in their relationship. She also wrote "who [what white woman] will sacrifice for your people, will take them with you, as their own," implying that she was the only white woman who ever would.[72] She also recounted a discussion she had with another woman about Ethel. According to Mary Roe, that woman described Ethel as not "charitable" or "loving," as well as "undeveloped, unsettled, even superficial."[73] Mary Roe's controlling behavior and paternalism allude to her belief that she was higher on the social evolutionary ladder and, thus, had the right to cross proper boundaries and interfere in the adult Cloud's romantic and emotional life.

At the same time, Cloud emphasized his masculinity and sense of strength to Mary Roe. For example, he described his attendance at a Thanksgiving alumni celebration at Mount Herman in a letter to her. The principal asked him to speak for all the alumni. While introducing him as a typical Mount Herman young man, the principal stressed Cloud's birth on a reservation, without any advantages. In his retelling of his experience to Mary Roe, Cloud asserts himself as a self-made man of importance, challenging Mary Roe's emasculation of him, treating him as a child, not as a proud Ho-Chunk man.[74]

The Roes' Christian socialization involved time management, piety, guilt, and the superiority of Christianity over other religions, such as the Ho-Chunk Medicine Lodge and the peyote religion. Cloud's antagonism with the Ho-Chunk Medicine Lodge and the peyote religion contributed to his feelings of loneliness. He had arguments with his Ho-Chunk uncle Arthur Cassiman, a follower of peyote, while he was working as a missionary on the Winnebago Reservation.[75] Because there were so few Christians living on the Winnebago Reservation when he started as a missionary there, he had few supporters. As his granddaughter, I was saddened to learn that he viewed Christianity as the only true religion, a colonial belief that followed his white, Christian training. In contrast, his daughter, my mother, had great respect for the peyote religion, the Medicine Lodge, the Sun Dance, and all other Native ceremonial traditions.

Cloud was especially vulnerable to his adopted white family's influence because he was an orphan and wanted desperately to have a mother and father again. He suffered horribly upon the death of his Ho-Chunk mother, father, and grandmother. He wrote to Mary Roe, "Since my mother of flesh and blood left me no one has seen my tears. They have been shed unseen. But you [Mary Roe] have seen them, because you have entered my innermost life."[76] In this letter Cloud discusses how he let down his protective mask, becoming vulnerable and expressing his emotions to Mary Roe. However, to open up emotionally in a settler-colonial relationship was, unfortunately, dangerous and must have taken a tremendous emotional toll.

Cloud performed a "good" Indian identity for whites, usually keeping his inner Ho-Chunk warrior self hidden and protected. His doubleness must have been excruciating at times, to camouflage his identity, while whites racialized him, treated him as lower on the social evolutionary scale, and saw him as a child, not a full-grown man. Because of power dynamics, Cloud would have to withhold his true thoughts and feelings—especially as he relied on the Roes for loans to pay his college education. Whites surrounded Cloud, so he had to see the world through their lens for his survival, which likely caused internal confusion and emotional trauma. The Roes' socialization of Cloud to have a settler-colonial view of Christianity, placed above Ho-Chunk spiritual practices and traditions, caused arguments between Cloud and his Ho-Chunk uncle, Arthur Cassiman, and potentially caused distance between them.

Fortunately, my grandmother, Elizabeth Bender Cloud, a White Earth Ojibwe, whom he married in 1916, helped him develop proper boundaries between himself and his white adoptive mother. Indeed, Cloud strengthened his Native kinship ties and married a strong and powerful Ojibwe woman. Elizabeth was a fluent speaker of Ojibwe, and her mother, Mary Razier, taught her to be independent. After my grandparents were married in 1916, Elizabeth wrote a letter to Mary Roe. She understood that Mary was very possessive of Henry and had difficulty accepting Elizabeth as his wife. She wrote, "I realize that losing a son has not come without a struggle and not without a bitter fight, but Henry belongs to you as much as he ever did." By offering to share Henry with Mary Roe, Elizabeth was also reminding Mary Roe of her pivotal role as his wife. In writing, "I shall not allow him to forget you and he never will," she emphasizes her power to influence Henry's feelings for Mary Roe.[77] As a result of my grandmother's positive impact, Henry's emotional dependence on Mary transformed into a relationship with more appropriate boundaries.[78] Here Elizabeth's diplomacy and cautiousness is likely an indication of settler-colonial power dynamics and Cloud's reliance on the Roes' for loans and the Roes' connection to a powerful, white, wealthy network that helped him found a high school, a Christian preparatory school for Native young men and boys.

Even though Cloud faced power dynamics in regard to gender, race, and class within his white adopted family, he was able to assert his distinct position. For example, he struggled to earn money to pay for his education and, as a result, the Roes offered him loans for his college expenses. Cloud wrote a letter to Walter Roe, outlining all of his bills, asking his adoptive father if his parents had paid for his college education. In his response, Walter answered in the affirmative that his father had paid for his college fees. He then wrote that Cloud could wait to pay Mary Roe back. Cloud's question emphasizes his subservient role, not a biological son, who deserved money as gifts, which likely motivated Walter Roe to give him extra time to pay off his loan.[79]

Why was Cloud so willing to be informally adopted into a white missionary family? One must remember the period and how difficult it must have been for him to succeed at Yale as the only Native American. Cloud's connection to whites made sense during this racist time. It must have allowed him to gain power and become successful in a white environment. There was not the strong Indigenous network that exists today, supporting Native college students, including Indigenous professors, staff, college-support programs, or available scholarships and other resources. Cloud faced continual racializing and emasculating dominant discourses, and he lived far away from his Ho-Chunk family and tribe. And so an alliance with white missionaries, who were connected to influential white reform groups, provided Cloud with a white network and reliable financial resources. Cloud told my mother and her sisters about his class anguish, like feeling awkward when he showed up in a tuxedo instead of a suit. The Roes could teach him how to blend into white upper-class culture, so that he would not have to feel so awkward. Furthermore, the Roes were Christian missionaries, a role he respected and wanted to emulate. His white informal adoption helped him lessen his feelings of loneliness, after the loss of his own mother, father, and grandmother. At the same time, this adoption could be understood through a Ho-Chunk cultural lens. When a child dies in a Ho-Chunk family, one will adopt another child to fill his or her place. Later in life, this is what Cloud did when his own son died at three years old. Following Ho-Chunk tradition, he adopted Jay Russell Hunter, the son of his Ho-Chunk friends John and Etta Hunter. Cloud's "taking the place" of the Roes' son, who died in infancy, made sense from a Ho-Chunk perspective.

Leslie Marmon Silko's novel *Gardens in the Dunes* provides some insight into Cloud's adoption into a white family.[80] A white couple holds "captive" an Indian girl, Indigo. In this story, Indigo does not become white. Thus, Silko reverses the usual captivity narrative in which Indians steal whites and these whites "go Native." Indigo travels to Europe with this white couple and learns about European culture, while maintaining her Native identity. Similarly, the Roes taught Cloud much about white culture. At the same time, Native culture and my grandfather fascinated the Roes. For example, the Roes hired seventy men and women to make beadwork, bows and arrows, tepees, and ornamental pouches.[81] Mary Roe wore a Native American buckskin dress. "Playing Indian," argues Philip Deloria, helps whites construct an American identity, displacing Natives as the true Indigenous people.[82] It also contributes to whites getting in touch with a savage freedom that Indians represent. By adopting Cloud, Mary Roe could finally play the role of mother, even though Cloud was a grown Ho-Chunk man in his twenties. It also brought her and her husband closer to a fascinating "savage other," whose cultural relics they wanted to preserve.

Cloud not only kept his Ho-Chunk identity strong but also taught the Roes Ho-Chunk beliefs. Indeed, Cloud adopted Walter Roe into his tribe's Thunderbird Clan, which challenged conservative Christian notions that his Ho-Chunk cultural ways were pagan. In a letter to Walter Roe, Cloud discusses that they must keep his adoption secret, because members of the mescal religion, now called the Native American Church, would say they were practicing pagan ideas.

> I am taking the privilege of sending you what I consider your very adoption into the bird [Thunderbird] clan of the Winnebagoes [Ho-Chunks]. The totem is the eagle. As you will see he stands in the midst of sleet and hail, defiant, and confident. . . . He is the king of birds. If I publicly adopt you . . . the mescal followers would laugh us to derision as reactionaries for they now consider such acts . . . as heathenism and obsolete. As a recognized and true member of the Bird [Thunderbird] clan of the Winnebagoes . . . "Hochunk" "The Big Voice," I "Wonagalohunka" the "Chief of the Place of Fear," herewith adopt you head, scalp lock, and body into the warrior clan.

This adoption shows that Cloud was not an empty vessel who lost his Ho-Chunkness while learning white culture. Quite the contrary, Cloud adopted Walter Roe to be a member of his Ho-Chunk clan and in the process taught Walter Ho-Chunk cultural ways.[83]

Cloud also gave his adoptive white family Ho-Chunk names, including Mary Roe and Bessie (Elizabeth) Page, his adopted cousin. He wrote a letter to Mary Roe and gave her a list of possible Ho-Chunk names and asked her to choose one.[84] He wrote a similar letter to Elizabeth Page: "I've got a lot of names for you. I submit them. You can choose the one you like. The first one's nearest to 'gift-to-God'—'Hi nook who kaw chunk ka,' means 'Consecrated Woman.' It's a regular Indian name. 'Wah cho gi ni wiu ga,' meaning 'leader' (women). 'Hamb goo mah ni wiu ga' meaning—'Coming dawn.' 'Wah nik shoo jay wiu ga'—meaning 'Red bird.' 'Ho chunk ki wiuga,' meaning 'Winnebago woman.'"[85]

Thus, Cloud transformed his white adoptive nuclear family into a Ho-Chunk sense of an extended family. Cloud not only gave his white extended family Ho-Chunk names but also told them Ho-Chunk stories.[86] He spent much time with Mary Roe's relatives while he lived on the East Coast. Rather than traveling to Oklahoma to be with Walter and Mary Roe during Christmas, he spent his winter vacation with the Pages, and he saw them on weekends when he was a student at Yale. Upon his death, my grandmother, Elizabeth, wrote to Bessie Page and told her how much her beloved Henry appreciated Bessie and her extended family.[87]

It is a wonder that Cloud, as the only Native American at Yale University, not only survived but excelled in an all-white, highly competitive environment such as this. Letters in the Roe Family Papers show that he supported his Ho-Chunk identity and culture, which helped him survive and succeed. Cloud connected to his sense of Ho-Chunkness by using both geographic and virtual Native hubs. His creation of Native hubs included changing his white adoptive family into a Ho-Chunk sense of an extended family.

Cloud transformed the woods around Yale into another Native hub, a geographic location where he could rejuvenate himself as a Ho-Chunk person. His connection to nature brought a sense of his Ho-Chunkness into an alien environment while living away from his family and tribe:

The other day I went into the woods to be alone. I found the loneliest spot of all the places I had visited. At one place I found a wet spot. Last autumn's leaves were laden with such moisture. I thought some spring must be beneath. The next I heard something beating the wet leaves as if it were a tiny switch. Looking around and up I saw a branch of a tree some fifty feet high and drops were coming from the branch. The next thing I did was to sprawl out my legs, bend back with my face straight up and mouth wide open; the drops splashed into tiny sprays on the end of my nose, cheeks and eyes before they found my wide-open mouth. In this way I drank a lot of it. I was on a ridge and the sun was just setting. It was a new sunset to me. The great fiery ball sank into the naked arms of some popular trees. . . . These two little experiences cheered me up for a whole week.[88]

In this moment drinking the water dripping from the trees and witness-ing the beauty of a sunset, my grandfather invokes the power of the hub by transporting a sense of home and his Ho-Chunkness into the woods thousands of miles away from his tribal homelands. Cloud used the trees, the water, and a vibrant sunset as a protector and a healer, a portrayal that differs greatly from colonial narratives of the past. From my grandfather's point of view, nature was not to be possessed but relied on in times of stress and disorientation. He imagined nature not as an object to be developed and tamed but rather as a place to heal. In this way, too, he claimed the woods as his own, a home away from home, where he gained a foothold, a sense of belonging, and rootedness in a time of uncertainty. This connection recharged and strengthened him to continue. At the same time, one could argue that the water provided him with a spiritual moment of cleansing, not only from a Ho-Chunk perspective but also from a Christian one. The use of water in baptism is integral to one's Christian rebirth. The water could have helped him reconnect not only to his Ho-Chunk but also to his Christian identity.

Another way he maintained his Ho-Chunkness while at Yale was by constantly telling others Ho-Chunk stories, an example of Native hub making that is not necessarily tied to a geographic location, a virtual hub. As a college student, Cloud shared his Ho-Chunk culture by telling traditional Ho-Chunk stories to white audiences for their delight and for a price. He used this money to help pay for his education. He certainly must have known that sharing his Ho-Chunk knowledge was a way to become popular in an all-white environment. It was a strategy for him to use his cultural difference by playing on dominant notions of himself as a tourist curiosity, a commodity, and an exotic Indigenous man for his own goals and objectives.

While Cloud was the first "full-blood" Native American to graduate from Yale University, in June 1910 there was not much recognition of his feat in the local newspapers. As his granddaughter, I am amazed at his accomplishment. He was the only Native American attending this elite university at the time. A sea of white students, who came from radically different class experiences and backgrounds, surrounded him. Even so, he was popular with his peers. They selected him to be a member of the Elihu Club, a prestigious secret society. He won second place in the Ten Eyck speaking contest. As a result, he was named the best orator on campus. Because of all of these accomplishments, the local New Haven paper named him as one of the three most interesting students in 1910 and singled him out as the most prominent man in the class of 1910.[89]

The speech he gave that won him second place in the Ten Eyck contest, "Missions to the American Indians," was published in the *Yale Courant*. He spoke in terms that whites would find pleasing, while embedding subversive critique in the narrative, another example of Cloud's double-ness. He begins his published essay speaking on behalf of a vanishing race, supporting a white rhetoric that Indians are indeed vanishing and supporting settler colonialism. He then inserts his own Native perspective, critical of whites: "Civilization, sure of its divine right, has extended the hand of fellowship to those outside its pale, only to let fall the mailed fist of the oppressor."[90] Then he switches back to white rhetoric" "Here in their feather and paint are gathered a thousand Indians who have gone back to the gloom of paganism. . . . With weird chant, swaying to the wild rhythm of that strange music, the long line takes up its barbaric march." At the end of the essay, he asks for more Christian missions, not more soldiers or government agents, to improve Natives' everyday existence. Unfortunately, calling for additional Christian missions was in support of settler colonialism, as Christianity represented assimilation of Natives into white notions of gender, sexuality, marriage, and hetero-patriarchal notions of the nuclear family.[91] While Cloud most likely is arguing for Natives' lives being "saved" in a physical sense, his discussing more Christian missions supported Natives potentially vanishing from a gendered, sexual, cultural, and identity perspective, supporting settler colonialism. Cloud uses white rhetoric to create a speech pitched to a white audience and still manages to include a short burst of Native critique to reach his goal, winning second place.

Walter Roe encouraged Cloud to speak about a Native topic when he was working on his speech for the Ten Eyck oratory contest. Walter thought an Indigenous topic would be more warmly received than a non-Native topic.[92] It points to Walter encouraging Cloud to perform a role as an "exotic" Native man for whites to receive him positively. Given his many years of experience dealing with whites, Cloud taught his children not to be "show Indians," Native Americans who performed Indianness without any substance. Teaching his children how to survive among whites shows his Ho-Chunk position. My aunt Marion was once put in this role her father warned her about. She was supposed to stand onstage in a buckskin dress, while a white person sang a stereotypical Native love song into a microphone. She vowed never to perform this kind of role again.

Being the only Native American at Yale definitely had its costs. He told a story to his children about his election to the Elihu Club. When his Yale roommate, Duncan, found out that my grandfather was elected and not him, he kept repeating, "What have you done? What have you ever done?" Duncan was very upset, because he had not been selected that year, and, as a result, he was trying to downgrade him. Cloud told his children he was not worried about getting elected into the Elihu Club, a highly prestigious organization and one extremely difficult to be accepted into, and didn't fully understand his roommate's disappoint-ment.[93] This example shows how he encountered disrespect by dealing with a roommate who did not value his abilities or accomplishments and alludes to how competitive Yale could be. It also points to how he experienced Yale from a distinctly Native perspective.

Auburn Seminary, Yale Master's Degree, and Society of American Indians

Cloud enrolled in seminary at Oberlin College in Ohio. Because Cloud had many ties with people on the East Coast, he decided to leave Oberlin College and attend Auburn Seminary in Auburn, New York. This school would enable him to become an ordained Presbyterian minister. Later in life he told his children that he learned to relate the training there to his own Ho-Chunk background. He had a dim view of missionaries who cut Natives off from their unique culture, attempting to force Natives to forget ourselves as distinct people.[94] He graduated from Auburn in the spring of 1913. The following year, in 1914, he graduated from Yale University with a master's degree in anthropology. He enrolled at both Auburn seminary and Yale Graduate School concurrently. He was able to complete both degrees, because his master's degree included not classes but rather directed readings with professors and a thesis.[95] His master's thesis was titled "An Anthropologist's View of Reservation Life."[96]

Cloud spoke twice before the Friends of the Indian, a white reform group, at Lake Mohonk, New York. His first presentation in 1910 backed taxation of Native lands to help provide money for public utilities. He argued in favor of taxes to support local governments, including criminal justice. Advocating for taxation of Native lands did not support tribal sovereignty as we know it today. By supporting the imposition of white laws on Native lands, as well as calling for the end of federal trust protection from taxation, he goes against tribal sovereignty.[97] Naturally, the reform group received this recommendation warmly. His argument was likely consistent with the views of the majority of members of the Friends of the Indian, including his white adoptive mentors, the Roes. All these factors could have influenced his speech. By relying on white rhetoric, he was supporting settler colonialism. Cloud's views on these matters, however, later changed and evolved. A little more than twenty years later, Cloud advocated in favor of the Indian Reorganization Act, which rejected the assimilationist Native policy and continued the trust status of allotted Native lands, including their exception from local taxation.

According to Lucy Maddox, Native intellectuals of the Society of

American Indians, a pantribal organization Cloud co-founded, worked to reshape the dominant popular white rhetoric to reach their own goals and objectives.[98] Their tactics were similar to the American Negro Academy, whose most well-known member was W. E. B. Du Bois. To strengthen their voice in the public sphere, both groups mixed the rhetoric of progressivism and racial uplift with their own distinct points of view. In a similar vein Cloud could have made the tactical decision to support dominant rhetoric about taxation of Native lands in one speech to garner financial support from white reformers to fund a college-preparatory school for Native boys in the future.

Cloud's distinctly Indigenous position, in contrast, is strongly present in his own personal writings, which I found in our Cloud family files, showing how he changed his intellectual position from white-centric to Native-centric, depending on his audience. In 1931 Cloud argued that rather than try to erase Native knowledge as part of the federal boarding school's civilization training, one should build on existing Indigenous knowledge:

> Certain government employees come into the [Indian] Service and look upon the Indian and his ways of thought as beneath them, and think [they] are so common as to merit very little respect and therefore anything that is Indian is not worth preserving and not given much thought. . . . The right way to look at this question of Indian philosophy is to examine it very carefully and see how it contributes to the happiness and satisfaction of this individual. You make it possible for the Indian to build on what he already has. You have to proceed from the known to the unknown. You bring him a new philosophy entirely unknown to him. This mistake is being made in the attempt to civilize the Indian.[99]

Cloud challenges the lack of respect federal-government employees had for Native thought and philosophy, while he argues against assimilation and instead for a flexible and fluid notion of culture where Natives combine Indigenous and white knowledge together. His flexible and fluid notion of culture is a radical departure from static notions of culture linked to settler colonialism and which classic anthropology and federal policies of assimilation relied on. Assimilationists assume that dominant culture would overpower subordinated culture. Assimilation was viewed as a one-way process in which the oppressed people will be forced to give up their culture and replace it with dominant culture and ideas.[100] Rather than erasing Native knowledge and thought, Cloud incorporates white knowledge along with Ho-Chunk culture and philosophy. In this way Cloud, who received a master's in anthropology at Yale, shows how his anthropological ideas and his notions of culture and identity were flexible, fluid, and pathbreaking.

In 1914 Cloud again presented to the white group, the Friends of the Indian. His paper, the "Education of the American Indian," was much more revolutionary and Native-centric than his first one. He wrote, "The first effort, it seems to me, should be to give as much as Indians are able, all the education that the problems they face clearly indicate they should have. This means all of the education the grammar schools, the secondary schools, and the colleges of the land can give them."[101] This is a radical statement at a time when the status quo was for Native Americans to be sent off to reservation boarding schools that taught only vocational education. His involvement in Society of American Indians could have moderated his earlier assimilationist and antisovereignty stance. This second talk provided a springboard for fund-raising to found his Christian college-preparatory school for Indian boys.

The recurrent themes in his early writings of individual self-help and self-support served as an intellectual precursor to his later ideas about Natives' need for self-sufficiency as a group. He used the popular notion of self-help to inform his Native policy recommendations. Cloud argued in 1913 that, rather than be dependent on the government, Native Americans should work to sustain themselves: "So long as we crowd the Government schools, where everything is given free, so long as we let ourselves depend upon the agency, so long will our status as wards continue. I assert that in a country of so great and multiplied facilities for schooling, almost all our Indians now in Government schools can earn their own education. . . . We must live the doctrines of endeavor and self-support and preach the same continually. It must be an internal movement. The faster the movement spreads, the sooner the shackles of the [government] system will fall off."[102] He argued that for Native Americans to become strong, they must free themselves from a dependency on the federal government. These ideas likely contributed to his later ideas of economic development and self-sufficiency for Native people.

In an undated paper found in our Cloud family files, Cloud, a Ho-Chunk intellectual, links Natives' need for liberation and self-support to our need to organize ourselves. He indirectly challenges and critiques the government's suppression of Native languages in the boarding schools. He discusses how Natives' maintenance of our tribal languages can help us express ourselves as well as serve as a mechanism to develop initiative and work toward freedom. In other words, he argues that maintenance of one's tribal language can assist in Natives' progress and development:

> What the Indian needs today is freedom. He needs to develop initiative. When you force him to talk this other language [English] which he does not know think of the state of mind you throw the [Native] child in. The attitude of the educators who made this rule is that the quicker he learns the English language the better for him. Years and years ago we were not permitted to speak the Indian language. I forgot my language while I was away at [government boarding] school but picked it up again after I returned home. I have not forgotten it to this day. I can express myself in Indian more adequately than I can in English. There are certain things I can say in Indian that I cannot possibly make known in the English language. Every language that you know enriches your vocabulary and gives you a means of expressing yourself. The Indian needs freedom. He needs to express himself in activities and attitudes. He needs to fly away and be free. He needs to bear responsibilities in order to develop his personality. . . . The Indian needs the ability for organization, for group activities. . . . What the Indian needs is a means of self support.[103]

Thus, Cloud transforms an individualized Eurocentric idea about self-help and self-support, including the need for Indigenous peoples to shoulder responsibility, into a Native-oriented strategy for growth. By bringing together Eurocentric ideas with a strong Ho-Chunk belief in the importance of tribal languages, he combines both white and Ho-Chunk cultures to imagine a better life for Native Americans. In this way he argues for cultural pluralism rather than assimilation, and Native Americans' right to be different and belong in American culture and society, an Indigenous cultural citizenship.

Winnebago Tribe of Nebraska

While Cloud was at Yale, he maintained his connections to his reservation in Winnebago, Nebraska. He visited his tribe often in an effort to convert other tribal members to Christianity. Because he was a tribal member and spoke Ho-Chunk, he had a definite advantage over other missionaries. Many of the traditional Ho-Chunks opposed him, especially members of the Medicine Lodge, the keepers of our tribe's traditional spirituality. Medicine Lodge ceremonies were secret, and membership was tightly controlled and usually hereditary. He wrote about the angry faces of the Medicine Lodge members who passed him on the street or attended his Christian services to demonstrate their antagonism. He discussed his happiness when he was able to convert some of the Medicine Lodge members.[104]

While reading letters regarding Cloud's delight about converting Medicine Lodge members to Christianity, I felt a strong sense of discomfort. My mother, Woesha, taught me to respect all religions, including the Ho-Chunk Medicine Lodge. The settler-colonial aspect of Christianity, which emphasizes that it is the only true religion, was something my mother always questioned. This shows how religious attitudes can change over generations.

Even though there was strong opposition from tribal members to Cloud as a Native Christian, he became a leader for his tribe and served on a delegation that visited Washington in 1912. Because of many removals, Ho-Chunks were divided. Half of the tribe was living in Nebraska, while the other half lived in Wisconsin, where we originated. The Nebraska tribe received most of the annuity payments from the federal government, while the organized Wisconsin tribal members demanded their fair share. Nebraska Ho-Chunks traveled to Washington DC to sort this out. The Nebraska Ho-Chunks also faced the end of the federal trust-protection period in 1912, which they wanted to extend. Federal trust protection meant that Natives did not have to pay taxes. This shows that Cloud, two years after his original 1910 talk to the Friends of the Indian, had changed his position. He did not support taxation of Native lands; he supported his tribe advocating for the extension of its trustee status.

Our Winnebago tribe chose Cloud to be one of the delegates. He assisted in drafting of the "Statement by the Winnebago Delegation on Behalf of the Nebraska Branch," given to the commissioner of Indian Affairs, Robert G. Valentine. He was one of the three signatories of their formal petition. He met with the commissioner and other Indian Service officers during his visit to Washington. In July 1912 he wrote to Commissioner Valentine regarding other tribal concerns. He came away from this experience as an advocate for his tribe. His position as a member of the delegation helped other tribal members view him positively.[105]

Modern Ho-Chunk Intellectual

Cloud's Ho-Chunk warrior identity influenced his analytical perspective as a Ho-Chunk intellectual, motivating him to challenge settler colonialism. In a 1915 letter to Mary Roe, he emphasizes his Ho-Chunk warrior identity by relying on "warrior talk" while examining Gen. Richard H. Pratt, the founder of the first government boarding school for Native Americans, Carlisle. It concentrated on vocational rather than college education, since Native Americans were assumed to be lower on the social evolutionary ladder and therefore not smart enough to handle college-preparatory education:

> General Pratt has shown himself a venomous creature and we need to treat him as such. The poor old man is to be pitied for his long lost fight for Carlisle and his *one idea*. He has the Indian Office in general against him; all the missionaries who know actual conditions are one against him. All he can do is to join forces with people of like mongrel faith and there are many of them—all willing to come down to the lowest kind of muckraking methods. I would not have anything to do with him. If he gets in my way, I'll hit him hard and knock him out and go on. The trouble with Pratt is—he is selfishly egotistical. . . . He would take the responsibility of recreating the Indian race if he

thought he had the power. He little realizes what great harm he has done the Indian race by posing as their greatest friend. He was the man who in the first place limited the Indian education down to the eighth grade.[106]

Cloud utilizes warrior language by portraying Pratt as the enemy of the Indian race, although I do not believe he would have physically hit Pratt but rather would have "hit him" with rhetorical blows if he got "in [his] way." Cloud condemns Pratt's paternalism, assuming he has the right to "recreat[e] the Indian race." Cloud also modifies the exceedingly racialized and white-supremacist word "mongrel" to employ against whites who backed Pratt and Carlisle and as a challenge against the negative influences of colonialism and racism on Indigenous people. This quotation shows how Cloud's warrior training was central to his anticolonial strategies, since this education taught him to defend his people and fight aggressively against the enemy. It also educated him to use a Ho-Chunk intellectual lens, which enabled him to criticize Pratt as paternalistic and disrespectful.[107]

In sum, Cloud was a great storyteller, continually telling Ho-Chunk stories and other humorous tales. He relied on popular white notions of the self-made man to assert his masculinity and avoid being viewed as a Native nonman. This creative strategy helped him increase his power in the public sphere while receiving political and financial assistance from whites, including the Roes. He relied on his Ho-Chunk warrior training, including fasting, storytelling, courage, pride, and self-control for amazing fortitude and success in the midst of settler colonialism. Cloud developed a modern Ho-Chunk warrior identity, combining his Ho-Chunk warrior education with white ideas. Thus, Cloud challenged assimilation and argued for flexible and fluid notions of culture and identity. As a Native and a Christian, he used both Native and white rhetoric in his oratory and writing to be heard in the public sphere during an incredibly racist time. He relied on Ho-Chunk–centric hubs at Yale to remain connected to his Ho-Chunk people, including adopting a white missionary family into his Ho-Chunk sense of community and telling Ho-Chunk stories. He was recognized as a Ho-Chunk tribal leader as a young man and a Yale student and even traveled to Washington DC to advocate for our tribe. The following chapter discusses how Cloud, as a modern Ho-Chunk warrior and intellectual, fought for Geronimo and his fellow Apaches, co-founded the Society of American Indians, and founded a college-preparatory Native Christian high school, the American Indian Institute.

CHAPTER 2

Society of American Indians and the American Indian Institute

This chapter examines Henry Cloud's activist and intellectual work as a member and founder of the Society of American Indians (SAI). Specifically, it focuses on his efforts to free Geronimo, an Apache, as well as his people—who had been imprisoned after their capture by the U.S. military in 1886—and his efforts to assist the Apaches who chose to stay in Oklahoma with their land-allotment struggle against the federal government.[1] It discusses how Henry applied his Ho-Chunk and Yale education to fight for the Apaches. Ultimately, Henry Cloud was a Ho-Chunk intellectual shaped by his Ho-Chunk warrior training. As such, he relied on the SAI as a pantribal hub to support the Apaches' struggle against the federal government.

In addition, this chapter considers Henry Cloud's powerful working and marital relationship with Elizabeth Bender Cloud, whom he met in Madison, Wisconsin, at the fourth annual SAI conference. Elizabeth's childhood on the White Earth Reservation and her white schooling encouraged her to use both virtual and geographic hubs to challenge colonial, assimilationist strategies to separate her from her Ojibwe family. As an Indigenous intellectual, like Henry, Elizabeth was subversive. Although she relied on settler-colonial rhetoric in her writings, she asserted Indigenous perspectives. Similarly, by working both inside and outside of the home, Elizabeth combined an Ojibwe sense of a gendered identity with white notions of domesticity. In fact, Henry and Elizabeth followed Native notions of complementary gender roles: Henry was often away fund-raising for the American Indian Institute, and Elizabeth stayed home and ran the school. Elizabeth and Henry worked together as a "power couple" in a respectful, nonhierarchal Indigenous partnership.

Society of American Indians

Henry Cloud was a founding member of the SAI, a Native pantribal hub of a select group of Native American leaders that supported dialogue regarding Native issues and ideas. Well-known members included Arthur C. Parker (Seneca), the first editor of the *American Indian Magazine*, and Charles E. Eastman (Dakota), the editor of *Collier's* and other eastern magazines, as well as John Oskison (Cherokee), Gertrude Bonnin (Yankton Nakota), Marie Baldwin (Ojibwe), and Rosa B. LaFlesche (Ojibwe). Non-Indians could be associate members, but they could not vote. One prominent non-Indian member was Gen. Richard Henry Pratt.[2]

By allowing only Native Americans to become full members, the SAI, unlike other Indian reform groups, emphasized that Natives themselves should solve the "Indian problem."[3] Native Americans developed the SAI's goals and objectives within a general public atmosphere of white reform groups and federally enforced paternalism. For example, the Friends of the Indian, a coalition of white reform groups and individuals, met annually at Lake Mohonk. Their members included the Women's National Indian Association, the Indian Rights Association, missionaries, and individual white reformers. The Friends of the Indian's mission was to save Natives from heathenism and transform them from savages to industrious American citizens.[4]

In October 1911 Cloud helped to organize the SAI's first annual conference in Columbus, Ohio. He was a member of the advisory board in 1911, 1912, 1917, and 1919 and chaired the board in 1912. From 1911 to 1912 he was also vice president of membership, recruiting Native members and non-Native associate members. As vice president of education in 1916 and 1918, he was the spokesman of the SAI's educational platform. Finally, from 1915 to 1917 he was a member of the editorial board of the *American Indian Magazine*, the SAI's journal.[5] The *American Indian Magazine* was a way for Native intellectuals to support this pantribal hub across geographic distance, maintaining a sense of Native community, identity, and belonging. It was a platform to fight for Indigenous concerns and rights.

Cloud never became president of the SAI, even though there was discussion about the possibility. In a written response to Parker's 1914 letter about him potentially becoming president, Cloud emphasized his lack of experience, since he was still in his late twenties.[6] He also declined because he was busy laboring to found a Native college-preparatory high school in Wichita, Kansas, the American Indian Institute. Cloud's work with a wide range of Indigenous leaders gave him not only the opportunity to learn from other Natives and discuss Indigenous issues but also the chance to meet my grandmother, Elizabeth, during the aforementioned SAI conference. They eventually had five children: Marion, Anne Woesha (my mother), Ramona, Lillian, and Henry II, who died from pneumonia when he was three years old. Indeed, both Elizabeth and Henry became important leaders in national Native affairs.

Cloud's Fight for Geronimo and His People

In 1908, while still an undergraduate at Yale University and in his early twenties, Cloud began his successful campaign to release the Chiricahua Apaches from Fort Sill. Cloud heard about the Apache situation from Walter Roe, his informally adoptive, white missionary father, who lived in Colony, Oklahoma, which was about forty miles from Fort Sill. The fact that Cloud learned about the Apache struggle from Roe shows how Cloud used a colonial relationship with a white missionary for Native goals and objectives. His Ho-Chunk warrior training as a member of the Thunderbird Clan taught him the importance of leadership and fighting for his people and certainly must have influenced his decision to support Geronimo and resist the federal government. The Chiricahua Apaches, the last survivors of Geronimo's people, had valiantly fought official U.S. governmental actions to move them onto increasingly smaller and smaller reservations. But, finally, after evading U.S. government troops for nearly a decade, they were captured in 1886. The Apaches were ultimately taken to Fort Sill, where they resided in terrible housing, were given insufficient rations, and endured severe weather.[7] The government initially refused to allow Cloud to work on behalf of the Fort Sill Apaches, since the Apaches had not granted him official permission. Geronimo met with Cloud and gave him authorization to act on their behalf. In 1933 Cloud explained that his training at Yale helped him fight for the Apaches' release.[8] In one of Cloud's Yale classes on the U.S. Constitution, he studied constitutional principles of attainder and corruption of blood. Article 3, section 3, clause 2, prohibits punishing descendants for the crimes of their ancestors. Cloud argued that by being detained, the children of the Apaches were being punished for their ancestors' behavior. And so, as a modern-day educated Ho-Chunk warrior, Cloud applied the U.S. Constitution to help him fight for Geronimo and his band's freedom.

The Dawes Allotment Act was a major strategy to dispossess Natives of millions of acres of land. It followed after the federal government forcibly removed Native Americans from their lands, including five successive Ho-Chunk removals in the 1800s. The Allotment Act was yet another settler-colonial tactic of land dispossession. It attempted to assimilate Natives into U.S. society by changing their communal connection to land to an individual one and by encouraging our Native ancestors to farm land allotments. The government marked the best land as "surplus" and set this land aside for whites. These superior lands had precious minerals and rich agriculture potential, while the land set aside for Natives was often insufficient for agricultural use and did not have water for irrigation. In addition, as discussed in the introduction, this land allotment supported patriarchal notions of the nuclear family: heads of household (meaning men) received 160 acres, married Native women received no land, single adults received 80 acres, and children received 40 acres. This distribution was the case until an 1891 amendment changed the terms so that any Native adult, regardless of family status, would receive 80 acres. The act attacked not only Natives' communal relationships to land but also their powerful feelings of spiritual, emotional, and physical connection to that land.[9] Therefore, it encouraged alternative, nongeographic networks of belonging in the form of Native hubs. Since Indigenous peoples were living apart from one another on individual allotments, these hubs—not based in geographic space—were a way to remain connected to their communal Native sense of identity and gender.

In the following sections, I discuss Henry Cloud's intellectual and activist efforts to support the Apaches' land struggle. The Apache prisoners of war, who refused to move to Mescalero, were pressured to leave Fort Sill as a condition of their freedom. At the same time, these Apaches insisted the government give them unused allotment lands from the Kiowa-Comanche-Apache reservation lands near Fort Sill.[10] In 1912 and 1913 Henry wrote to the commissioner of Indian Affairs, Cato Sells, to complain that the government had not provided the Apaches with rations and land allotments as promised.[11] On October 7, 1913, he met with the Apaches again, who were still imprisoned at Fort Sill, and learned more about the land-allotment struggle. Although government officials had promised the prisoners 160 acres of improved land, they were reneging on this promise: they informed the Apaches they would receive only 80 acres of good agricultural land for each head of household. Cloud also learned why government officials had reduced the number of acres from 160 to 80 acres; they believed the Apaches would lease the land and "debauch themselves with laziness and drink," a rationale reflecting racist and colonial assumptions of this period. Cloud, after meeting with the Apaches, began crafting a brief to support their fight against the government. On October 16, 1913, Cloud outlined the key facts of the case:

> While at Pahuska, Okla. I had a long interview with Special Agent Ellis on the Apache matter. . . .
>
> If the appraisements [of] $3200 for 160 acres is correct, (and such are the *average* appraisements for 160 acres and 80 acres respectively), the $100,000 is barely sufficient to give 80 acres of good agricultural land for each man, woman and child.
>
> The reading or wording of the law relating to the Apaches is subject to the general allotment act of 1887 where it specifies 160 acres of grazing land or 80 acres of agricultural land for each man, woman and child.
>
> The law leaves the whole matter to the discretion of the Sec. of Int. and Sec. of War as to detailed arrangements. Whatever they (the sec. of war and sec. of Int.) decide upon are called *rulings*.

[Ernest] Stecker claims that *rulings* are for either 160 acres of grazing land or 80 acres of agricultural land. If all this is true of course we can only have recourse to new legislation, which is a difficult matter.

Granting that the appraisements are reasonable both to the Kiowa-Comanches and to the Apaches and granting that the law is fixed as specified above, the three men, in my opinion are acting in good faith and are doing the best possible under the circumstances.

But . . . let me state the other side so far as I have come.

In all three hundred thousand dollars were appropriated for the whole Apache band, $200,000 at first and $100,000 later. It does not take, it did not take all of the $200,000 to move and settle the Apaches in Mescalero. A portion of that sum belongs to those who chose to remain at Fort Sill.

This ought to increase the $100,000 immediately available to at least give some of the men at Fort Sill 160 acres of good agricultural land.

The understanding all along has been for 160 acres of good agricultural land.

No farmer unless he irrigates can hope to make a living on 80 acres and it is doubtful on 160 acres.

I have the facts to support B and C and will get the data for condition A.

D) The Indians have proved themselves capable of stock farming. They have had an experience of 25 years or more.

In my telegram to you I did mention the fact that I laid the whole case before [the white reformers and members of the Indian Rights Association] [Samuel] Brosius and [Matthew] Sniffen. . . . The next step for me is to go to Washington and determine how the $300,000 appropriated is to be apportioned and to lay the matter before both the Sec. of Interior and Sec. of War. I shall see the Commissioner about . . . the Fort Sill matter also.[12]

This letter shows how insightfully Cloud understood key elements of both sides of the case, including the central importance of the Allotment Act of 1887.[13] Cloud alludes to the progressive identity of the Apaches, who were choosing to stay in Oklahoma, writing they had "proved themselves capable of stock farming." In support of the Apaches, Cloud argues that the secretaries of the interior and war ultimately had discretionary power regarding the number of acres the Apaches would receive. In contrast, Ernest Stecker, a government official, argues that the number of acres was fixed; meaning only new legislation could increase the Apaches' allotment to 160 acres of improved land. At the same time, Cloud agrees with government officials that only 80 acres would be available if indeed the number of acres was set, and the Apaches, Kiowas, and Comanches accepted the land appraisement.

On the Apaches' side, Cloud challenges government officials' claim that only $100,000 was available for the purchase of land, arguing that it was insufficient, that there was money left over from the Apaches' resettlement to Mescalero, and that $300,000 in total had been appropriated. Moreover, this letter demonstrates how hard Henry worked in support of the Apaches, including meeting with government officials and traveling to Washington DC to talk to the secretaries of the interior and war, establishing his place on the national stage as a young man. He was able to combine his Ho-Chunk education—which motivated him to bring Indigenous perspectives to bear on government affairs and taught him oratory skills—with his Yale training, which educated him in colonial strategies of argument and important legal concepts. And Cloud used this dual education to systematically and quickly gather evidence in support of the Apaches' side of the case—only nine days passed between this letter and his initial meeting with the Apaches. Finally, this letter points to Cloud's work with the white reform group, the Indian Rights Association, as well as his work with the Society of American Indians.

Cloud, Apaches' Land Struggle, and the SAI

Cloud brought the Apaches' land-allotment struggle to the SAI, an important and powerful pantribal hub, so the organization could lobby the federal government on the Apaches' behalf. The society unanimously supported a brief Cloud wrote, and copies were sent to the secretaries of war and the interior, the commissioner of Indian Affairs, and Congressman C. D. Carter.[14] On October 25, 1913, Cloud presented his brief, "The Case of the Fort Sill Apaches Again," to the SAI and asked for their support. In other words, Cloud shared his Native intellectual ideas with a pantribal hub of Indigenous intellectuals. Through this hub Cloud could receive feedback on his struggle in support of the Apaches from a powerful network of Indigenous intellectuals. Therefore, thanks to the pantribal platform of the SAI, Cloud did not work in an intellectual vacuum but instead gained support and insight from many astute Native intellectuals.

In his Native-centric brief Cloud recounts how an exhausted group of Apaches surrendered in New Mexico in 1886 to Indian scouts rather than to the U.S. military. The Apaches were then forcibly taken to Forts Pickens and Marion in Florida; the Mount Vernon barracks in Alabama; and finally to Fort Sill, Oklahoma. After twenty-seven years of penal servitude, an act of Congress freed the prisoners and then became law on June 30, 1913. Notably, Cloud discusses that $300,000 in total was allocated to help provide land for the Fort Sill Apaches' resettlement. Ultimately, 176 Apaches resettled in Mescalero, New Mexico, and 80 chose to stay in Oklahoma. Cloud wrote,

At a Council meeting ordered by the Secretary of the Interior on December 1st, . . . 1912, . . . it was proposed to buy 160 acres of improved land for each head of family. . . . 160 acres of good agricultural land at least for each head of a family was the intent and purpose of the law under which these Indians are now being allotted. . . . Actual land conditions . . . make it impossible to make a living on 80 acres. . . . In a letter . . . of October 14th, 1913, the President of the Cameron State of Agriculture . . . a man who knows the region . . . says: "It is my . . . firm belief that the average farmer cannot nor does not make a living on a farm of 160 acres land in this southwestern country. . . . The Apache Indians have been trained as stock-raisers. They have shown fitness for such a life. . . . As to the fitness of these Indians let me read you portions of a letter written by R. A. Bellinger, then Secretary of Interior, to Moses E. Clapp, Chairman Committee on Indian Affairs, United States Senate, under date of February 18th, 1910: "During the fifteen years that the Apaches have lived at Fort Sill, under the supervision of the Military authorities, they have become prosperous, peaceful and contented: they have been taught to care for themselves in large measure as agriculturalists, stock-raisers and mechanics: they individually cultivate considerable pieces of land: they own and brand their own cattle as individuals."[15]

Cloud encourages others to prompt action. He shows his sensitivity to the Apache warriors' experiences by describing their surrender, emphasizing their decision to submit to Native scouts rather than the U.S. military, an allusion to their warrior pride even in defeat. Cloud also employs various rhetorical strategies to argue in support of the Apaches. He recalls the government promise of 160 acres of improved land and the purpose and intent behind the law. He cites an agricultural expert to prove the harsh, unacceptable conditions of the land that was provided, and he cites a military expert to bolster his Native-centric argument about the Apaches' "fitness" to receive 160 acres of improved land. In fact, Cloud's use of the words "fitness" and "individually" shows his ability to utilize the colonizers' categories against them by emphasizing the Apaches' progressive identity as assimilated Natives living the life the federal government intended for them. Thus, Cloud challenges government officials' negative, racist assumptions that the Apaches would lease the 160 acres and "debauch themselves with laziness and drink."[16] He ends the brief pleading for the full 160 acres of good agricultural land, summarizing the main points of his argument and reminding the federal government about "treaty stipulations," "fair dealing," and "justice." All these astute rhetorical strategies demonstrate Cloud's Ho-Chunk intellectual prowess enhanced by his Yale educational training. While at Yale, he studied debate, oratory, and the colonizer's own arguments. In these ways Cloud indigenized his colonial training to fight for the Apaches and against the federal government.[17] And this act of indigenizing shows his subversive Ho-Chunk strategy of doubleness speech. Cloud combined white and Native rhetoric for Indigenous goals and objectives.

Soon after Henry brought the Apaches' land struggle to the SAI, Elizabeth sent a letter to the society on behalf of Margaret Giard, an Ojibwe, in support of her claim for an allotment on the White Earth Reservation:

The mother's name was Margaret . . . Giard. They settled here around 1885 and settled on a certain piece of land. Soon after that Mrs. Giard was put on the roll and allotted this piece of land. Then for some reason she was taken off the roll and was told to allow two nephews of hers to hold it and after she could definitely ascertain her rights she would be given the allotments again. But when she was again put back on the rolls her original allotments could not be obtained. She has lived here for twenty-seven years and now that the nephews are growing to manhood, the son Pete Giard wants to put them on this improved piece of property. I consider this an injustice as these boys could have obtained allotments elsewhere. Mrs. Giard is a widow and should this be allowed she will be turned out of a home that has been improved by years of hard labor. They asked me to write to the Society on behalf of their rights as Indians. . . . As a member of the Society I believe in doing good for any worthy Indian family and if the Society can in some way help them it would be for the good of the race.[18]

In this letter, as a modern Ojibwe warrior woman, Elizabeth acts as this elderly woman's protector, challenging the behavior of Giard's nephews. Elizabeth also emphasizes the unpredictable and gendered nature of settler-colonial allotment policy; one moment Giard had land, and the next moment her male relatives had her land instead. Initially, according to the Allotment Act, married women were not entitled to land, but this changed with an 1891 amendment, as discussed earlier. It seems that the Allotment Act affected Native women in arbitrary and unfair ways, since Native males could be given land that once belonged to an older female relative. Much like Henry's use of the SAI to back the Apaches in their fight for land, Elizabeth used the SAI as a vehicle to support the rights of an Ojibwe elder to receive her land allotment. Therefore, the SAI was a Native, gendered, intellectual, and activist hub that the Clouds relied on to fight in support of Indigenous land and interests.

It was Elizabeth's and Henry's mutual involvement in the SAI that brought them together. There are many potential reasons why Elizabeth and Henry became a couple. Both suffered through the federal boarding schools, excelled academically, read voraciously, had a deep commitment to their people, and, most important, were devout Christians. In the following section I discuss Elizabeth's Ojibwe childhood, her training in white schools, and how she, like Henry, used Native hubs to maintain her tribal identity and her connection to her Ojibwe people.

Elizabeth Georgian Bender's Childhood and White Schooling

Elizabeth Georgian Bender was born on April 2, 1887, in Fosston, Minnesota, near the White Earth Reservation.[19] Her Ojibwe name was Quay-Zaince, meaning a twin, and Elizabeth's twin sister died at birth. She learned about the Ojibwe world from her mother, Mary Razier, a "full-blood" Ojibwe with an Ojibwe name of Pay Sha Deo Quay. Mary had some white schooling but preferred to speak Ojibwe, and she taught all her children to speak Ojibwe fluently. Mary was a healer, a midwife, and the daughter of a medicine man. Albertus Bender, her husband, a German American, lived and worked in the logging camps. He had blazing blue eyes and married Mary when she was around fifteen or sixteen.[20] He learned to speak Ojibwe before he married Mary Razier, so Elizabeth grew up in an Ojibwe-speaking home. They had three daughters, Anna, Elizabeth, and Emma and seven sons, John, Frank, Charles, Albertus, Fred, George, and James.[21]

My mother, Woesha, loved her grandmother profoundly, until Mary's death at seventy-three years old. She told me stories of the log-cabin home, where Mary lived alone in her old age. It was ten miles from the Canadian border, in countryside covered with evergreen trees, except where the land was cleared for farming. And my grandfather, Henry Cloud, also loved Mary dearly. She treated him like a son, and he enjoyed helping and supporting her, including building her the cabin she lived in until she passed away.[22] Woesha traveled with her family every summer to visit her grandmother Mary. They gathered all kinds of berries around her cabin and saw many animals, including bear and porcupine. Mary kept her log-cabin home immaculate, decorated it with her craftwork, and set up her loom outside in a tent. During Elizabeth's childhood Mary tended a garden that kept her family happy and satisfied with vegetables, fruit, and flowers; she also canned meat for the long, cold winters. My mother once told me, with a glint in her eye, that Mary could shoot a deer and skin it with one hand tied behind her back. As a child, I would imagine this elderly Ojibwe woman, with a shotgun in her hands, peering down the long barrel and firing. Mary was an independent, strong Ojibwe woman who was able to fend for herself after her husband passed away. Indeed, Mary, early in her marriage, lived near Albertus's relatives, but she was unhappy there. So she returned to the White Earth Reservation with her children in tow, and Albertus followed her. Mary and Albertus lived on Mary's 160-acre allotment, where they built a house, a granary, and a farm.[23] Mary taught Elizabeth not only to speak the Ojibwe language but also to live as an Ojibwe woman.[24]

Traditionally, Ojibwe men and women held complementary roles. Women tended the gardens and prepared the meat and fish that men brought home from the hunt. Women undoubtedly directed and managed their own activities. The men who helped did not oversee the women but played assisting roles. Ojibwe women not only prepared the venison and bear's meat but also had a voice in determining who would receive the divided portions. Fur traders mentioned bartering directly with Ojibwe women for processed furs. Ojibwe women's power—especially in terms of their control over the ownership and distribution of resources—should not be underestimated.[25]

Furthermore, in the nineteenth century U.S. government sources described three Ojibwe women as leaders of their bands: "The head chief of the Pillagers, Flatmouth, has for several years resided in Canada, his sister, Ruth Flatmouth, is in her brother's absence the Queen or leader of the Pillagers: two other women of hereditary right acted as leaders of their respective bands, and at the request of the chiefs were permitted to sign the agreement." In 1889 government negotiators were encouraged to explain to Congress why Ojibwe women were permitted to sign official arrangements and settlements. Ojibwe women leaders did not seem to present a problem for Ojibwe people, but only for whites.[26]

My mother, Woesha, did not remember Elizabeth saying anything more about her German American father, Albertus. My aunt Marion, like her sister Woesha, described spending every summer with her Ojibwe grandmother, Mary. But Marion saw her German grandfather only once, when she was six years old. Elizabeth always privileged the Ojibwe aspects of her identity, over the German American one. She maintained a close connection with her Ojibwe mother, Mary, and her siblings, but not with Albertus. Also, Elizabeth had white cousins, her father's relatives, somewhere in Minnesota, but she never looked them up.[27]

As a child, Elizabeth helped her parents with chores both inside and outside of the home, challenging white gendered notions of female domesticity and showing she was taught a flexible and fluid Ojibwe notion of gender. Elizabeth wrote, "I used to help my mother in the housework and also used to help my father with the outside work when it was necessary; there was nothing I enjoyed as much as working out in the open air."[28] By discussing her childhood in a fund-raising letter for Hampton Institute (a boarding school she later attended), Elizabeth performs Ojibwe hub making through storytelling, making a connection to her Ojibwe family while away at a boarding school.[29] Indeed, Elizabeth's discussion of gender as a child on her reservation challenges the domesticity training she had at Pipestone and Hampton boarding schools, which emphasized that girls should be confined to the domestic sphere.[30] Many years later Woesha encouraged her mother, Elizabeth, to write her life story. One day, as the two of them sat together talking, Elizabeth said proudly to Woesha, "My father said I was as good as any of my brothers. I could clean out the barns (around the cattle stalls) as well as any boy."[31] This is an extremely significant comment about Elizabeth's fluid sense of Ojibwe gender identity and her interest in working outside the private sphere.

At the age of nine Elizabeth attended her first white school, the Sisters School of Saint Joseph, a Minnesota Catholic school about 150 miles away from the White Earth Reservation. She wrote, "I stayed there for two years and then came home and spent two years at home."[32] After this she spent the next four years at Pipestone, a federal boarding school that was established in 1893. In a 1905 letter Elizabeth wrote,

When I was ten years old I was sent to an Indian government school in Minnesota, called Pipestone Industrial School. The school consists of a large school building, dining hall, boys' building, girls' laundry, a large red barn, and a few teachers' cottages. The girls and boys go to school only half a day the whole year round, the other half being devoted to manual training, such as girls working in the sewing room, laundry, kitchen and baking, and the boys working in the tailor shop, carpenter shop and on the farm. . . . I had two sisters and two brothers there, and we spent four years in going to school there. . . . We had to spend a term of three years there before we were allowed to return home![33]

Even though Elizabeth wrote this letter to a "friend" of Hampton Institute (another boarding school she later attended) to fund-raise for the school, there is camouflaged critique of Pipestone. Her use of the word "only" in her description of going to school "only half a day the whole year round" points to an indirect criticism of the lack of academic rigor in her Pipestone boarding-school training. Elizabeth also assertively places an exclamation point in the narrative. In this way she critiques the federal boarding-school policy that separated Native children from their families for long stretches of time. The exclamation point speaks volumes about her negative feelings toward this boarding-school practice. It was necessary to camouflage her criticism during a time when Native people suffered much racism and could not truthfully express their points of view. In a 1900 letter she mentions that she "liked" Pipestone federal boarding school.[34] She very well could have felt forced to write she liked the training there. Thankfully, her sisters and brothers accompanied her to these coercive surroundings. Thus, despite the hostility of the colonial environment, her tight family network enabled Elizabeth to create an Ojibwe family—centric hub, which could act as a buffer to some degree.

In her Hampton fund-raising letters, she discusses the lands and people of White Earth. She wrote, "I live on an Indian reservation, and it is situated in a very beautiful spot, among hundreds of small and large lakes. Every fall the Indians find a great pleasure hunting wild ducks on these lakes."[35] Her writing expresses a deep sense of connection to her land and people. She transforms a fund-raising letter, a potentially tedious boarding-school assignment, into a memory of beauty and an ancestral connection to an Ojibwe sense of place. Leslie Marmon Silko writes, "Our stories cannot be separated from the geographical locations, from actual physical locations on the land. . . . And our stories are so much a part of these places that it is almost impossible for future generations to lose them—there is a story connected to every place, every object in the landscape." According to Silko, Indigenous peoples maintain a connection to the stories of their people, a sense of a Native oral tradition, through maintaining a connection to land.[36] By remembering an Ojibwe sense of place, Elizabeth accesses the stories of her people, her Ojibwe identity, hundreds of miles away, from a white-controlled boarding school. Elizabeth challenges the settler-colonial strategy of separation by creating an Ojibwe hub and maintaining a sense of connection.

When Elizabeth describes the experiences of other Native girls and boys at Hampton whose families are far away, she again contests the colonial treatment of family separation: "I came in the fall of 1903 with twenty-three other Indian girls and boys. They all had come from their western homes to go to an institution that they had heard so much of. Some of them were rather homesick and lonesome after arriving here, but I was rather fortunate in having a big sister here. Hampton is just like a home with plenty of room for a big family, and I couldn't get lonesome if I tried."[37] Here Elizabeth is being subversive by emphasizing how other children felt homesick and lonesome because they were very far away from their families. She indirectly critiques the boarding-school policy of separating Native children from their parents. At the same time, she emphasizes again how the presence of her siblings created a cushion for her in a colonial boarding-school situation. Her description of Hampton as a home away from home once more shows how she and her siblings created an Ojibwe family hub in the midst of colonialism.

Elizabeth's white father, Albertus, encouraged her to go to Pipestone federal boarding school and later to Hampton Institute, but her Ojibwe mother did not. Elizabeth wrote,

When I went home [from Pipestone], and told my parents of my intentions [to go to Hampton], my father approved, but my mother did not. I told her of the beautiful things I had heard about Hampton, but she said, "It's far, far away from the land of sky-tinted water." Of course, she said this to me in the Indian language (Chippewa when translated this is what she said). I finally persuaded her for me to come, and I hated to leave home. My parents felt dreadfully bad the day I left, but my father said, "I want you to study hard, and be a good girl." I have tried hard to live up to the parting advice he gave me.[38]

Elizabeth emphasizes her parents' opposing views of white schooling. Her Ojibwe mother wanted Elizabeth to stay home with her people, while her father wished her to attend white schools. These opposing viewpoints must have been difficult for Elizabeth. Her writing combines her parents' wishes. On the one hand, she wants to "study hard, and be a good girl" for her father, but she also emphasizes her deep attachment to her Ojibwe home and mother by emphasizing that she "hated to leave." She also mentions that she understands her mother speaking to her in Ojibwe. Thus, through storytelling, Elizabeth participated in Ojibwe hub making, maintaining a connection to her Ojibwe mother, identity, and language—even while hundreds of miles away from the White Earth Reservation.

While Elizabeth felt a close connection to her parents, her older sister, Anna, did not. Anna's white schooling started earlier than Elizabeth's. At age six Anna was sent to the Lincoln Institute in Philadelphia, a federal boarding school. Two of her brothers, Charles and John, went to the nearby "Educational Home on forty-ninth street," Lincoln, a boarding school for Indigenous boys. After seven years at the school, when it was time to return home to Minnesota, Anna "had no reason for wanting to go home," she wrote, "except that other students went to theirs. I seldom heard from my parents and was so young when I came away that I did not even remember them." She continued,

How miserable I felt when the time came to go! It was to me the leaving of a home instead of returning to one. . . . My mother met me at the station bringing with her my two younger sisters and two younger brothers whom I had never seen. They greeted me kindly but they and everything being so new and strange that I burst into tears. To comfort me my mother took me into a store close by and bought me a bag of apples. . . . As we gathered around the table later a great wave of homesickness came over me. I could not eat for the lump in my throat and presently I put my head down and cried good and hard, while the children looked on in surprise. When my father returned from work he greeted me kindly but scanned me from head to foot. He asked me if I remembered him and I had to answer no. He talked to me kindly and tried to help me recall my early childhood, but I had never known many men and was very shy of him. At last he told me I had changed greatly from a loving child to a stranger.[39]

Anna's beautiful prose describes the heart-wrenching experience of my grandmother's sister, my ancestor, no longer remembering her parents and never having met her younger siblings. Her mother, Mary, bought her a bag of apples to distract her from something so horrible, from not recollecting her own mother. Her father, Albertus, spoke harsh words to his own child, telling her she had transformed into an outsider.

Anna's sad recollection of returning "home" to strangers, her own Ojibwe family, shows the deleterious impact of separating a young child of six years old from her closest relatives for many years. To feel connected to one's home and family, one must have regular contact. The Native boarding schools' policy of separating young children from their families was agonizing for the entire Bender family. In this context Mary's strong reluctance toward Elizabeth leaving to go to Hampton boarding school was reasonable and understandable.

After becoming reacquainted with her sister Elizabeth, Anna felt less lonely than before, but she stated, "I had much to learn and much to endure those next few months that I cannot tell you here." As her descendant, I wonder what Anna had to endure while she was home at White Earth. She very likely was struggling with feelings of disconnection and confusion regarding her place within her own loving family. Anna spent about three months at White Earth and then prepared to leave for Pipestone, accompanied by her brothers and sisters. "I will remember the day my brothers and sisters and I went away. It was a bitter cold day and we were six miles away from the station. We did not know that a team was coming for us so we started off early in the morning and got three miles before the team came and picked us up, and we went on to Pipestone we [and] two other students."[40] Anna's description of their departure for boarding school, a scene of children walking together in the bitter cold, expresses a sense of sadness and loneliness.

Anna had already determined before she left Pipestone that she would go to Hampton Institute unless her family needed her back home. A teacher at Pipestone, a former Hampton Institute student, encouraged her to attend Hampton. This teacher "could do almost anything when anybody was sick she could take their places from office work to cooking including sewing[,] matron, nursing and teaching. We used to call her Jack of All Trades and I used to think to myself, 'If that is the way they educate people at Hampton, there is the place I want to go,' so the next fall I boarded the train for Hampton." Anna's description of her decision to go to yet another white boarding school was consistent with settler-colonial strategies to encourage Natives to move from one colonial environment into another and to focus on vocational rather than college-preparatory training. Anna's goal at Hampton was to become a typist, and she sought a "general education" in the program.[41]

Hampton Normal and Agricultural Institute was at first a boarding school for African Americans. It started to enroll Native students only in 1878. Samuel Armstrong, son of missionaries, established Hampton. Its Indian department was a forerunner of a federal boarding-school system, a colonial-educational process created to assimilate Natives into American society. The purpose of the private, nondenominational school was to train "the hand, the head and the heart" of youngsters, teaching them to be models and teachers of their people. In many ways Hampton was similar to other settler-colonial, off-reservation federal boarding schools. Hampton snatched students away from their far-off reservation homes; controlled and regulated every single aspect of their education; highlighted white "civilized" religion, culture, and language instead of Native cultural ways and education; launched a summer outing system where students were put in white homes to continue learning English and white culture; and regulated students in military style, with divisions, inspections, and drills.[42]

Hampton Institute, however, was different from federal-government schools in multiple ways. The school's roots educating African American students shaped the school's subsequent program for Natives. The mission was to train Native students to be examples who would train other Indigenous people. Hampton had a more moderate stance in regard to assimilation as compared to other schools, such as Carlisle, whose motto was, "kill the Indian, save the man." Hampton did not want its

Native students to merge with white society but rather to return to the reservations, where they could teach their people. Hampton worked to encourage a "missionary sentiment," and it was not under control of the Bureau of Indian Affairs. Initially, its Native students were supported through private donors, which explains why Elizabeth was encouraged to write fund-raising letters. But once their educational program proved successful, the institute received federal support. Because of the concern that students would "go back to the blanket" or return to tribal ways as soon as they returned home, Hampton's employees maintained contact with alumni. Follow-up correspondence reinforced the education Natives had received at the school. It convinced critics that Hampton graduates continued to practice the lessons they had learned, and it proved to potential funders the importance of appropriating money for Indian education.

Both Elizabeth and her older sister, Anna, were exemplary students at Hampton, who attended there along with their siblings Emma, Fred, and George.[43] Being together with siblings at Hampton must have softened the emotional blow of being away from their parents, enabling them to create an Ojibwe hub in the midst of a white boarding school. Elizabeth and Anna excelled academically and were active in a number of organizations. They were members of the Josephines, a female literary society, and they wrote for the student-run school newspaper, *Talks and Thoughts*. The school officials even asked them to visit rich whites and fund-raise for the school. At Hampton students were encouraged to celebrate Native American and African American art forms. This relative openness to cultural difference (as compared to Carlisle and other boarding schools) helps explain why much of Hampton's *Talks and Thoughts* was devoted to Native American folklore. The school's founder, Armstrong, encouraged students to write about their cultural traditions in the newspaper. Armstrong's openness, however, in no way changed his judgment of more fundamental deficiencies of Native people.[44] Only hard work and proper Christian training, according to Armstrong, could eventually remedy Natives' shortcomings. The Bender sisters were encouraged to sing in their Ojibwe language in front of white audiences for fund-raising purposes. Even though Hampton emphasized the civilization of Native students, school authorities referenced the students' tribal past whenever it proved helpful for obtaining financial support for Hampton. Elizabeth and Anna were subject to whites viewing them as exotic and as living proof that they had been transformed from "savage" to "civilized" Natives.

Elizabeth wrote in *Talks and Thoughts* about hers and Anna's fundraising trip for Hampton, but she leaves out any description of hers and Anna's parlor performances for white audiences. One could view her decision not to focus on their presentations as a moment of resistance, a desire to not dwell on their experiences being used as Native exotic objects for the benefit of Hampton. While in the earlier fund-raising letter, Elizabeth places an exclamation point as a subversive challenge to policies of separation, this time she writes about the smiles on the faces of boarding-school students. This potentially shows that Elizabeth felt less comfortable being truthful while writing for the student-run paper. In her article Elizabeth concentrates instead on her sightseeing trips to Carpenter and Independence Halls in Philadelphia and to the zoological garden, aquarium, and the Museum of Natural History in New York City. Her discussion of her sightseeing trip emphasizes her status as a Native intellectual and her desire to expand her mind. The Museum of Natural History was the most interesting, according to Elizabeth, because "it contained so many Indian ornaments, weapons, domestic utensils, medicines, and I believe every imaginable thing that the different tribes of America used."[45] In her description of the wide range of Native artifacts, Elizabeth created a Native hub, connecting to her Indigenous identity both in a geographic place, the museum, and virtually, through writing. It was also a way for her to show pride in Native history and Indigenous peoples' accomplishments.[46]

The Indian Service

Many of the Ojibwe students at Hampton, like Elizabeth and her sister Anna, worked in the Indian Service.[47] Hampton encouraged graduates to serve as examples and teachers for their people, to spread the school's colonial training.[48] In her time with the federal Indian Service, Elizabeth occupied a complicated role as a colonial agent. At the same time, she used her role as a teacher to critique the government, expose the widespread trachoma situation, and improve education for Native students.

Elizabeth taught on the Blackfeet Reservation. She complained that the "Indian Service is not a 'bed of roses' by any means and there are some features that are very discouraging. There is a certain class who are incompetent; who possess no love for the work they are in; only as a means of livelihood." Elizabeth calling her Indian Service colleagues "incompetent" was a strong indictment of the Indian Service overall. When Elizabeth first came to teach on the Blackfeet Reservation, the school provided instruction only until the fourth grade, and later school officials added instruction until the seventh grade. Elizabeth wrote, "We try to follow the state course as near as possible, considering we do not use the state books. But we aim to make our grades correspond to the grades of the state so that our children may enter the same grade should they enter a public school."[49] This attempt to improve education for Native children, trying to provide them with similar education as white children received in the public schools, was another challenge to colonialism. Elizabeth believed that the Society of American Indians could help improve the Indian Service for the better.[50]

While Henry was busy fund-raising for the American Indian Institute, Elizabeth discussed her experience at the Indian Service during her address, "A Hampton Graduate's Experience," at Hampton's anniversary in 1915, which was later published in the Southern Workman. Elizabeth courageously exposes the rampant trachoma on the Blackfeet Reservation: "This brings me to the horrors of trachoma and my observation among the Plains Indians. It is a disease that without medical attention gradually impairs the sight until blindness results. Upon the examination of one hundred and fifty children in our school, forty-three were found to be afflicted with trachoma. The Government sent out specialists about three years ago, and they found that, out of the Indian population of 300,000, 50,000 had trachoma." Elizabeth helped treat the trachoma cases before she was transferred to work at the Fort Belknap Reservation, where the trachoma situation was even worse. Someone told Elizabeth that it was the "one-eyed reservation," and she felt it was almost true. She continued, "I cite these instances because I feel so strongly these problems that are confronting our people; and they are problems that we can all help to remedy, whether our vocation in life is that of a teacher, carpenter, nurse, or blacksmith. If you cannot get a doctor to treat this disease, be interested enough to treat the cases in your own community. Think of it! Nearly thirty percent of all Indian children are in danger of becoming blind. Nearly 17,000 Indians boys and girls are in danger of complete blindness." At this point in her talk, she was directly addressing the Native students in the audience, encouraging them to become leaders and actively work to deal with the terrible disease. At the beginning of her address, she anticipated health problems on the Blackfeet Reservation: "On the bench was an Indian mother, cuddling in her arms a sickly looking baby and trying to soothe its fretfulness. I learned afterward that they were all of the same family, and were there to take a midnight train in order to see if they could get medical aid which the government doctor could not adequately give the sick infant."[51] Here Elizabeth sharply criticizes the government health services for their inadequate health care on the Blackfeet Reservation.

As a Christian woman, Elizabeth spoke out against the "horrors of the grass dance, the sun dance, and the use of mescal" during her Hampton address.[52] Elizabeth, like Henry, criticized Natives' use of peyote. In fact, all the members of the SAI organized against the Natives' use of peyote. In contrast, my mother, Woesha, taught me to respect all religious traditions, including Indigenous ceremonies. Woesha drove our family to watch the sun dance on the Pine Ridge Reservation when it was no longer illegal. Reading Elizabeth's description of Indigenous spiritual traditions as "horrors" is disturbing, although it is an accurate reflection of her time.

Elizabeth resigned after her second year teaching on the Blackfeet Reservation. Instead, she decided to pursue health care, following in her mother's footsteps. She took a nurses' training course in Philadelphia at Hahnemann Hospital until she was convinced by her former co-workers and pupils to resume teaching in Browning, Montana.[53] Henry, "her sweetheart," visited her:

Henry Roe Cloud dropped in on us this morning between trains. When the doorbell rang I was surprised to see him standing there, hat in hand, and that pleasant smile. This all happened at the hospital where I am detailed now, and we were having quite a Hampton party in Lavina's [surname unknown] room. There we sat, Angel, Carmen [surname unknown], and I talking and discussing war, cards, Carlisle and then Mr. Roe Cloud joined us. . . . He wanted to stay longer but had a meeting with Dr. McKenzie and D. Jones at five o'clock in Washington. He certainly is a busy fellow.[54]

This gathering together of Indigenous people—a Native hub—occurred in the room of her Indigenous friend, Lavina. Here Elizabeth expresses her deep sense of pride in Henry, who had many important meetings to attend, in regard to fund-raising for his Native college-preparatory high school. Elizabeth's letter also points to a network or hub of Native intellectuals, who gathered together, and met at Native boarding schools, including Hampton and Carlisle.

Elizabeth mentions her friend Angel, who most likely was Angel Decora, the Ho-Chunk artist and intellectual. Decora taught at Carlisle and was an established artist, already published in *Harper's Magazine* and with studios in New York and Boston. In Decora's autobiography, published in the 1911 issue of the *Red Man*, Carlisle's newspaper, she discusses that young Indians had a talent for pictorial art, Natives' artistic knowledge is worth recognition, and Natives at Carlisle are developing these talents and may contribute to American art.[55] Decora emphasizes Natives' inherent artistic talent, the value of Indigenous art, and its prominent location in American art—challenging dominant perceptions of Native cultural achievements as lower on the evolutional scale than those of whites. She also discusses Emma, who was most likely her sister, who attended their Native hub gathering, showing how Elizabeth maintained connections with her Ojibwe family.

In 1913 the Indian Service transferred Elizabeth to Fort Belknap School in Harlem, Montana. She taught Assiniboine and Gros Ventre children in Harlem for a year and then returned to Hampton to resume postgraduate work in home economics. In 1915, two years later, Elizabeth was once again teaching—this time at Carlisle Indian School, the first federal boarding school, founded by Richard H. Pratt in Pennsylvania, as already mentioned. In 1916, while at Carlisle, Elizabeth wrote about white notions of womanhood in the Carlisle paper, *Red Man*. Her article, "Training Indian Girls for Efficient Home Makers," begins in a covertly subversive manner: "DO NOT intend to tire the reader with long drawn out stories of

Fig. 4. Henry and Elizabeth at the center of the photo. Elizabeth's sister Emma is to the left, and Carmen, a friend, is to the right. Photograph courtesy of the Cloud family.

broken treaties, the misappropriation of Indian money, nor do I intend to dwell on the subject of how we have been starved . . . on various reservation[s]. . . . We hear a great deal about developing leaders for leadership and are apt to forget that our girls are to be the sources of such leadership, too, for they represent our homemakers and homekeepers." Even though Elizabeth emphasizes that she will not discuss the terrible impact of colonialism on Natives (by using capital letters), she still rebelliously reminds the reader of past abuses. Elizabeth argues that Native women are important sources of leadership, while emphasizing Indigenous women's role within the domestic sphere, as taught in federal boarding schools.

However, insofar as subservience—as opposed to leadership—was foundational to white notions of domesticity, Elizabeth creatively combines Ojibwe and white notions of gender. At the same time, her article reproduces gendered, colonial ideas about domesticity. Since "the home is the very core of civilization," Elizabeth argues that Native Americans' successful integration into U.S. society was in the hands of Indigenous women. She portrays the reservation as places where "unkempt homes which are breeding places for filth and disease outnumber the homes of cleanliness and Christian training, and thousands and thousands of acres of Indian land rich in undeveloped resources, are lying idle."[56]

Elizabeth follows settler-colonial and racist ideas that Natives' homes were dirty and in need of Christian influence, and she follows colonial notions that Indigenous lands lay idle and needed to be developed. She, regrettably, also wrote, "Can we expect to develop great, strong Christian leaders in spite of such home conditions? Yes, we can. We can take our youth away from home, send them off to such schools as Haskell, Carlisle, or Hampton for a period of years, and have them associate with high minded instructors who shall teach them that the home is the very core of civilization, that the ideal home shall permeate its environment and bring it into keeping with that of their school." Here Elizabeth follows gendered, settler-colonial strategies for civilizing Native women through the imposition of white, female gender norms. In this article she agrees with the policy of separating Native children from their families, which is very different from her subversive use of the exclamation point in one of her early Hampton fund-raising letters, in which she underscores how difficult it was to be away from her family for so long. This diametrically opposed change in perspective could reflect how her audience of white Carlisle officials influenced her writing, encouraging her to communicate in a very gendered, settler-colonial manner. She wrote this article while she was a teacher at Carlisle, possibly feeling compelled to write something her superiors would have agreed with, to keep her job.

Furthermore, according to Lucy Maddox, Native intellectuals during this time often combined white and Native rhetoric to be heard in the public sphere. Like Henry, Elizabeth mixed Indigenous and settler-colonial perspectives in her writing and speaking, which enabled her to be heard in the public domain during a very racist and colonial time.[57] At the same time, Elizabeth praised Carlisle for creating a "model home cottage" that instructed Native women "how to cook over a common stove, take care of kerosene lamps, and prepare three meals a day in the most wholesome and economical way . . . to learn the art of cooking cereals, vegetables, eggs, fish, bread, cake, and pastry, besides the proper setting of a table and the preparation and serving of family meals."[58] Here Elizabeth again supports white notions of women's domestic roles, criticizes reservation life, promotes assimilation, and, even more painfully, encourages the allotment of Native lands.

Unfortunately, in this article Elizabeth's Ojibwe warrior woman identity was mute, covered and camouflaged by white-centric rhetoric. Instead, she spoke primarily from a "good Indian woman" voice, a voice that points to the reality of working and living at a bastion of settler colonialism, Carlisle Indian School. As Elizabeth's granddaughter, reading this article, imbued with settler-colonial notions of gender and supporting assimilation and allotment, was indeed difficult, agonizing, and challenging. It was also surprising since later Henry, as a modern Ho-Chunk intellectual and warrior, fought back against allotment in his role as coauthor of the Meriam Report and the Indian Reorganization Act of 1934.

Reading this essay, I remembered that central to my work of decolonization is confronting the hard truths of colonization and discussing how my grandparents, at times, were complicit in settler colonialism. My work to face these excruciating colonial moments is integral to my Native feminist ethic. At the same time, I remembered their Native intellectual contemporary Luther Standing Bear and his simultaneous support and rejection of the assimilation campaign against Natives.[59] In his book *My People the Sioux*, for example, he discusses traveling to recruit fellow Lakotas to attend the federal boarding school, Carlisle, and paints a positive picture of Carlisle. In contrast, in his next book, *The Tragedy of the Sioux*, he discusses how he was a bad Indian, a hostile; he does not discuss any desire to stay at Carlisle or portray this federal boarding school in such a positive light. This ambivalence between Native and settler-colonial perspectives in both Elizabeth's and Standing Bear's portrait of Carlisle gestures at how Native intellectuals, during this racist and colonial period, were strongly encouraged to mimic white culture and discourses. Consequently, they were not comfortable expressing total honesty about their experiences or perspectives. Instead, they used doubleness, camouflage, and masking to protect themselves. It seems that Standing Bear became more comfortable being honest in his later publications as compared to his first book.

Henry and Elizabeth Get Married

My grandparents, Henry Roe Cloud and Elizabeth Georgian Bender, announced their engagement in 1915 and married on June 14, 1916. They got married at the home of Charles and Marie Bender, Elizabeth's brother and his wife, in Philadelphia. Charles Albert Bender, who was a great pitcher for the Philadelphia Athletics, was eventually inducted in the 1953 Baseball Hall of Fame. Later on Henry described his relationship with his wife, Elizabeth, to a good friend of his, Harold Buchannan. He told him that he was happily married to Elizabeth, he was deeply proud of her, and he was proud to be her life partner. He told Harold that Elizabeth had often been his guidepost.[60]

In 1916 Henry described the racism he and his new wife, Elizabeth, experienced. He discussed their visits with affluent whites for the purpose of fund-raising for his college-preparatory high school for Indian boys. A letter to Mary Roe demonstrates the positive influence of Cloud's published autobiography, which underscores his identity as a self-made man:

That noon in going to the hotel for lunch we were taken for Negroes and sent to the kitchen for our lunch. When I asked for the ladies wash room and toilet room the proprietors pointed to a slop bucket and told me to wash there. When I asked her if that was all they had, she said "yes." Needless to say we did not eat in the kitchen nor wash in the slop place. We ate in the dining room with all the members of the Harvard club. Elizabeth and I felt pretty blue for two days. The first time she went with me to make an appeal [for money] I got such brusque treatment and such insult from piggish folk.

The world has its two sides but Christian philosophy melts it all. We took it as part of the game. We visited the McCormicks and I shouldn't be surprised if they give us as much as $3,500. One of the finest experiences in my life came after this affair at Lake Geneva. Mr. McCormick invited Elizabeth and me to dinner. To my great surprise he said, "We will drive over to my mother's place and see her [for] five minutes!" As soon as she came out she said, "Why, Henry Cloud I know all about you. I have read [about] your beautiful life in the *Southern Workman*. I am so happy to meet you and Mrs. Cloud."[61]

Henry highlights his feeling of power as an educated Native man by sharing how he rejected eating in the hotel's restaurant because of racist treatment, deciding instead to dine at the Harvard club. He emphasizes his and my grandmother's resilience and strength, quickly recuperating from feeling "blue" and viewing their racist experience as "part of the game," while stressing their exceptional fund-raising skills. Cloud highlights two sides of white society—one racializes him, and the other gives him respect. Rather than seeing my grandfather through a racist lens, Mrs. McCormick discusses his published autobiography and portrays my grandfather's life as "beautiful." Henry attributes his respectful treatment to Christianity, since the McCormicks were Christians. Indeed, his rhetorical use of the self-made man and his Christian identity most likely supported the elderly Christian woman's positive impression of him.

American Indian Institute

Henry Cloud's desire to improve Native education motivated him to found the American Indian Institute, originally named the Roe Indian Institute (after his white adopted father, Walter Roe), an early Native college-preparatory high school for Indigenous boys. According to my mother, Woesha, her parents wished the school could have also included Native girls, but funders were not interested. My grandparents were living in an intensely sexist time, when men and young boys were privileged over women and young girls. Dominant society was following patriarchal notions of gender. Therefore, males were encouraged to attend college more often than females.[62] As late as 1918 the Commission on the Reorganization of Secondary Education argued for a two-track system. White girls and girls of color were encouraged to train for vocations, while students, mostly boys, were guided to take college-preparatory courses. It was not until 1932 that this sexist policy was supposed to change at the school. It was announced in the *Wichita Beacon* newspaper that a cottage was to be built, because Native girls would be admitted soon to the American Indian Institute.[63] When I found this newspaper article in our Cloud family archival material, I was surprised to discover the school planned to admit girls, since my mother, Woesha, did not tell me this. I wondered if this really came to pass and hoped that it did.

From 1910 to 1931 Henry Cloud fund-raised for the school, developed its curriculum, and co-ran the school with his wife, Elizabeth, starting in 1915, when the school opened its doors. Henry must have received valuable educational advice and counsel from his wife, as she was trained as a teacher, an experience and profession Henry did not share. His later involvement in the Meriam Survey taught him that his own abusive educational experiences in a government boarding school were not isolated, but common throughout Indian Country. Federal-government schools for Native Americans offered vocational training that was of little use to their students, both on and off the reservation. Even the education provided at the famous Carlisle and the Hampton Institute was heavily vocational. Cloud chose Wichita, Kansas, as the school's site, because of its central location, to encourage Native students from all over the country to attend.

During the first few years, Native students were able to utilize classrooms in Fairmount College's basement and lived in a small cottage. Once new buildings could be financed and built, the main campus was situated at Wellesley Avenue and Twenty-First Street in Wichita. The school included one large dormitory; a smaller two-story dormitory with five bedrooms on the upper floor, a kitchen, dining room, bathroom, and a library; a one-story cottage; a driveway with two stone gates; and a flagpole. The cottage was big enough for a teacher's apartment and to house five students. A barn, agricultural structures, and wheat fields were part of the campus too.[64]

My aunt Marion Hughes described her early years at the school. "When I was small and growing up, we lived on campus, which later became the home of other people who worked at the school." Later, she described, her dad bought property to the east of the school, a home and forty acres. The school was on a hill, then there was a valley, then the Cloud home, with a barn and outbuildings at the house. She continued, "We used to play in that barn, and in the hay. The field to the east was always put in wheat. . . . My sisters and I sure used to play on the haystack. It was out from the city [of Wichita], five minutes into town, but we didn't grow up in the city. It was on the east side of Wichita. It was pretty flat towards Colorado [Street], but there were hills to the east, the Flint Hills, which went more than 200 miles northeast."[65] My aunt Marion also discussed how she and her sisters always considered these Native students their big brothers. Marion's description shows how the school provided a warm, fun Native home and hub for my aunt and her siblings. Furthermore, Marion and her siblings always appreciated the visits of their cherished Ojibwe grandmother, Mary Razier, Elizabeth's mother.

The school opened in September 1915, with seven students enrolled, including George Martin of Alaska (tribal affiliation unknown), William Ohlerking (Cheyenne and Sioux), Harry Coonts (Pawnee of Oklahoma), Walter Laslay (tribal affiliation unknown, of Iowa), Robert Chaat (Comanche of Oklahoma), David C. Hamilton (Cheyenne of Oklahoma), and Burney O. Wilson (Mechoopda of California). During the second year, enrollment increased to fourteen.

Because the American Indian Institute served a relatively few number of Indigenous students, class sizes were small, and students could receive an excellent college-preparatory education, including, for example, science, history, language arts, and foreign-language courses. Henry Cloud hired Native teachers—an early form of Native hiring preference—who

Fig. 5. American Indian Institute, originally called Roe Indian Institute—the small sign in the photo uses the original name. Photograph courtesy of the Cloud family.

could act as Indigenous role models while providing first-rate instruction. James Ottipoby, a Comanche and a graduate from Hope College in Michigan, taught history. Roy Ussery, a Cherokee, was the science teacher, and Robert C. "Charlie" Starr, a Cheyenne-Arapaho and a graduate of Oklahoma State University, was an instructor of agriculture. Because it was a Christian nondenominational high school, students also received biblical history instruction. As the school increased in size, a three-story dormitory was planned. There was not enough money for this building until May 1921. It was named after a benefactor from Chicago, Elizabeth Voorhees and was therefore called Voorhees Hall. It was large enough to house thirty to forty students. There were two apartments on the bottom floor, and the rest of the building included two big meeting rooms that were used for study hall in the evening.[66]

Henry Cloud provided Native leadership education for Indigenous boys. He hoped that his school could educate a new generation of Native American leaders by giving Native American boys a Christian-based, nondenominational high school education. Harry Coonts, a Pawnee

Fig. 6. Henry holding his eldest daughter, Marion, on his lap. In the center of the photo is Elizabeth's mother, Mary Razier. Elizabeth holds her daughter Anne Woesha on her lap. Photograph courtesy of the Cloud family.

who attended the school, explained his understanding of the leadership training he received there: the American Indian Institute "taught Christian leadership, that is to say an Indian man was to fight for his people to get justice."[67] Cloud encouraged his students to transform a Christian, individualized, masculine identity into one that incorporated an educated warrior identity, encouraging them to fight for the well-being of tribes, to be of service to Native Americans, and to right the wrongs of the federal government.

Harry Coonts, who became the president of his tribal council, is an example of the American Indian Institute's successful Native leadership training. The following is his testimony to Cloud, regarding his tribal situation:

> We, the Pawnees—the members of the Pawnee Council, are the eyes of this Tribe. . . . You [Cloud] used to say that the removal of the Pawnees constitutes one of the saddest marches ever in this land. We then numbered 10,000, now we are only 800. In the treaty of 1857 we ceded

to the United States 25 to 26 counties a record of which will be found in the Omaha Cession 1856 and 1857 section: all lands lying north of Platte River to the point west where the two forks of the Platte River separates. . . . Within this tract of land was reserved for Pawnees thirty miles east and west and 15 miles north and south. The United States Government promised, by treaty, to pay Pawnees $30,000 annually. That is what we are receiving today. The government also promised to educate Pawnees in the same treaty. A school was to be turned over to them after the fulfillment of the treaty. I want you to understand today that the government owes an education to the Pawnees. The Pawnees have been loyal to the Department. The Pawnees have ceded a great territory to the United States. . . . In 1917–1918 a Competency Commission came from the District of Columbia. This Competency Commission issued patents to individual Indians because they could speak a little English. . . . Not one of those so called competent Indians has a foot of land left today. This business of declaring Indians competent to take care of themselves has made a very hard road for the Pawnees. . . . When you get to Washington D.C. tell the Secretary of the Interior that you were with the Pawnee council, that one of them was your first students to come to your school, that he was telling you the real facts about the trust period needs to be extended to these people, that the government must not turn them loose upon their resources, that it would be nothing less than a crime. . . . So, on behalf of the Pawnee Council say that the tribal sentiment is strong for the extension of the trust period.[68]

Demonstrating his Cloud-inspired educated warrior skills, Coonts exposes the abuses of the federal government, including forcing the Pawnees on a horrific march, and implies that this removal caused the loss of many of his ancestors' lives. He argues that the government owed the Pawnees an education in exchange for the Pawnees ceding massive amounts of land. Coonts uncovers the often terrible cost of being declared competent, precipitating the loss of even more Pawnee land, and the importance of the government extending the trust period (rather than losing trust status and no longer having Indian-specified legal status and rights).

Indeed, Coonts discusses how Cloud taught him Native-centric history, helping him understand the government's injustices.

The federal government established Competency Commissions to determine whether individual Natives were competent enough to use their lands allotted to them during the General Allotment Act of 1887. Individuals, who were determined to be competent, were issued fee patents regarding their land. While a fee patent gave power to the allottee to decide whether to keep or sell the land, the enormous loss of Native lands was almost inevitable and unavoidable, given the harsh economic reality of the time and lack of access to credit and markets. Department of the Interior officials knew that virtually 95 percent of fee-patented land would eventually be sold to whites, supporting more Indigenous land dispossession.[69]

Later, in the 1949 commencement speech for graduating Mount Edgecumbe Alaska Native students, Henry Cloud discussed other pivotal educated Ho-Chunk warrior values, which he must have taught his American Indian Institute students, including pride and courage. By encouraging his students to become educated warriors for their people, Cloud defied the federal boarding-school training that taught Natives to be ashamed of their tribal identities, cultures, histories, and philosophies and focus on subservience rather than Native leadership. Motivating Native students to feel a sense of pride and courage was an antidote to the colonial boarding-school regimen of shame and subservience. Therefore, Cloud worked from a traditional Ho-Chunk educational perspective to encourage Native students to regain a sense of prideful, Indigenous humanity; to become motivated by ancestral warrior courage; and to stand up and fight for Native people and challenge colonialism. Similarly, Paulo Freire emphasizes the importance of regaining one's humanity while experiencing oppression as an empowering aspect of working for social change.[70] Notably, reclaiming a sense of Indigenous pride is paramount to becoming tribal sovereign peoples. According to Cloud,

And the [Indian] race needs pride in your origin. Never be ashamed that you are an American Indian or Native of Alaska. Never be ashamed. I am thinking of the Iroquois [Haudenosaunee] tribe in the States. They had self-government. . . . They had a constitution followed upon that of the clan organization. . . . . Benjamin Franklin took lessons from their tribal organization and put [these lessons] in the US constitution of the United States of America. Your [Indian] race has accomplished things of that sort of world import. You should lift your head and be proud that you are a Native American. And then you should have courage. The Indian race despises a coward. . . . There is philosophy among my [Ho-Chunk] people when the smoke of battle clears away let the enemy see the scars on your face [not] on your back. Face forward in the fight [against] all odds and costs. That is applicable to your vocation and anything you propose to do in this life.[71]

In this quote Cloud opposes the colonial notion that Natives were an inferior race by emphasizing that these young students should not be ashamed of their Alaska Native identities, but instead very proud. He disputes the settler-colonial historical narrative about a heroic struggle between good and evil, viewing Indigenous peoples as evil and settlers as good. Cloud critiques this good-versus-evil binary by arguing that one of the founding fathers of the United States, Benjamin Franklin, learned from the Haudenosaunee constitution and introduced Native concepts into his formulation of the U.S. Constitution. In Cloud's historical rendering, Natives were not evil, but instead they had ideas of "world import" that were so powerful they influenced the writing of the U.S. Constitution.

In this way Cloud portrays Natives as intellectuals in their own right, who had systems of government that were equal (if not better) than the colonial government. Cloud also emphasizes that the Haudenosaunee had "self-government." The idea of "self-government" has a settler-colonial connotation in which tribal governments become subsets to the U.S. colonial nation as part of the Indian Reorganization Act of 1934. Regardless of the colonial meaning of the word, Cloud's discussion assumes that Natives had their own powerful governments and were sovereign nations before the advent of the colonizers. Cloud's analysis is a pathbreaking Ho-Chunk intellectual insight about tribal sovereignty and nationhood that predates later Native studies scholarly discussions, including Vine Deloria Jr.'s and Clifford Lytle's important 1984 book,

The Nations Within.[72] This was a strong prosovereignty stance, strikingly different from his earlier speech to the white reform group, Friends of the Indian (see chapter 1). His divergent and opposing viewpoints allude to two diverse audiences, the ultraconservative white reform group and the young Alaska Natives. These viewpoints must have been influenced by Cloud's age while delivering these two speeches—at the time of the first speech, he was in his twenties, and the second, his sixties—and the influence of the racist years of the early twentieth century. Furthermore, Cloud emphasizes a Ho-Chunk warrior philosophy that revolves around summoning courage, confronting fear, standing up, and facing all challenges. He encourages Native students to rely on these Ho-Chunk educational values and philosophy to attain a modern vocation. Cloud, therefore, inspires Native students to combine traditional and modern identities. Cloud was a modern educated Ho-Chunk warrior and an intellectual, and he encouraged these Alaska Native students and, I am certain, American Indian Institute students to follow in his footsteps.

Cloud described founding the American Indian Institute to graduating Alaska Native students at Mount Edgecumbe High School in Alaska in 1949:

I founded the American Indian Institute for young [Indian] men in the states. And there I taught them the work system. They had to work, rich or poor—that was the life of the institution. An Osage boy came [to the school] from the Oklahoma country and he had money from oil, royalties. We had him work along with the other boys. We harvested great fields of wheat. He stood at one end of the field of wheat and looked way down yonder and had to shuck this wheat. After perspiring heavily at the end of one row, he turned to me and said, "I now know what goes into a loaf of bread." He had been receiving $3000 every three months. He did not have to work, but after graduation he took a job just like any boy would and rose in that job until he became an official in the Greyhound lines.[73]

In this quote Cloud discusses the importance of labor for Indigenous students, while arguing that one's upper-class status should not stop a Native person from benefiting from work experience. Cloud's belief in the white idea of the work system was consistent with his Ho-Chunk warrior training regarding the significance of hard work. It was also similar to traditional Ho-Chunk education regarding the importance of working hard and fast. Helene Lincoln, director of the Ho-Chunk Language Renaissance Program in Winnebago, Nebraska, discussed how Ho-Chunk traditional education revolves around the concept of "waresak." "Ware" means work, and "sak" means fast, and "waresak" also means enjoying work and doing it well.[74] Thus, Cloud combines a Ho-Chunk notion about the importance of hard work with a white idea regarding labor, ultimately building on his traditional Ho-Chunk educational training.

While working at the school, Henry Cloud maintained strong ties to his Ho-Chunk people. Consequently, Ho-Chunk students attended the American Indian Institute, including Moses LaMere, David Whitehawk, Curtis Beaver, and George and Walter Snake. Ho-Chunk families traveled to visit the school and frequently would spend the night there. Cloud would offer them gifts for making the journey to visit and would feed them.[75]

Cloud's goal of providing a high school education for Native American boys was an unusual one. During this time many argued that secondary education was not needed for everyone. Most of the high schools served urban and suburban white populations—only a few included African Americans and even fewer admitted Native Americans.[76] As previously mentioned, Cloud wanted to include Native females, but others did not agree with him. Even so, his decision to focus on Native males was problematic, since Native women and their need to be trained as leaders was not addressed, potentially contributing to power imbalances between males and females in tribal communities. These power differentials were partially caused by government boarding schools, where patriarchal notions of gender norms were emphasized, teaching Indigenous females to be subservient to Native males.

The American Indian Institute held powwows at the school. My mother, Woesha, wrote, "While very small, I listened with rapt attention to the beat of the drum being played by one of 'the boys.' Hearing the sounds of drum and song became a natural part of my being. Every so often there were social gatherings by the willow-bordered ponds to the northern edge of the pasture. A picnic and dancing followed by [tribal] stories told by my father was the usual program. The dances by the campfire were stomp or snake dances, the two-step, the round dance. Games included [the] moccasin game. My father enjoyed especially telling love stories."[77] In her autobiography my mother emphasizes how Native culture, including powwow dancing and Indigenous stories and games were an integral part of the school's educational curriculum. By telling Ho-Chunk stories, Cloud provided his students a traditional Indigenous education, following in his Ho-Chunk grandmother's footsteps, who taught him the stories. These social get-togethers also supported the development of Native hubs, both based in geographic space and virtually, not tied to a specified location, where each student could relate to their tribal identity and culture while away from their tribal homes. Hearing Cloud discuss Ho-Chunk stories, for example, could stimulate students' memories of fellow tribal members sharing their own tribally specific culture, supporting a Native hub not based in geographic space. Singing powwow songs could remind Native young men and boys good times at powwows on their home reservations. Gathering together on the American Indian Institute grounds was a geographic location that created a pantribal hub.

Furthermore, the school promoted the study of Native language arts.[78] Celebrating Native culture was definitely a radical approach to education during this time, when government boarding schools destroyed everything Native American. In fact, as part of the American Indian Institute's Literary Society, the students were encouraged to examine the relationship between Shakespeare and traditional tribal stories. Students would meet in the Clouds' home once per week to discuss white writers and tribal stories. This Native-centric educational approach helped the students to connect their college-preparatory education with their tribal backgrounds. Elizabeth Cloud's involvement in Hampton's Literary Society, the Josephines, must have influenced the creation of the Literary Society, except with a pivotal difference. Henry Cloud could tell Ho-Chunk stories and their related importance as Indigenous philosophy and as instruction in encouraging positive behavior and action.[79] This Ho-Chunk-centric educational approach assisted the students to understand difficult and complex Eurocentric stories.[80] At the same time, placing traditional tribal stories on an equal footing with Shakespeare was a revolutionary educational method. Boarding-school officials, in contrast, viewed Native stories and folklore as less developed than white literary works.

Similarly, in 1931 Cloud's critique of the Indian Service (see chapter 1) points to his motivation to develop Native-centric educational curriculum at the American Indian Institute. Cloud taught Native culture, history, language arts, and philosophy together with white philosophy and ideas, supporting cultural pluralism rather than assimilation. Cloud challenged the lack of respect federal-government employees had for Native thought and philosophy.[81] He argued against assimilation and instead for a flexible, fluid notion of culture where Natives combine Indigenous and white knowledge. His flexible and fluid notion of culture was a revolutionary departure from static notions of culture, which the federal-government's policy of assimilation was based on.[82]

Moreover, Henry Cloud's Indigenous-oriented intellectual training, curriculum, and perspectives regarding Native leadership, history, culture, philosophy, and language arts are examples of Native-studies curriculum and approaches.[83] His Ho-Chunk-inspired educational work could be viewed as an early precursor to later Indigenous-studies curriculum and training developed in Native-studies programs on college campuses.[84] The school's use of Native-oriented curriculum was an example of the Clouds' belief in cultural pluralism and Indigenous cultural citizenship: the right to be different and belong in tribal nations and U.S. society.

Elizabeth Bender Cloud, Co-Principal

While Henry was the principal, founder, and fund-raiser for the American Indian Institute, Elizabeth ran the school while he was away fund-raising. Elizabeth wrote, "Henry is away so much and when he is away, I am 'chief cook and bottlewasher,' in other words all the responsibility of school affairs seems to fall on my shoulders." In this way Henry and Elizabeth were following Native notions of complementary gender roles between couples, rather than white notions where women are confined in the domestic sphere and subservient to their husbands. Elizabeth, for example, did financial accounting, wrote fund-raising letters, and accompanied Henry on recruiting trips for the institute. In a letter to Miss Andrus, a Hampton school employee, Elizabeth attempts to recruit some of the Native boys who would not be returning to Hampton for the American Indian Institute: "I am loyal to Hampton, but with so few [Native students] there it seems to me everything bears on the negro problem and they are a long ways from home to feel the real touch of the Indians' need for leadership."[85] Here Elizabeth emphasizes the differences between Hampton and the American Indian Institute. One main difference was the institute's purpose to encourage Native young men to be leaders rather than be subservient. Another difference was the school's focus on the education of Native young men rather than an emphasis on educating African Americans. Her mention of Hampton being far away from Native students' homes was an oblique critique of the school's separation of Indigenous children from the so-called negative influences of their tribes and families.

My father, Robert North, described Elizabeth's relationship with Henry and her role in the American Indian Institute:

She [Elizabeth] was a remarkable woman, and it was very fortunate he [Henry] had her. . . . He generated ideas, interesting ideas . . . but she was the practical one, and she kept the family together, and furthermore, particularly in the early years, after their marriage in the early 20s, when he was head of the school in Wichita, he had to spend an enormous amount of time raising money, so he'd be gone for months, and just at the time when the girls were being born, and when little Henry was born, and she was really running the school, and there was a lot to run. . . . But there were also all kinds of crises, as you can imagine with youngsters of that age: they were always being swept by measles or chicken pox, and the boys would all get it, and then the girls would get it, and they were always short-handed, and you know I've seen her letters that she wrote to him during those years, and she was always cheerful. She was always patient, but she'd insert little signals here and there, that she could do with a little help.[86]

My father, Robert, discusses the challenging role my grandmother, Elizabeth, had running the school, being both a mother and the unofficial head of the school. She bridged private and public spheres, while following a fluid sense of Ojibwe gender. In this quote my father describes

Elizabeth as the "practical one" and Henry as the idea person. I would argue that Elizabeth also generated ideas along with Henry, and labeling Henry as more intellectually astute than Elizabeth could be a sexist categorization.

Elizabeth also discusses the challenge of juggling multiple responsibilities, including her serving as a cook, attending a conference, and maintaining their home:

> This fall we were without a cook for two months and as much as I hate to cook I pitched in and cooked for about thirty until the holidays. . . . I could not have done it, had not my mother been here, but she looked after our household and kept the house spick and span. We have so much company dropping in from all parts of the country. I try above everything else to keep my home cozy and neat, but am not a slave to housework. . . . Henry and I attended the Student Volunteer Convention in Des Moines, where we went as delegates.[87]

Here Elizabeth challenges the white colonial notion taught in Native boarding schools that Indigenous women must be confined in the home, exclaiming she was not a "slave to housework" and hated to cook. At the same time, she emphasizes how her mother kept her home "spick and span," an important lesson girls learned in the Native boarding schools. Elizabeth also highlights how her Ojibwe mother traveled from the White Earth Reservation to help her run her household, showing how she maintained a close connection with her mother and how her home became an Ojibwe hub, since her mother Mary could provide an Ojibwe cultural influence on her children.

Elizabeth was always available to support Henry during political crises and issues at the American Indian Institute. In 1920 Elizabeth wrote in a letter about how the white race, including Mary Roe, who was on the institute's board, viewed my grandfather as a child, who was not fit to be the principal of the college-preparatory high school for Native boys:

> I suppose mother [Mary Roe] wrote recommending you be the one to raise the money on the outside while perhaps someone else to be put in charge of this school to have direct charge. . . . There is this

thing about it dearie. If you are not made principal of this enterprise and people do not think you have the ability to head this enterprise for our people, then the graceful thing for us to do is to step out. It is evidence enough that the white race [including Mary Roe] still thinks the Indian in the childhood stage of development and *Henry Cloud* is not meant for the leader of his people.

She discusses Mary Roe's recommendation of putting him in the role of fund-raiser for the school rather than as principal. She aligns herself with her husband, while expressing her love for him, calling him "dearie" and saying that she will also leave, since she, along with Henry, worked at the school. By emphasizing his name, Henry Cloud, and not including the surname Roe in the middle, she prioritizes his Ho-Chunk identity above his connection with his white "parents." Her underlining points to her understanding and her compassion for his suffering from racist treatment, while respecting his worth as a Ho-Chunk man, even without the Roe name. My grandparents could share the difficulties of living in a racist world, including the colonial beliefs of those close to them, such as Mary Roe's. As this example reveals, Henry's marriage to Elizabeth was central to his resilience in the face of colonial adversity.[88]

In another letter about Mary Roe, Elizabeth analyzes why Mary was not supporting Henry in his bid to become school principal: "After you wrote what she said, 'Letting Henry down easy, etc.,' I just felt that I do not want to even see her again. . . . Mother loves very intensely or else does everything in her power to undermine who she has loved if she thinks her love is being cast aside. If she comes down here when school is nearly out, I do not want to see her and I will go down on our family farm if she does come. I wish she had never come into our lives."[89] Elizabeth discusses Mary Roe's belief that my grandfather had "cast aside" his informally adoptive mother's love, again showing him drawing a boundary between them as a protective strategy. This letter once more demonstrates my grandmother's commitment to stand by her husband during moments of incredible difficulty and strain caused by his relationship with his white "mother."[90] Her loving support and intense rejection of Mary Roe points to how enraged Elizabeth was and how challenging this maternal relationship could be.

Earlier, in 1919, Mary Roe wrote a letter to my grandfather, complaining about his behavior toward her. She wrote, "Therefore, dear, whenever, hereafter I seem not to respond or to turn away remember my own assertion of finding a dual personality in you, one of which draws one by the bonds of a tender, a pure, and a faithful affection, one that dishonors no one; while the other repels me and can win from me no understanding or cooperation."[91] Mary Roe's discussion of Cloud's "dual personality," alludes to his mixed feelings toward her. On the one hand, Cloud treated her positively and dutifully. On the other, he used a defensive strategy, drawing a boundary between himself and Mary. This letter also shows her attempt to use rejection as a reprisal for his self-protection.

The importance of this school was deeply etched in my childhood memory when my adopted Ho-Chunk uncle, Jay Russell Hunter, invited our family to attend the First Annual Wichita Powwow. There the Hunters honored the American Indian Institute. My uncle was a student at the school, and his parents, John and Etta Hunter, worked at the American Indian Institute. The Hunter and Cloud families have always been close, since John Hunter and Henry Cloud were best friends during childhood. Cloud would always visit John and Etta Hunter on their farm in Winnebago. Indeed, Etta would take care of my mother and her sisters while my grandmother, Elizabeth, assisted in running the school. Etta taught my uncle Henry II our Ho-Chunk language before he died at three years old. Following Ho-Chunk tradition, my grandparents adopted the Hunters' son Jay Russell as a way to soften the terribly painful emotional blow of losing little Henry. We traveled to Wichita and attended the honoring ceremony. At the powwow I heard a brief history of the American Indian Institute broadcast over the loudspeakers. My uncle, Jay Russell Hunter, called us out into the arena to dance around the circle in honor of the school.

These childhood memories not only demonstrate the importance of the American Indian Institute to those who attended and worked there but also show how Henry continued practicing his Ho-Chunk culture and language. Henry would converse often with John Hunter in our Ho-Chunk language. My aunt Marion remembered how much her dad,

Henry, enjoyed talking to his close friend John in his tribal language.[92] Henry's decision to invite John and Etta Hunter to work at the American Indian Institute was a way to transform the school into a Ho-Chunk hub. Besides following Ho-Chunk tradition and adopting Jay Russell Hunter, Henry encouraged his son to learn Ho-Chunk. When my aunt Marion was around eleven or twelve years old, she was also supposed to spend a summer with John and Etta Hunter, and only Ho-Chunk was to be spoken. At the last minute Elizabeth decided her daughter Marion could not go, because she was the oldest and had many family responsibilities. Cloud continued speaking his Ho-Chunk language throughout his life, ultimately challenging conservative Christian doctrine as well as the assimilationist policy of the government's Indian boarding schools that punished Native children for speaking their tribal languages.

My mother, Woesha, described how much she missed her dad during this period, when he traveled to fund-raise for the school:

> So the homecomings [of her father] were very, very joyous and [a] happy occasion, and there were times when we would spend, regardless of the hour of the night or day, we'd have an hour or two with the parents when my father was reviewing all that happened while he was gone. As I say, we would have liked very much to have him home all the time but . . . that would have been too much to expect. And he was a person who valued his family so much. He was a very romantic type and displayed his love for his family quite openly; [he was] very, very affectionate. Mother, when she went on her speaking engagements, as I grew older she would take me with her, so there was no great feeling of loss in that sense.[93]

In this quote my mom describes the difficulty of having her dad gone so frequently. In contrast, Woesha's mom, my grandmother, Elizabeth, represented a reliable presence in her life. In a sense my own mom sacrificed her need for her father to be home more, understanding his responsibility as a public figure. Her memories of her dad's affection

Fig. 7. Etta and John Hunter with Henry II, youngest child of Henry and Elizabeth Cloud, at the American Indian Institute. Photograph courtesy of the Cloud family.

shows a personal, familial side of Henry, which is often missed in other portrayals of him.

Elizabeth's role as a school leader is underscored in a 1933 newspaper article in the *Wichita Eagle*: "The powwow is an annual event at the American Indian Institute. This year, in the absence of Dr. Henry Roe Cloud, head of the school, who is in Washington on business, it was managed by Mrs. Cloud. . . . Then Mrs. Cloud gave a short talk, welcoming the guests and outlining the purpose of Indian education."[94] Elizabeth acted as the school's principal in Cloud's absence.

In 1931 Henry Cloud, who was tired of constant fund-raising and the difficulties of running the American Indian Institute, decided to accept a position as an Indian Affairs field representative at large, with duties revolving around Indian education. He took a one-year leave of absence, while he continued as the unofficial principal of the school through 1931. At this time Elizabeth assumed more of the school's fund-raising and administrative duties. She continued as a matron of the school, teacher, and local administrator. Cloud argued for his wife to be the school's next principal, since she knew the operations of the school firsthand. He advocated for her, as she was a Native American, and he felt that an Indigenous person should assume leadership of the school. He also tried to deal with the church's potential concerns of putting a woman in charge: "Many women have become prominent in educational work in our country as deans, presidents as well as founders and leaders of many and diverse types of educational institutions among the white people. I am thinking of the Berry Schools. I am thinking of the many presidents of great women's colleges in the East."[95] Elizabeth was denied the role due to her gender. Because the school was primarily for Native American boys (even though there was a plan to start admitting girls in 1932), it was viewed inappropriate for a woman to be principal. Elizabeth's leadership in running the school and Henry's support of her involvement showed that neither believed in the Eurocentric model of subservient female behavior taught in the Native boarding schools. Henry Cloud resigned in 1932, and Elizabeth Cloud followed suit on September 15, 1934. This finished the final chapter of my grandparents' work running an early Native-run college-preparatory high school for Native youth.

Fig. 8. Henry looking happy with his four daughters swimming. The eldest daughter, Marion, holds onto her father's elbow. The second eldest, Anne Woesha, is to Henry's right. Henry holds the youngest, Lillian. The second to the youngest, Ramona, stands in the front. Photograph courtesy of the Cloud family.

Fig. 9. John and Etta Hunter on the left in the back row. Henry is holding a movie camera on the right. Anne Woesha is the tallest daughter. The Clouds' youngest daughter, Lillian, is also wearing a hat and stands in front of Anne Woesha. The Clouds' youngest, Henry II, stands in front, and Marion is next to her father, Henry. Photograph courtesy of the Cloud family.

Fig. 10. The Cloud family at the American Indian Institute. Henry has his arms around his wife, Elizabeth, and his daughter Anne Woesha. The Clouds' oldest daughter, Marion, stands next to her mother. In front of her parents is the youngest, Lillian. Ramona, who is the second to the youngest, is next to her grandmother, Mary, who is positioned on the right side of the photo. Photograph courtesy of the Cloud family.

In sum, this chapter is a Ho-Chunk–centric analysis of Henry Cloud's involvement in the SAI and his successful activism and intellectual work in support of Geronimo and his people. Cloud's Ho-Chunk warrior identity was central to his intellectual abilities, enabling him to look at the world from Native perspectives, while energizing him to fight for Ho-Chunks and Native Americans overall, including the Apaches. I discuss how Cloud combined his Ho-Chunk and Yale training, transforming a colonial education into Native-centric intellectual firepower to fight in support of the Apaches' struggle against the federal government. It is also an Ojibwe-centric analysis of Elizabeth, who, like Henry, relied on

Native hub making to maintain a connection to her tribal identity and family, used Native and settler-colonial perspectives in her writing, and combined Indigenous and white notions of gender. The chapter, furthermore, argues that Henry Cloud's Native-oriented educational methods at the American Indian Institute included leadership training, Native history, culture, philosophy, and language arts, encouraging Indigenous boys to become educated warriors for their people. Henry Cloud's development of Native-studies curriculum and approaches was not only a radical approach to Indigenous education but also a harbinger of later Native-studies programs at colleges, such as University of California at Davis and Berkeley and San Francisco State University campuses. The Clouds' supporting students' tribal identities was a direct challenge to their settler-colonial Native boarding-school training and demonstrates their belief in cultural pluralism and Indigenous cultural citizenship. The chapter also examines the work, activism, and marital relationship of Henry and Elizabeth Cloud, arguing they practiced a Native notion of complementary gender roles. Elizabeth and Henry were a "power couple" who shared equally the running of the American Indian Institute. The next chapter discusses Henry's decision to take a break from the American Indian Institute to become the only Native member of the survey team investigating the Indian Service; co-write the Meriam Report and, according to available evidence, the Indian Reorganization Act of 1934; and accept the superintendent position at Haskell, a federal-government boarding school.[96]

CHAPTER 3

Henry Cloud's Role in the Meriam Report, the Indian Reorganization Act, and the Haskell Institute

This chapter examines Henry Cloud's involvement as the only Native American on Lewis Meriam's ten-member survey team. Cloud and the other team members undertook and completed an exhaustive investigation of Indian affairs — the basis for a 1928 study of the socioeconomic conditions of Native Americans throughout the United States and the Indian Service. The Brookings Institution's Institute for Government Research, a privately run research group based in Washington DC, commissioned the survey team's efforts. In 1928 the survey results were made public and were commonly called the "Meriam Report" and officially titled "The Problem of Indian Administration." This powerful report documented governmental neglect and inefficiency in the Indian Service and exposed extensive poverty, health issues, and bad conditions on reservations and in federal boarding schools.

As part of the survey team, Cloud was central to the investigation of Native conditions. Cloud wrote unfavorable reports, exposing the horrific conditions in the Rosebud and Yankton federal boarding schools. The Meriam Report's release led to the passage of the Indian Reorganization Act (IRA) in 1934. According to available evidence, Cloud assisted in drafting the IRA and encouraged tribes to agree to the act's conditions.[1] As a result of his involvement in the Meriam Report, Cloud was considered for the position of commissioner of Indian Affairs, but his colleagues blocked his nomination and potential appointment by portraying him as "puzzled" and emotionally weak—objections that point to racist assumptions.[2] Cloud instead built on his Native-studies curriculum work at the American Indian Institute and advocated for Indigenous culture, history, and leadership training at Haskell federal boarding school and for Native cultural citizenship—the right for Natives to be different and belong in U.S. schools.

Cloud and the Meriam Report

Cloud played a major role on the survey-staff team of the Meriam Report. As a Yale-educated Ho-Chunk intellectual, principal of the American Indian Institute, and founder of SAI, he was perfectly positioned to serve on such a high-profile survey team. Cloud understood Native reality and conditions: he was born and raised on the Winnebago Reservation, attended Native federal boarding schools, was well connected to Native Americans across the United States, had traveled to many reservations, and had already conducted investigations of federal boarding schools.[3] According to Meriam, Cloud was remarkably well versed in such fields as health, education, and community life and law. Meriam highlights Cloud's noteworthy accomplishments as part of the survey team:

> In all announcements of the arrival of the survey staff at a jurisdiction, the fact was featured that the staff included one Indian. What is commonly termed the Indian "grape vine telegraph" also worked. Add to these aids was the fact that Mr. Cloud has a wide acquaintanceship among the Indians of the United States and had been active for years in constructive work on their behalf. The result was the one hoped for, namely, that the Indians would come to him. Thus conferences with Indians and Indian councils became a regular part of the work of the survey.[4]

Because of Cloud's involvement and presence, the survey staff was able to acquire essential information. Many Natives came to Cloud to discuss their particular problems.[5] His involvement meant they could finally talk to a Native professional who understood their plight and had the power to improve conditions.

Cloud's role in the survey team was far beyond, as Meriam describes, that of a contact person and mediator between white administrators and Native communities. In fact, Cloud's perspective was crucial to the team's understanding of Native conditions throughout Indian Country. Two highly critical reports of federal boarding schools, which Cloud wrote, had no dates in our Cloud family files. They expose the horrible abuses Indigenous children suffered. These reports could have been written as part of his work in the Meriam Commission or for other investigations of federal boarding schools he had previously conducted in 1914 and 1915.[6] In his report of the Rosebud federal boarding school, he wrote,

One of the worst schools I have seen has been the Rosebud Boarding school at Mission, S.D. [South Dakota]. . . . Evidence of maladministration was on every hand,—in buildings, grounds, farm and in the character of the student body. The boys' sitting room was shown me at one end of the basement playroom. Furniture strewn about everywhere. Coats and trousers in tangled heaps, covered the dust laden floor. The toilet arrangements were bad. . . . The floor of the laundry was dirty and the ceiling and the walls were literally black with soot. The four walls were covered with scratched names. This laundry is a shame to any institution.

The bakery and kitchen were also in poor condition. In the room where bread is made, coal is stoked into the stove so that the floor is covered with coal dust. . . . The kitchen is poorly equipped. Utensils were of the rudest sort and kept in very cramped quarters. Dishes had to be washed in the dining room. I stood throughout one meal in the school dining room. Everywhere the children would hold up their plate high in the air for more food.

The sheds in the barnyard were tumbling down and the fences were dilapidated. . . . More serious than the condition of the buildings is the moral atmosphere of the school that must have long prevailed before Supt. McGregor took charge. James Farmer, one of the present larger boys was a "tough" in the school. He smoked cigarettes and chewed tobacco constantly. In an altercation with the engineer of the school he knocked him down. According to Mr. McGregor, in eighteen years three boys froze to death by running away. This year three girls ran away. For such an offense as this under the former administration one girl was made to carry a ball and chain around her ankle, and push a wheel-barrow for hours in front of the whole school.[7]

Cloud exposes the shocking abuse and unhealthy conditions of the Rosebud boarding school. The buildings were poorly maintained, and the school was filthy, making it a dangerous, unsanitary, and unhealthy place for young Native children to live. The Native girl's abusive punishment for running away—being shackled with a ball and chain around her leg and being forced to push a wheelbarrow for hours in front of the school—was similar to the punishments in prisons at that time, not the punishments in educational institutions. Cloud's discussion of the moral environment of the school points to his training as a Christian Presbyterian minister, emphasizing that smoking and chewing tobacco is a moral failure, not just unhealthy behavior. Cloud also highlights how dangerous these federal boarding schools were for Natives' safety, threatening Native children's lives, by recounting how three boys froze to death after running away. This boarding school was such a terrible place for Native children to inhabit that these boys risked their very lives to escape the ghastly living conditions. Indeed, running away took much courage, as the winters are severe in the Dakotas. It was a valiant act of resistance to run away—a challenge to settler colonialism. And Cloud's own searing critique of this boarding school is an extension of these Native children's anticolonial resistance.

In the Cloud family files I found an additional undated report Cloud wrote regarding Yankton Indian School:

I cannot say very much that is favorable to the Yankton Indian School. The boy's matron and the girl's matron were both negligent in their duty. . . . The washroom was disorderly. The attempt to have the boys use the tooth brush was becoming a danger rather than a help. All tooth brushes were placed in pockets along the wall with no designation as to owners and every one was dirty and repulsive. The boy's clothing, corduroys, coats, sweaters, etc., were all piled into a huge box indiscriminately. There were no separate places for each boy's belongings.

On examining the girl's dormitory, I was shown around by the boy's matron. I stepped down into the basement to see the toilet and bath arrangements. It was pitch dark down in there although it was midday. I stumbled upon a heap of what seemed to be a big pile [of] rubbish. While I was thus groping about I heard the girl's matron berating the boy's matron for bringing me over to her quarters without first warning her. She said, "I wouldn't do that to you." I found that the thing I stumbled over was a tangled mass of girl's dresses left upon a dirty basement floor.

The campus was strewn with papers everywhere. The wind blew the papers against the fence in front of the school so that it became a wall of rubbish and weeds.

When it rained, the water fell from the eaves, there being no down pipes. As the boys ran in and out and around the building, its immediate vicinity became a mire.

Close by, about eight yards, there was a large pig-pen. From this pen half a dozen sows roamed at large over the campus. The stench, when the wind blew from that direction, was strong.[8]

Cloud critiques the matrons as derelict in their duties and not providing a safe or healthy environment for Native children. He describes the unhealthy practice of dirty, communal toothbrushes, a ripe vector for the spread of disease to young children. The matrons did not even ensure Native children had access to clean clothing, and the clothing was not organized or separated for each child. Instead, their clothing was dirty and strewn across the floor. Cloud also discusses pigs wandering around the school premises—another vector for spreading diseases.

These two reports prove that these two federal boarding schools were filthy, unsanitary, abusive, and poorly run. Cloud's description of the horrific environments of these schools was a microcosm of the entire federal boarding-school system and is a challenge to settler colonialism; federal boarding schools were a colonial apparatus developed to erase and eliminate Native children's distinct cultural identities and allegiance to their tribal nations.[9] Once Native children no longer felt an attachment to their tribes, they could then possibly become willing to give up their

Native land to the federal government. Land dispossession is integral and central to settler colonialism.[10] Cloud describes in depth the extreme punishment of a Native child he witnessed, revealing the suffering of children in these schools. Cloud's exposure of the appalling abuse and unsanitary conditions at these two federal boarding schools demonstrates his anticolonial intellectual stance and ability to wage a powerful critique of the federal boarding schools and the Indian Service—a skill that must have shaped his contribution to the Meriam Report.

Survey Team and Commissioner of Indian Affairs Discussion

As a result of Cloud's work on the Meriam Report survey team, his name was seriously considered as a candidate for the commissioner of Indian Affairs. Lewis Meriam, technical director of the survey team, believed that for the recommendations of the survey staff to impact Native Americans, the Indian Service needed to undergo extensive reform. In a 1928 letter to Edward Dale, professor of history at the University of Oklahoma and another member of the survey team, Meriam discusses that the country needed a commissioner of Indian Affairs who was an effective adminis-trator and able to accomplish his goals and objectives. He praises Cloud's work with the survey of Indian Affairs and deliberated on suggesting him for the high-level position of commissioner of Indian Affairs:

> Henry might be awfully unhappy in that office [as commissioner of Indian Affairs]. I do not think any one of us ought to accept it unless we are positive that we shall have the active support of the President of the United States and that public opinion is sufficiently behind us so that we are going to have appropriations. Unless Henry were sure of this I do not think the position would bring anything but bitterness and disappointment. He would be subject to pressure and demands of a kind which he has not previously encountered and his experi-ence would not furnish any guide as to how to handle them. I am not sure but that might be an asset rather than a liability but I fear that they would be the part of the job that would make life miserable unless they were counterbalanced by a feeling of real advancement and achievement. The job would be a deadly one, and particularly

to Henry whose feeling of responsibility would be far greater than that of any of the rest of us because he would feel that tremendous responsibility to his own race.[11]

Meriam argues that Cloud was inexperienced and did not possess the thick skin necessary to execute this high-level position. He mentions Cloud's race as one reason he is unfit to be commissioner: Henry would feel too much responsibility to his own race. This racialized reasoning is problematic since whites become administrators in the U.S. government and serve their own white constituencies, and their race is not held against them. Meriam's evaluations of Cloud repeatedly point to racist assumptions. He views Natives as not equipped emotionally to handle the suffering of our own people. This problematic logic is discussed by Iris Marion Young, a feminist philosopher, who argues that people of color and women are assumed to be inferior to (rational) white men because they are unable to handle emotions appropriately, especially in the public sphere.[12]

In his response Dale confirmed Meriam's analysis of Cloud's potential efficacy as commissioner of Indian Affairs:

Frankly and confidentially, I do not think that Henry is the man for the job. I know you will not misunderstand this, for everyone in our group must know that I love Henry like a brother and have the highest admiration for his remarkable qualities of mind and heart. I do not believe, however that he is fitted either by temperament or training for such a task. I feel as you do that he might be unhappy in such a position and would undoubtedly be subject to pressure and demands that would be very puzzling to him. In addition, I do not think he knows much of governmental administration or of the organization and workings of such bureau as that of Indian Affairs.[13]

In this letter Dale evaluates Cloud as unfit, in terms of temperament and training, for the task of commissioner. His description of such a high-level position being "puzzling" to Cloud reveals Dale's condescension toward Cloud and his abilities—a condescension that must be viewed through the lens of racism. The word "puzzling" implies Cloud, as a Native man, lacks an intellect, ability, or fortitude strong enough to weather the pressures of the job. This assumption is a curious one, since Cloud survived many immensely difficult pressures, such as an impoverished childhood on a reservation, being forcibly taken to and living within an abusive environment of a federal boarding school, and, as an adult, somehow excelling in the intense academic environment at Yale.

At the same time, Cloud, who most likely was not aware of the Meriam-Dale correspondence, had written to Meriam recommending that the survey staff catapult him into the position of commissioner of Indian Affairs.[14] Meriam wrote an October 26, 1928, letter to Cloud, saying that he had long thought of the possibility of catapulting him into the position of commissioner. Meriam responded honestly to Cloud that the job was an impossible one, where he would "encounter so much inertia and active opposition that he will fall short of his goal." In addition, Meriam argued that no "young or middle aged man who has his own way to make [should] take the position at this time. It is too likely to break his spirit if it does not discredit him." Finally, Meriam highlighted that even though he would be "thrilled to see Henry Roe Cloud Commissioner, and I know others wound, but I don't want to let my enthusiasm lead me into catapulting my friend into a martyr's job." He articulated to Cloud that he possibly will "render such great service in other ways that to put [him] in that office seems a needless sacrifice."[15]

The same thoughts that E. E. Dale shared with Meriam were echoed to Cloud, who Dale thought was not "fitted either by temperament or training for this particular job." Dale also wrote to Meriam, stating that it would be a wonderful thing to see Cloud reach his ambitions but that it would not be good for him personally to land the job.[16] Later, in a letter of February 21, 1929, Dale wrote to Meriam, discussing why Cloud was not up to the job of commissioner of Indian Affairs:

Certainly, one of two things is going to happen, either we are doomed to have more years of Indian Service like the present one, improved and strengthened, of course, to a certain extent, our report and the publicity it has received, but essentially the same old system after all, or else we are going to have what we all hope—a rather complete change of viewpoint and somewhat wholesale reorganization of the Bureau along the lines we have suggested. If we are to have the first, Henry would be very unhappy in the job. He would find himself in a maze of technicalities and red tape for which he would have little understanding. He would see himself helpless to do the things that he wanted to do and would suffer very keenly when he saw the interests of helpless Indian children traded off for other things desired by members of Congress. He would find himself up against a brick wall without any power to make a single dint on it. On the other hand, if it is to be a far reaching organization, Henry is not the man to make it. He has not the training, the experience, nor the understanding of government and governmental affairs that would fit him to assume the leadership of such a work as reorganization. Of this, I am sure. I confess that the matter has not disturbed me, however, for I am frank to say that I do not think he has a ghost of a chance of ever securing that appointment.[17]

While some might argue that Lewis Meriam hoped to become the next commissioner of Indian Affairs, his letters demonstrate that he would not have accepted the position. Meriam wrote, "I fear that John Collier has included my name on the list of persons of his group [he] is considering for the commissionership. My own feeling is that I should be regarded as entirely out of it because I think I can do more good on the outside than I could possibly do on the inside [of the federal government]."[18] While Meriam was not interested in the position, Dale gave Meriam his hearty endorsement as "the only man [on the survey staff] fitted for the position of Indian affairs": "At the same time, I cannot help feeling that if there is to be a reorganization along the line suggested, you are the best qualified man in the United States to do the job. Your training, experiences, and knowledge of government and governmental problems plus your knowledge of Indian affairs and your keen interest in the problem would make you the ideal man for the place."[19]

After reading these letters, my mother, Woesha Cloud North, argued that Dale was "apple polishing," telling Meriam that he would make a good commissioner. She said, "So they would not endorse him [Cloud] in any way. . . . So my father did try for it [to be commissioner], and it's true—you need to play the political game. And he had hoped his friend and [Yale] classmate, Bob Taft [son of former President William Taft], would throw some weight towards the nomination, but he just didn't have enough political clout to do it, and if he couldn't get his so-called friends that he worked with to back him . . . and you need all the political backing."[20]

It is odd that Dale endorsed Meriam so strongly and discounted Cloud's abilities and experience, arguing that Cloud was not fit for the position of commissioner. Donald Critchlow, a historian, portrays Meriam as an "efficiency expert," who was less interested in changing current governmental Indian policies than in ensuring streamlining existing policies through a properly organized administration and well-trained specialists. The Meriam Report, Critchlow argues, called for an improvement in the administration of the Indian Service, but it did not look ahead to a "New Deal" for American Indians, a revamping of Native policy discussed by John Collier and others. John Collier and the critics of the Indian Service, on the other hand, pushed for a radical shift in policy—away from Natives' individual land ownership and toward tribal incorporation of Indigenous land.[21] In other words, Critchlow argues that Meriam and his supporters lacked innovative ideas that could contribute to Native policy reform—his lack of originality a detraction from his suitability for commissioner of Indian Affairs.

In the letters between Dale and Meriam, neither emphasizes Cloud's unique expertise. Cloud had educational credentials equal if not superior to the other investigators. And because of his experiences with Native Americans as an investigator, missionary, and educator, he had more firsthand knowledge of Native peoples than the rest of the survey team. The only other member of the team with any real knowledge of Native Americans was Fayette A. McKenzie, another cofounder of the Society of American Indians. Also with a master's degree from Yale, Cloud was the only trained anthropologist on the staff. Cloud's education, experiences, knowledge, and perspective made him a valuable member of the survey team.[22] But Cloud's strengths are not reflected in these letters. Rather, he was judged as "puzzled" by bureaucracy. Cathleen Cahill, in her book *Federal Fathers and Mothers*, discusses how the opportunities for Native Americans working for the Indian Service were limited to tasks believed to be appropriate for their race. There was a glass ceiling that Native Americans could not rise above, due to the strong racist environment. Therefore, the position of commissioner of Indian Affairs was not a possibility for Cloud or other Natives at that time. Following Cahill, Dales' and Meriam's discussion of Cloud alludes to the underlying racist attitude that Native intelligence was inferior to that of whites.

Four or so years later, in February 1933, the Navajos wanted Cloud to become commissioner of Indian Affairs, but their political efforts never reached fruition.[23] In the early twentieth century, the United States was not willing to have a Native American as head of the Bureau of Indian Affairs. It was not until the 1960s that a Native became commissioner of Indian Affairs.[24]

During the summer of 1927, once the fieldwork portion of the Meriam Report survey was finished, Cloud and our family found a place to stay in Kensington, Maryland, so he could assist in writing the report. Elizabeth's sister, Emma, a registered nurse who worked at Hahnemann Hospital in Philadelphia, went with the Clouds to Maryland. Lewis Meriam had found a house for them close to where he lived. Every day Cloud traveled to the Indian Affairs survey headquarters in Washington DC to contribute to writing the report. Cloud's daughters went swimming, rode bicycles on the street, or played croquet on the grassy lawn. And everyday Henry II somehow knew exactly when his father would arrive home and waited for him on the edge of the walkway.[25]

Death of "Little Henry"

After the report was written, the Clouds returned to Wichita and to running the American Indian Institute. The following year, 1929, was an incredibly painful one for our Cloud family. First, Cloud's fervent desire to be the commissioner of Indian Affairs was never realized. Then the Cloud family suffered the death of Henry Roe Cloud II, their only son and brother, who died of pneumonia at three years old in Wichita, Kansas. Little Henry experienced heart problems, and his doctor had taken out his tonsils. The doctor, Henry, and Elizabeth were all afraid that "Little Henry" was going to suffer from acute ear infections. He stayed in the hospital for close to three months. On March 25, 1929, the day before his death, Little Henry played with stuffed animals and toys for the first time since entering the hospital. The doctor informed the Clouds that they were "through the crisis." Then, at about four in the morning the phone woke up the Cloud family. It was Henry Sr. He told Marion, the eldest, "Instead of Uncle John [Hunter] taking you to school this morning, I want you and your sisters to come to the hospital. He'll bring you down." Marion answered, "Oh my, that doesn't sound very good to me." Henry responded, "Well, we'll talk about it when you get here."[26]

Little Henry's sisters arrived at the hospital, and their dad took them by the hand one child at a time to be with their little brother. As Henry guided Marion down the hall, he started to cry. This was the very first instance that Marion had witnessed her dad cry. Henry told Marion, as she was the eldest, why he had asked for them to come to the hospital. Sadly, he wasn't certain if their little brother would survive or not. He told her, "He just, all of a sudden, is worse." First thing in the morning Little Henry could recognize his mom and dad. Unfortunately, when his sisters came, around ten o'clock, he couldn't identify any of them. Even though he was awake, he was no longer able to recognize his family. Afterward he drifted off to sleep. His brief life ended at ten thirty, and our family's intense and overwhelming grieving started.

Henry and Elizabeth created a memorial for their son. In the Cloud family home at the American Indian Institute, there was a huge fireplace. Etched in the dense marble was carved, "To the memory of 'Little Henry' and the glory of all childhood." Below was the following engraving: "When the long shadows at eventide fall, to play, to love, to rest."[27]

Cloud's Impact on the Meriam Report

Despite the Cloud family's great loss, the operation of the American Indian Institute continued, as did Henry's intense and constant efforts to make the world a better place for Native Americans. The previous year the Meriam Report had been officially submitted to the secretary of the interior. Cloud's indelible impact on the report can most clearly be seen in the section on education. The subsection "A Special Curriculum Opportunity" discusses the importance of bringing Native history into the schools and integrating it into the curriculum. The numerous references to Santee Indian Mission School, an institution only Cloud was familiar with, confirms his input. His contributions can also be seen in the reports of what worked at the American Indian Institute. Because Cloud was one of the few who remained in Washington DC, and he played a role in all phases of the investigation, I argue that he played a larger role in writing the Meriam Report than commonly recognized.[28]

My father, Robert North, discussed Cloud's diminishing political influence with the change of presidential administrations from Herbert Hoover to Franklin D. Roosevelt and the increased involvement of John Collier, who was hired as the commissioner of Indian Affairs:

> While he [Cloud] was under the Hoover administration with the Meriam Report where he apparently was a key figure, he was the tie of all of these eastern or Chicago intellectuals and academics with the Indian cultures, he was a key man on that committee. But as soon as Roosevelt came in, and Collier became the key thinker, he was immediately in trouble. I think it took no time at all for him to realize that. I don't remember my chronology exactly now, I haven't thought about these things for a long time, but when he was put in charge of Haskell, well that, they were getting him out of the way. It was the first step in a letdown, and they continued to use him, because he was—he could go into any reservation anywhere and immediately know people and be accepted. But he was also distrusted because in the eyes of many of these people on the reservations, he just represented the Bureau [of Indian Affairs].[29]

North describes Cloud as a "key figure" for the Meriam survey team and the link between East Coast intellectuals with Native cultures. North's portrayal challenges Meriam's and Dale's patronizing depiction of Cloud's abilities. Cloud's position as a key figure would have made him an excellent candidate for commissioner of Indian Affairs. At the same time, Native Americans as a constituency were not as politically powerful as compared to John Collier's political backing, and Cloud receiving the position was not feasible.[30] Furthermore, as a member of the Republican Party (not a democrat like President Roosevelt), Cloud's chances to be chosen to become commissioner of Indian Affairs were slim. North emphasizes that the federal government used Cloud because he could gain the trust of Natives. Therefore, Cloud, according to North, was being taken advantage of on two levels—his incredibly sharp intellectual ability and his identity as a Native man. But rather than receiving just reward for his hard work and intellectual prowess, according to North, Cloud was pushed "out of the way" with his placement as superintendent of Haskell. North also notes that Natives distrusted Cloud because he represented the arm of the federal government, a settler-colonial power.

Cloud, Superintendent of Haskell

In 1933 Cloud accepted the position of superintendent of Haskell, the federal government's largest boarding school in the Midwest, while Elizabeth continued to work for the American Indian Institute. Cloud, according to his daughter, Marion Hughes, took the position with the understanding that he could make changes to the curriculum because, at the time, the federal boarding schools did not provide Natives adequate educational preparation.[31]

Despite the position not being his first choice, it was a prestigious one. Natives congratulated Cloud for his lofty appointment as superintendent of a federal Indian boarding school. For example, Samuel Anderson, a Haskell alumnus who had helped the Meriam survey team travel from Okmulgee to Seminole, congratulated Cloud for his appointment: "You have set a shining example of what an Indian can do, which is an inspiration to older Indians as well as to our younger Indians who have yet to decide what their objective is in life." He said Cloud's admirers wanted him to be considered for commissioner of Indian Affairs. He also wrote, "I attended Haskell for a short time in 1910 and during 1911 to 1912. I admit to you I was not a howling success so I silently slipped away one nite [sic], never to return."[32] In this congratulatory letter Anderson explains his decision to run away many years before Cloud became superintendent of Haskell, as a result of his not being a "howling success." Running away was a common occurrence at Haskell Institute and many federal boarding schools, as these schools were extremely traumatic and abusive environments for Native students. Here we see another act of resistance

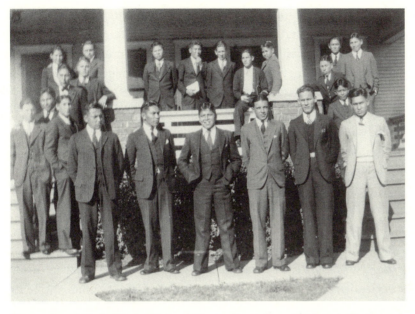

Fig. 11. American Indian Institute students of 1931 (see chapter 2). Photograph courtesy of the Cloud family.

and a warrior challenge to the oppressive, settler-colonial situation of a federal boarding school. Anderson fled an assimilationist environment that endeavored to stamp out Native identity and break the students' attachment to their land.

Closing the Jail

When Cloud began his new appointment, the first thing he did at Haskell Institute was close the jail. Jails were common in federal boarding schools, and they were used to punish Native students for various infractions, including running away. Closing the jail, Cloud took a clear stance against the settler-colonial approach to punishing children. Before Cloud's arrival Native children were treated similarly to today's incarcerated people. When Native children ran away, these employees would work to capture runaways, issue alerts to authorities in the nearby towns, and ask sheriff departments to issue arrest warrants. As a punishment for running away, students were locked up in the school jail for two nights.[33]

White reformers founded Haskell federal boarding school in 1884, supporting a strict curriculum for Native students. They demanded total submission and assimilation to white culture. Settler colonialism occurred not only on the battlefields but also within the intimate places of homes and the public spaces of schools. These boarding schools offered an emotionally laden atmosphere where one group (white reformers, teachers, and missionaries) could coerce their own values on a subordinated group (Indigenous peoples) and force them into transforming their behavior and appearance.[34] If colonial projects delineated racial classifications, Ann Stoler argues, then schools created an atmosphere "where relations between colonizer and colonized could powerfully confound or confirm the strictures of governance and categories of rule."[35] These relations are the "intimacies of empire."[36]

Cloud worked to change Haskell for the better. During a commencement speech at Haskell, Cloud used Native-centric ideas to communicate to his Native audience and challenged settler colonialism. He discussed the oppressive influence of white teachers who tried to force Native children to abandon the culture and spirit of their ancestors. Cloud contests the colonial force of assimilation and instead argues for cultural pluralism and a modern Native identity, retaining important aspects of Native culture while becoming part of American society. In this way he argued for a Native cultural citizenship, the right to be different and belong in the American educational system. In his address Cloud alluded to Haskell's shadows as a federal boarding school:

> A conquered race must meet the fate of exploitation. The bulwarks of racial integrity have been broken down. Faith has been violated. The once great and glorious past of the race has been held up disparagingly by many white teachers thinking thereby to coerce the young Indian student to abandon this reigning spirit of his forefathers. Mistakenly teachers of the past believed that this was the only method left open for advancement into the white man's civilization. Happily we are abandoning this ignorant method. We cannot afford to commit further social wrong in this fashion, we are to reinterpret to American

society, Indian values. We are to save superlative values, attitudes, ways of life and preserve them for the achievement of the larger goal.

Cloud said, "Haskell Institute is definitely committed to the preservation of Indian race culture," and he argued that no dominant race has the right to destroy the past of any people. He drove home the point that teaching Native American history helps us understand our present circumstances. He further argued that Haskell's purpose was to develop Native leaders, and these future leaders needed to understand the government and critically analyze the operations of power. He said, "the student in these halls should know why kings ruled the masses in the days gone by, why millions of the common people supported these kings over long stretches of years, why intelligent men and scholars for decades were denied a share in government, why no voting had been permitted to the people."[37] Rather than encourage the students to learn only a trade, even though Haskell was a vocational school, Cloud motivated them to become leaders of their tribal communities, similar to the American Indian Institute. This stance departed radically from the subservience usually taught in federal boarding schools.

In another radical shift, Cloud implemented a policy of Indian hiring preference, as he did at the American Indian Institute, and argued that Native students were more willing to learn from Native instructors. For example, he hired Robert C. Starr, an Arapaho who had taught at the American Indian Institute.[38] At Haskell Cloud also supported the use of Native languages, organized Native dances, and updated a reprinted book of Native American stories and legends. Cloud's pedagogical approach at Haskell built on the one he used at the American Indian Institute, pushing the federal boarding school to become more Native-centric than before and supporting the incorporation of Native studies curriculum. Because of his involvement in the IRA, however, Cloud's tenure at Haskell lasted only two years.

As superintendent of Haskell, Cloud used his position to brainstorm with E. C. Little, a member of the General Federation of Women's Clubs, about ways to improve the dire health conditions for Native Americans in Kansas:

I recall with pleasure your visit with me the other day. At that time, I outlined to you many things which the Federation of Women's Clubs could do for the Indians. . . . The health of the Indians in Northern Kansas, in the Mayetta jurisdiction where we have the Potawatomi, Kickapoo, Sac & Fox and Iowa Indians is in bad condition. What they need there is a general clinic to be held sometime, say in the next six months.

As to ways and means, I can get such of the Government doctors and nurses to cooperate as are already assigned to this jurisdiction, but the number is exceedingly limited and besides they are not experts along certain lines such as eye, ear, nose and throat; tuberculosis, trachoma, heart, etc. For these extra specialists we would need to seek outside medical help and such medical help must be paid for, as you know. One idea I have for raising money is to stage a football game between Haskell Institute and some other university, to be sponsored by the Kansas Federation of Women's Clubs, the proceeds to be used for health work among the Indians of this jurisdiction. This game can only be a post-season game and the possibility of raising at least $2,000 and possibly considerably more from such a game is very attractive, indeed.

You probably know that no general clinic to any great extent has ever been carried out among any tribes in the United States. There have been clinics restricted to teeth, trachoma, and possibly including eye, ear and nose in other jurisdictions, but this plan for a general clinic grips my imagination and I believe with persistent effort and careful planning we would put it over and it would be a great piece of work which the Kansas Federation of Women's Clubs can claim credit for.

The other possible method is to get some rich person or persons to contribute money to bring experts to such a clinic, but you know even the richest people in America are hard pressed in these times.[39]

In this quote Cloud shows his strong commitment to improving the health conditions of Native Americans, his thorough knowledge, and his creativity for finding money and resources from a Haskell football game and locating rich donors for a Native health clinic. Cloud demonstrates his political savvy by telling a representative of a mainstream women's club that her organization could take credit for improving Native health conditions, while emphasizing the shocking reality that there was no general clinic available for Native Americans. Thus, Cloud works to improve health conditions of Native peoples and their right to live healthy lives—another act of Native cultural citizenship.

As the superintendent of Haskell and a member of the Winnebago Tribal Council, Cloud used his new government position to support and advocate for our tribe and address our peoples' concerns with the federal government. In a letter to the commissioner of Indian Affairs on November 24, 1933, he wrote, "I have just received the enclosed list of complaints from members of the Winnebago tribe. I am passing it on to you because I really believe there is a great deal of truth about the complaints against this man Hess at Winnebago Agency. Searching investigation ought to be made of this man and he should be turned out if these complaints are well founded."[40] The letter Cloud received from three members of the Winnebago Tribal Council and other tribal members explained the overall issue and complaint. Elsie Ross rented Charles English's allotment and had not paid for five years, meaning he owed a total of $666.21. The letter explained that Elsie Ross was a county commissioner and that agency employees favored him without regard to the federal government or the Winnebago Tribe of Nebraska. Farmer Hess was the agency official who was assigned the task to make sure the rent and taxes were paid."[41]

On November 23, 1933, Cloud wrote to Albert Hensley, a fellow Ho-Chunk and Winnebago Tribal Council member, to discuss his actions in support of our tribe. Cloud had made an exhaustive report regarding the conditions of the Winnebago and Omaha Reservations, addressing their complaints and proposing possible solutions to the commissioner of Indian Affairs.[42]

Indian Reorganization Act of 1934

In February 1934 the commissioner of Indian Affairs, John Collier, asked Cloud to encourage tribes to accept the IRA, an act that marked the change in federal policy from assimilation to cultural pluralism. Cloud agreed. He must have been well aware that the Native landholdings had diminished from 138 million acres in 1880 to less than 48 million acres in 1934.[43] During meetings with tribes Cloud attacked the Dawes Act, a settler-colonial tool to dispossess Natives of millions of acres of land. In a speech on the Pine Ridge Reservation, for example, he said,

> I have been trying to show the Indians that there is a close relationship between that loss of land and the health and prosperity of the Indian people. Now, the sure result of losing lands is the high death rate among Indians. It has been estimated that the death rate among the Indian people is two to one with that of the whites. Where one white man dies among one thousand white men, two Indians die among a thousand of their population. That death rate is too high. One explanation is that the Indians have become poorer and poorer with the inevitable loss of the vast acreage they had at one time. When they become poor they have less to eat and less to wear and no shelter. Their children are being brought into this world with a poor start in life. Malnutrition and bad housing conditions tuberculosis and other diseases are killing the Indians.[44]

In this quote Cloud astutely links the dispossession of Natives' land with a high death rate, emphasizing how our loss of connection to our land—and the resulting lack of food, clothing, and shelter—contributed to our people contracting diseases at alarming rates.[45]

In 1934 Cloud spoke at a meeting held in Wanblee, South Dakota, again condemning the impact of the Dawes Act on Native Americans and discussing how we lost our land:

> What are we going to do when those of us who have this 20 million acres of good land left—when that's all gone? . . . Now, we are going to lose that land in three or four ways. I'll tell you how. When one of our fathers dies he leaves that land to his children. There may be three, four, five or six children. These children find that the land is divided in small pieces and they can't farm it so they get together with the superintendent and sell it and spend the money. If one of the children had lots of money and could buy it all and farm it, that would be all right but usually we don't have the money that way. There's one thing we cannot do and that is to prevent the death of

our fathers. When they get old they die. And another thing we can't prevent and that is to keep his land from being split up because the law says that they shall all have equal shares of their father's land. In my country when our fathers die and we inherit his land and we grow up and have children and on down, sometimes 200 people have an interest in a single piece of land. When the rental on that grandfather's land is collected and they send me a check, I get 3 cents, the price of a stamp. That's what I get for my grandfather's land. So we all get together and say let's sell my grandfather's land. This 3 cents doesn't do me much good. So we sell it and soon the white man gets it and it is gone. That's one way we leave our land behind us and a white man comes and picks it up.

Now, the second way is to give an Indian a fee patent to his land and the next day or week he sells it to a white man.

I was looking at your map at the Pine Ridge Agency two or three days ago and there on that map are great red places all over it. The red places show the land that is sold. That is just like the young man who left his meat on the ground and the wolves got it. In this case the white man is getting it.

The third way the Indian loses that land is that: The Indians pay taxes on that fee patented land and by and by the tax collector comes around and the Indian hasn't any money to pay and after awhile the country comes and takes it away from him. In my country on many reservations where I have been where the land is fee patented a good amount of it is being lost today.[46]

In this quote Cloud astutely analyzes the Dawes Allotment Act as a settler-colonial tool to dispossess Natives of our land by describing a map, including the checker boarding of reservations, where whites owned some pockets and Natives owned other pockets, as well as the continual dividing up of land, Natives' inability to pay taxes, and the fee-patent policy. The Allotment Act divided Native land into 160 acres, 80 acres, and other parcels to Natives, making millions of acres available for white settlers. Fee patents, also known as certificates of competency, were "awarded" to Natives, who were determined to be "competent" (in other words, civilized enough) to sell, lease, or mortgage their land independently of the Bureau of Indian Affairs. Furthermore, being considered competent meant the federal government removed one's land from trust status, and then the competent Natives had to start paying taxes. In most cases we could not afford the taxes, and so our land was confiscated. Altogether, millions of acres of land were lost, as Natives sold their land or could not pay taxes.[47] Cloud connects to his Native audience by telling stories about the extensive land dispossession from a Native perspective. He uses words such as "my country" and "our fathers" to emphasize that this land dispossession happened to him and his own Winnebago tribe. Cloud's ability to connect to Native audiences and educate and advocate for the Indian Reorganization Act to tribes quite likely contributed to its successful enactment in 1934.

In a 1934 speech on the Pine Ridge Reservation, Cloud encouraged Natives to embrace economic development, which is for economic profit and requires that the entrepreneur use labor, capital, and resources.[48] The Indian Reorganization Act, Cloud argued, was a chance for Native tribes to rebuild their lives and reclaim their manhood and sense of victory through economic development rather than remain stuck in inertia with no hope for improvement:

> Now, when this situation takes place, you have the three things necessary to bring about industry among your people, namely: Land, labor and capital. The Government will give you the land, loan you the capital which you have the privilege of paying back in thirty years without interest, and you supply one, the labor. After you get started in this industry, some other things get started at the same time. You start the growth of your heart which means character. You start the growth of your mind which means education, and you start the growth of health which means good stamina, a good physical body. Having started all those things, you have developed your own personality. You have now reached a stage in your life where success appears on the horizon. Before that you had no land, you had no capital, no means of improvement. You simply woke up in the morning and passed the day and when night came on you went to sleep. You were making no

progress. Now that you begin activity; you are wide awake, living, and resourceful. You have more initiative than you ever had and the sum total result is an Indian people who stand up like men with victory in their hearts. That is the way I see it. I hope you will be in favor of this Bill and that it will become a law.[49]

In this quote Cloud encourages Natives to embrace economic development by emphasizing how industry will strengthen their mind, heart, character, and personality. Cloud argues that the government will provide Natives with the land, while loaning the capital, and Indigenous peoples themselves can provide the labor, so Native men can "stand up like men with victory in their hearts." Cloud alludes to the settler-colonial tactic of treating Native warriors, who were trained to be proud and defend their tribal nations, as nonmen and children. Instead, he encourages Native warriors to reclaim their manhood and rise up victorious and no longer suffer the pain of defeat, causing a lack of motivation and a sense of hopelessness. Cloud's message of using land, labor, and capital encourages Natives to embrace a modern identity and become successful economically by entering the marketplace of capitalism.

Coauthorship of the Indian Reorganization Act of 1934

My mother, Woesha, always told me that her father, Henry, coauthored the Indian Reorganization Act. During a radio program, *Northwest Neighbors*, in 1945, he claimed coauthorship of the IRA. He said that he was one of the ten experts who developed the Meriam Survey "and later laid down the new policy for Indian Affairs for the Bureau of Indian Affairs." He emphasized that the IRA—which radio host Art Kirkham called the Indian Bill of Rights—was his brainchild: "Yes, I drafted it. . . . Most of the things I outlined had been adopted. I wanted the Indians to stop selling their lands, and a two-million-dollar fund was established so they could buy back their land. There were a number of things, such as a $25,000 scholarship fund, increased to $250,000, for Indian youth for vocational education, but perhaps the most important was the opportunity for the Indians to become self-governing. By vote of their tribal councils they could adopt a constitution and become a self-governing body. About three-fourths of the Indians have accepted this."[50] The act had four parts: Title 1, Indian Self-Government, granted Indians the right to organize for local self-government and for economic activities. Title 2, Special Education for Indians, directed the promotion and financial support of the study of Indian civilization, including arts, crafts, and traditions. Title 3, Abolished the Allotment System, restored existing "surplus" lands to the tribe and appropriated $2 million per year for the purchase of new lands. And, finally, Title 4, Court of Indian Affairs, created a special court of Indian affairs, which would serve as a court of original jurisdiction for cases involving Indian communities and its members.[51]

Based on the available evidence, it makes sense that Cloud assisted in drafting the Indian Reorganization Act of 1934.[52] Well before the act was passed in 1934, Cloud supported Native students' Indigenous identities, languages, and cultures in the American Indian Institute. He co-authored the Meriam Report, which documented poor economic conditions throughout Indian Country, the loss of land caused by the Dawes Allotment Act of 1887, and the severe problems of the federal boarding schools and the Indian Service. He argued for the importance of Natives supporting themselves economically. These ideas are necessary precursors to current discussions of tribal self-determination and sovereignty. Cloud could have helped draft the different titles of the IRA.

The IRA, however, was a settler-colonial tool, creating tribal governments that mimicked white corporations rather than traditional political structures. As a result, it encouraged tribal governments to become inherently colonial and male-dominated. Indeed, Cloud had difficulties with the federal government's tribal constitution-making process as part of the IRA. During a speech he delivered as a superintendent for the Umatilla Reservation at the Northwest, Inter-mountain, and Montana Superintendents' Conference in Pendleton, Oregon, in September 1941, he said,

> Herein lay a golden opportunity for the government to draw up constitutional forms of government consonant with natural concepts of [tribal] government reading back into the centuries. Being one of the appointed Field Agents or constitution makers, I drew up a form of government according to my tribal clan system and proudly showed

Fig. 12. Henry Cloud, a Ho-Chunk man, always sharply dressed when he went to work. Photograph courtesy of the Cloud family.

it to visiting traveling officials from the Washington Office. I was promptly told to throw this into the wastebasket as they had just what was needed for our Winnebago Constitution. Then they handed me a long list of so-called "powers" and "land provisions," filling several pages. The use of these definitive powers and land provisions was made mandatory then and there for every so-called "long constitution." Not withstanding the fact that such insertions into every constitution would render them alike and subject to the charge of uniformity, we obeyed orders. Strange as it may seem, every field Agent was taken severely to task later for uniformity of Constitutions.[53]

Here Cloud critiques the top-down nature of the constitution-writing process and disparages government officials' contradictory instructions. On the one hand, his supervisors threw his unique Ho-Chunk constitution in the wastebasket. On the other hand, the same government officials gave him specific powers and provisions to include, while reprimanding him and other field agents for developing uniform constitutions. In fact, Cloud's astute criticism of the IRA's constitution-making process is a pathbreaking intellectual insight elaborated in the 1980s by Native scholars, including Vine Deloria Jr.[54]

Native scholars argue that IRA constitutions (which are not based on tribal political structures) lessened the power of tribal governments rather than support and strengthen tribal sovereignty and self-rule. These constitutions involved limiting clauses, such as requiring a Bureau of Indian Affairs review or secretarial approval of tribal council actions. Therefore, many tribes who accepted IRA constitutions lost political power. Ironically, John Collier wrote, "it is imperative that we set the feet of our Indian friends on the path that leads to self-government," when the Rosebud, Pine Ridge, and other tribes, according to Richmond Clow, already had tribal constitutions and the right to self-government.[55] The so-called self-government of the IRA was steeped in paternalism and colonialism. The idea of the IRA "granting" Natives the right to self-government was based on the assumption that the settler-colonial state had that power, thus ignoring Natives' inherent right to sovereignty.[56] Cloud challenges settler colonialism by alluding to tribal nations' vexed and complicated position of being "nations within a nation" and "domestic dependent nations."[57] Despite tribal nations' preexisting political structures, the IRA instituted white, corporate political practices.

In 1944 Cloud waged his critique of the Indian Service to a room filled with white superintendents. He showed his strength, courage, and willingness to strongly advocate for his analysis and beliefs—while face-to-face with colonial power. In this meeting Cloud fulfilled his Ho-Chunk name as "War Chief." According to my aunt Marion Hughes, because of Cloud's continual criticism of the Indian Service, he was demoted and sent to work as an Indian agent on the Umatilla Reservation, suffering a major cut in pay.

Despite the IRA's settler-colonial implications, it led to a number of positive changes: many federal boarding schools closed; policy shifted from assimilation to cultural pluralism; Native land bases were reestablished through the compulsory return of lost lands resulting from the Allotment Act; and statutory persecutions of most Native religious ceremonies ended.[58] Cloud was the only person who was involved in so many aspects leading to the passage of the IRA, including investigating the Indian Service, co-writing the Meriam Report, and, according to available evidence, co-drafting the IRA and encouraging tribes to support the IRA.[59] Cloud, however, was not recognized for his pivotal contribution with either a career promotion or further involvement on the national stage.

In September 1935 Henry Cloud was honored with the Indian Achievement Medal of the Indian Council Fire of Chicago. The committee selected Cloud from various nominees, representing twenty-five tribes, including John Collier; A. C. Monahan, assistant to the commissioner and acting director of Indian education; Roberta Campbell, president of the General Federation of Women's Clubs; Dr. Charles Eastman; author Lew Sarett; Senator Lynn J. Frazier; ethnologist John N. B. Hewitt; Dr. B. D. Weeks of Bacone College; and Francis Densmore, a scholar of Native American music.[60]

After Haskell and his involvement in promoting the IRA to tribes, Cloud's new job was supervisor of Indian education at large, and his duties included various tasks. In 1935 and 1936 he studied the history of Ho-Chunk land ownership in Wisconsin. He lived in Tomah, Wisconsin,

Fig. 13. Cloud talking into a microphone, possibly during a radio program in 1945, when he claimed that the IRA was his brainchild and that he assisted in drafting it. Photograph courtesy of the Cloud family.

at a small public-health hospital that included housing for government employees. Henry journeyed to different old homesteads and county seats. Harold Buchannan, a Ho-Chunk, was his driver. Robin Butterfield, my cousin, interviewed Buchannan, who shared how much he admired Cloud, describing his composure, humor, charisma, and other positive qualities that enabled him to fit into any situation. Buchannan said Cloud loved his Indianness. He told Buchannan that when he was away, he missed our people intensely. Cloud said, "You know, Harold, I get streaks of longing . . . for my people, especially their activities. The climax of this would be if I could only hear even a drum beat. I love to see them enjoy themselves. I went a lot as a child [to participate in various Ho-Chunk events]." Later Cloud returned with his family, including his four daughters and his wife, Elizabeth. Henry and Elizabeth enjoyed playing tennis and golf at the Tomah Country Club. They laughed and teased each other about who won and how they played sports. Elizabeth kidded Henry that he couldn't get his second wind, so she could beat him.[61]

Years later, in 1949, Buchannan visited with Henry Cloud when he was invited to address graduating Mount Edgecumbe students at a large federal boarding school in Alaska (see chapter 1). Buchannan asked Cloud to have dinner with him. In 1953, after Henry died, Buchannan visited with Elizabeth Cloud, and she described Henry's love of animals. He especially loved his horses. She discussed how, during the last weekend she shared with Henry before he passed away, they went to feed the horses, and he talked to the horse, saying, "Turn around! You know you are supposed to. . . . It is the other end, where your mouth is." Elizabeth remembered Henry's humor as fun, thought-provoking, and sharp.[62]

In sum, Cloud was the only Native member of the Meriam Report and played a pivotal role, co-writing the exhaustive survey of Native health, education, and welfare conditions throughout Indian Country. He also, according to available evidence, assisted in drafting the Indian Reorganization Act of 1934.[63] His powerful reports criticizing federal boarding schools prove his power and courage as a Ho-Chunk intellectual and activist, exposing the abuse suffered by Native children. He was considered as a potential candidate for commissioner of Indian Affairs, but his colleagues, basing their opinions on racist assumptions, blocked his nomination. As a Ho-Chunk intellectual and activist, he used his position as superintendent of a federal boarding school, Haskell, to challenge settler colonialism, including closing the jail; incorporating a Native-studies curriculum, such as Native language arts, culture, history, and leadership training; and working toward Native cultural citizenship. Rather than be rewarded for his efforts to improve the Indian Service and change federal policy from assimilation to cultural pluralism, Cloud was transferred to become an Indian agent on the Umatilla Reservation in Oregon, another major let down from his prominence on the national stage.

CHAPTER 4

The Work of Henry and
Elizabeth Cloud at Umatilla

As a boy, general council chair of the Umatilla Reservation, Antone Minthorn, recalled seeing Henry around his Indian agent house—a two-story, white wooden-framed house on the west end of the tree-shaded Bureau of Indian Affairs (BIA) grounds. He would watch Henry practice his golf drive, and sometimes Antone would go looking for the lost balls. Viola Wocatse, receptionist at the Yellowhawk Clinic, also remembered Henry. She said he did a lot for the young people, encouraging them to work in the summers. She described him as both strict and nice, inspiring those around him to learn about their world. Sonny Picard, a refuse-truck driver, said that if you got in trouble, Henry would be right there and get you out of jail. Margarite Red Elk recollected Cloud as a very helpful superintendent: he got around among the people—and this marked a change from the former superintendent's distancing himself from Umatilla Natives. Elizie Farrow remembered one day when a government car pulled up with a big Indian as its passenger. Henry introduced himself and said he hoped to be the next superintendent.[1]

In August 1939, after Cloud's involvement in the Indian Reorganization Act (IRA) and his short-lived tenure as superintendent of Haskell, he suffered a significant demotion. His pay plummeted, and he lost his platform on the national stage. The downgraded position was agency superintendent, or Indian agent, of the Umatilla Reservation in Pendleton,

Oregon. The Umatilla Reservation includes Umatilla, Cayuse, and Walla Walla tribes. The federal government, according to Cloud's daughter Marion Hughes, offered him the job with the hope he would quit and as a punishment for his critique of the Indian Service.[2] Cloud's decade or so as an Indian agent of Umatilla was challenging. Federal-government officials thrust him into the midst of factional reservation politics: issues around hunting, fishing, timber, and agriculture, as well as land-lease problems. Although his Yale education had served him well—providing him with powerful networks and funding sources—it also linked him to white, settler-colonial forces. In other words, Cloud's identity as a well-educated modern Native put him in the middle of reservation politics. Cloud's identity and Indian agent role could also place him on the side of his white predecessor, Omar L. Babcock. Cloud's tenure as Indian agent, however, diverged from Babcock's. Cloud challenged white racist attitudes, supported Umatilla Natives in their struggles over fishing and hunting rights, combined white and Indigenous rhetoric in his writing and speeches, worked to be transparent regarding his goals and objectives, and ultimately supported tribal sovereignty. Meanwhile, Elizabeth founded the Oregon Trail Women's Club for Umatilla women, an Indigenous and gendered hub that boosted Native women's pride in their tribal identity, developed a modern Native identity, and encouraged college education.

The Umatilla Reservation is in the Umatilla River Valley. On the western edge is the city of Pendleton and toward the east are the Blue Ridge Mountains of Oregon. White settlers traveled west along the Oregon Trail, plowing the ground, erecting homes, and building up their colonial infrastructure—all to settle and stay in land belonging to Indigenous people. Around 80,000 acres of land of the reservation was farmland of wheat or peas. About half of the reservation had transferred into white ownership, because of the Allotment Act of 1887 and the forced removal of Natives onto the Umatilla Reservation after the signing of the treaties of 1855. The BIA held the remaining 30,000 to 40,000 acres of Indigenous land in trust for Native owners. Land ownership looked like a checkerboard, with white and Native parcels of 160, 80, and 40 acres intermingled. Natives owned portions of land, sometimes sharing each parcel among six or more adults and children. Most of the Indigenous-owned farmland was leased to white farmers, who owned sprawling and expansive ranches surrounding the reservation.[3] Native Americans had difficulty farming their own land, often lacking the funds to purchase the necessary equipment. And since they needed money to survive, Indigenous peoples were compelled to lease land, once again suffering land dispossession and settler colonialism—leasing land to white settlers ultimately eliminated Natives from access and use of their own land.[4] Even further, Umatilla Natives received exploitatively low land-lease payments, while white farmers reaped the land's profits. With such limited access to money and land, Umatilla Natives barely survived, forced to rely mostly on hunting and fishing, low land-lease payments, and government assistance.[5]

As a result of the Indian Reorganization Act of 1934, many tribal governments were forced to follow non-Native models of political decision making and economic distribution. Tribal-government leaders often occupied—and still occupy—challenging positions as go-betweens. Leaders, once elected, must work with the settler-colonial institutions of the BIA and Congress. Cloud, as a "good" Indian and an Indian agent, represented an instrument of the state, the BIA. He was implicated in the very governmental apparatus created to keep Indigenous people dependent on colonial institutions—a role that ultimately pitted him against "bad" Indians. In other words, "traditional" Natives often saw Cloud as their enemy.

Cloud's oldest daughter, my aunt Marion Hughes, explained why her father was transferred to Umatilla after working on the national stage:

> When he [Cloud] was in the Indian Service . . . he never kept quiet with criticism. . . . That was one reason they offered him the Pendleton job at [the] Umatilla reservation. . . . They thought he would quit and they were trying to get him out of their hair and he said, "I'll take that job. I love that country," which shocked the wits out of them. Their ploy didn't work. So, he was there ten years and he did a whale of a difference in Pendleton. . . . [Whites] had previously used the Umatilla and Nez Perce Indians for the Roundup parade.[6]

After taking this job, Cloud suffered a major cut in pay. At his previous position he earned $4,600, and, as an Indian agent, he received $3,200.[7]

According to Cathleen Cahill's book *Federal Fathers and Mothers*, the Indian Service often employed Indigenous peoples, and their superiors encouraged them to model the ideals of assimilation (e.g., submission to whites) to "bad" Indians. But when Natives became critical of the Indian Service or their loyalty to superiors was in question, they would be transferred to another location in the Indian Service to work.[8] My aunt Marion's description of Cloud's reassignment to Umatilla shows how he was punished for being a bad Indian, who was critical of the BIA. Cloud's transfer emphasizes his Ho-Chunk warrior identity—he fought his superiors, who wanted him to leave the Indian Service. Instead, he told the Indian Service, "I love that country." This declaration alludes to his Native connection to land and his making another Indigenous hub—a sense of connection not based in geographic space. Relying on his identity as a Ho-Chunk warrior, Cloud taught his daughter to fight rather than surrender.

Cloud's sharp intelligence, expertise, and connections had been relied on regarding the investigation of Native conditions throughout Indian Country, the writing of the Meriam Report, and later the development and passage of the IRA. And now, as punishment for his critique of the Indian Service, he was sent to the Umatilla Reservation as an Indian agent. His new, paternalist position meant fellow Natives could easily hate him. At the same time, to keep his job, he had to listen to and implement his superiors' goals. Although criticizing the Indian Service was in his comfort zone, other Indigenous peoples despising him was not. Federal officials, rather than rewarding him for improving the BIA and helping change government policy from assimilation to cultural pluralism as part of the IRA, demoted him. He was no longer in the national spotlight and was forced into the challenging settler-colonial position of Indian agent.

The Bureau of Indian Affairs buildings were positioned under gigantic old trees. My mother, Woesha, and my father, Robert, lived there with Henry and Elizabeth in the Indian agent's house after my father returned home from military service when World War II ended. In a 1988 interview my dad discussed how challenging Cloud's role on the Umatilla Reservation was. "But he [Cloud] also had trouble—during the three months that essentially I was on the [Umatilla] reservation in Pendleton where he was addressed as 'The Major' because in the old days when the Army ran the reservations it was always a major who was the superintendent . . . some of them just hated his guts." My parents witnessed how incredibly difficult Cloud's role was as representative and arm of the federal government and how tribal members—especially the older ones—loathed him.[9] Natives at Umatilla saw Cloud as either an assimilated Native or "white." As an Indian agent, he wore a suit, drove a government car, and played golf—markers or masks of a modern, assimilated, and even white status. Cloud dressed impeccably, wearing a three-piece suit every day, which very well could have alienated him from the impoverished Natives of Umatilla. In addition, his middle-class, Yale-educated status could represent many negative white attributes to other Natives. His clothing style and education most likely supported tension between him and other Indigenous people. Among whites, in contrast, his modern Native attributes could help him perform a "good" Native role and mask his underlying warrior identity.

Undeniably, these class markers are still relevant in Native communities today, both on the Winnebago Reservation in Nebraska and for tribal members of the Ho-Chunk Nation in Wisconsin. In an August 2011 interview, John Blackhawk, tribal chair of the Winnebago tribe of Nebraska, discussed his choice to wear jeans and a T-shirt as he went about his work as tribal leader. He wanted members of his tribal council to focus on the work at hand rather than get distracted by issues of hierarchy.[10] In contrast, during an August 2011 interview, Jon Greendeer, tribal president of the Ho-Chunk Nation, discussed his decision to dress professionally, claiming his professional attire did not negate his respect for Ho-Chunk culture. He argued that one can wear professional dress *and* maintain traditional elements of Ho-Chunk culture.[11] While today one can be viewed as Native while dressing professionally in tribal communities, during Cloud's tenure as superintendent, a suit and tie could easily represent whiteness.

Henry Challenged Racism and Settler Colonialism

When Cloud took his job as superintendent of the Umatilla Reservation in August 1939, some businesses displayed signs in their windows stating,

Fig. 14. Cloud wearing a three-piece suit as Indian agent of Umatilla Reservation. Photograph courtesy of the Cloud family.

"No Indians allowed."[12] These signs were in restaurants, bars, and card rooms. Leah Conner, the daughter of the Clouds' close friend and employee Gilbert Conner, babysat Cloud's granddaughter, my cousin Gretchen. In 1988 Conner discussed how in the town of The Dalles, when Indigenous peoples went to the movies, they had to sit in the balconies. They were forced to sit there, because they lived at Celilo Falls, a salmon fishing site, and whites complained they smelled of fish.[13]

Cloud challenged this sort of racism. He gave several sermons to this effect at a Presbyterian church in Pendleton. Within a year after Cloud's arrival, according to his daughter Marion, there were fewer signs of Native prejudice.[14] For example, sometime during World War II, Henry brought the Umatilla Indian Young Peoples' Choir to church, and in his sermon he said,

> They are organized to rally the Indian youth to the Standard of Christ, to carry forward the torch which the Nazarene, a mere youth himself, passed on to adventurous youth for each succeeding generation. They speak the tongue of their people. They know how to reach the hearts of their people. These Indian youths, out in quest of the larger, richer life, know the thought-life of their people. They know the actual living conditions of the whole Umatilla Reservation. They know that there is vast need for improvement in the life of their people. But they also know, and this is important, the many good things prevailing among their people come down to them from ancient times. They know that without the teachings of the white man a great many of their families from generation to generation have lived the hygienic principles of cleanliness as nature taught them, have been faithful to old custom marriages surpassing by far the average moral code practice of the general white population. These achievements form the true index to their pride—a racial characteristic.

Cloud finished his sermon by saying, "These young people, because of their Christian faith, will be the true interpreters of their people by word and example. They have faith in the future of America. They are supporting our national defense 100 percent."[15] As a Ho-Chunk intellectual, Cloud contests the racist, settler-colonial notion that Indigenous peoples are inherently dirty by emphasizing that Umatilla elders had taught these young, Christian Native young men to be clean and that this cleanliness was an inherently racial characteristic. Portraying Natives as dirty, primitive, and uncivilized was a way for white settlers to justify stealing Indigenous land and work to eliminate our tribal identities in federal boarding schools—both acts of settler colonialism.[16] He also disputes the gendered settler-colonial Christian notion that Indigenous peoples' "old custom" marriages were immoral. Gendered settler colonialism involved U.S. policies regarding the federal boarding-school system, which worked to destroy Native kinship systems, trying to supplant them with the heteronormative, patriarchal Eurocentric model of the nuclear family.[17] By emphasizing that Native custom marriages far surpassed the average morals of whites, Cloud challenges the white Christian practice of looking down on Native marriage practices.

In addition, Cloud discusses that the young people knew the "tongue" of their people, meaning they knew their Native languages, which challenged the federal government's attempt to eradicate Indigenous languages. Cloud, as a Native Christian man, highlights that these Christian, young men are the ones who will lead their people into the future and challenges the racism and marriage practices of white settlers. Thus, he brings an Indigenous Christian perspective to bear on colonialism. He emphasizes that these Indigenous peoples supported national defense, showing Natives were "good U.S. citizens," not just "bad Indians," who were not Christian and "primitive." One could argue that his Christian faith was an example of an oppressive religion. Certainly Christianity has been involved in many settler-colonial processes, including creating federal boarding schools and forcibly inserting the white nuclear family into Indigenous family relations. Cloud's discussion shows a complicated response: he challenges settler-colonial practices while emphasizing the importance of Christianity. Thus, Cloud was a "good" and "bad" Native simultaneously. Cloud highlights that Native Americans can have a complicated identity too—Christian and a veteran and still be Indigenous.

In 1940 Cloud defied Pendleton's white community by writing to John Collier, the commissioner of Indian Affairs, complaining that the Indigenous community at Umatilla was being used as a tourist attraction as part of the Pendleton Round-Up. In his letter to Collier, Cloud challenged racism on a national level:

> By financial inducement and privileges bestowed in one form or another approximately 1,000 of our Indian people in full Indian regalia, comprising men, women and children, are led to participate in the "Pendleton Round-Up." It is universally admitted that this Indian participation and the Indian section is the heart and central attraction for the white population. Some go so far as to say that were the Indians left out of it, that immediately the "Pendleton Round-Up" would become a gigantic flop. . . . The outstanding impression one receives is the commercialization of the Wild West in which the Indian plays the chief role. . . . The "Happy Canyon" performance in the evenings is a little piece of Indian pageantry combined with a portrayal of pioneer-village days and life with some true historical flavor along with characteristic gambling features that used to obtain in all the towns of the Pioneer West. "Happy Canyon" and the "Pendleton Round-Up," however, at their best, cannot be said to be of real educational value for the Indians or the citizens in general.[18]

The Natives of Umatilla suffered from severe poverty and dressing up in their traditional Native dress for white audiences' money and enjoyment was certainly an important way for them to support themselves economically and put food on the table. In this quote Cloud emphasizes how whites profited from Indigenous peoples' performances of their Native identities, implying whites' marketing of Native American identities was central to the financial success of the Pendleton Round-Up. In this way Cloud points to whites taking advantage of Indigenous peoples' poverty. These two events were not Indigenous-controlled and Indigenous people did not receive the lion's share of the profits from their own performances. Cloud's description of the Pendleton Round-Up as a "commercialization of the Wild West" recalls Buffalo Bill Cody making

Fig. 15. Cloud in Pendleton, Oregon, at Pendleton Round-Up, serving as grand marshal. He is the rider wearing the dark shirt. His horse was called "Snippy." Photograph courtesy of the Cloud family.

cowboys into heroes during Wild West shows. In these performances moving west and killing Native Americans were associated with moral, cultural, and racial progress. Furthermore, BIA officials discouraged Natives' participation in Wild West performances a few decades before because they worried it undermined assimilation.[19] Indeed, Cloud's letter to Collier is a challenge to the "commercialization of the Wild West" through public performances, especially insofar as it naturalizes settlers' colonization of the land and genocide of Native people.

Beginning in 1910 the Round-Up is Pendleton's most cherished rodeo event, central to the town's identity and a powerful symbol of the settler heritage of the white residents. Surrounding Native communities have always been encouraged to participate, and many looked forward to their annual involvement. Each year Indigenous peoples set up camp on the Round-Up grounds and participate in the rodeo. During their first year of involvement, organizers invited Native Americans and U.S. soldiers to perform a pretend battle using blank ammunition. But the Natives refused to be shot at with blank ammunition and the soldiers could not come.[20] Symbolic violence was not the only kind of violence. The rodeo can be dangerous, with riders and animals injured and killed. In 1913, for example, three Indigenous women died in a horse race. Dorothy McCall wrote that, in response to these women's tragic accident, a man in the stands said, "What's the matter with you people? After all, they're only Indians!"[21] This comment points to racist whites' assumption that Native women are not fully human, and our death is of no concern.

"Happy Canyon Indian Pageant and Wild West Show" continues today under the guise of a cultural performance about the settling of the American West. It begins with a portrayal of the Native American way of life prior to the coming of the white man. Then Meriwether Lewis and William Clark arrive and, soon after, so do the prairie schooners of the pioneers of the Oregon Trail. Fighting breaks out between Indigenous peoples and white settlers, and peace returns only when Indigenous peoples are taken to live on the reservation. The performance concludes with a reenactment of a frontier town's noisy and disorderly Main Street mishaps, and, ultimately, Indigenous peoples disappear.[22] The title "Happy Canyon" points to the underlying settler-colonial purpose of this Wild

Fig. 16. Cloud at the Pendleton Round-Up. He wears a long dark coat and is being honored with feathered regalia, according to our cousin Susan Freed-Held. Photograph courtesy of the Cloud family.

West show: the outcome is a happy one, where, as a result of colonialism and dispossession, white settlers and Natives are content. The Happy Canyon performance fits within frontier symbolism and narratives that emphasize the heroic acts of the first pioneers and the explorers' "discovery" and settlement of the region. The narrative structure of these frontier histories tells of a heroic struggle between the forces of good and evil. Violence is taken for granted and viewed as the motor that drives history-as-progress. In other words, the violence is accepted as the natural progression of the "good" white settler—who must kill "bad" Indians, the impediments to civilization. And ultimately white settlers emerge as the rightful inheritors of the land and resources.

Cloud offered an alternative to the settler-colonial narratives reinforced by the Pendleton Round-Up and Happy Canyon. Cloud's request of Collier's support for a change in Indigenous peoples' involvement included "the totality of Indian life. . . . To do this, it is necessary to present the arts and crafts along with all the historical features of the aboriginal American, involving the antiquity of [the] Indian on this continent so far as archaeology will reveal, his racial history . . . and the Indian's particular ethnological background along with the distinctive features of his own culture." Cloud discussed that exhibits highlighting Native culture and ethnology were possible and that "with proper organization and management," Indigenous painters, artisans, and singers could be encouraged to perform, turning the Round-Up into a wonderful Indian educational event. He emphasized a growing interest in Natives and wrote, "A study of the cultural background of the Indians has so much of social implication to our modern day civilization loaded with maladjustment of one kind or another. May not America discover something in the evolution of American Indians here on this continent for the last 30,000 years."[23] Cloud's idea of transforming the Round-Up and "Happy Canyon" from a Wild West show and tourist attraction into an educational event challenged the federal government's assimilation campaigns. Cloud's educational events could have encouraged participants to understand cultural relativism and respect Native cultures as equal to Western culture. At the same time, it is likely that the cultural performances he imagined did not expose the colonialism that had caused so much damage to Native Americans.

Cloud worked to open up lines of communication with Collier, who was also trained as an anthropologist, by using their shared discipline's settler-colonial assumption that one could learn from Indigenous peoples' cultures—and that this knowledge could help to correct the "maladjustment" of modern society and improve modern culture. In this way Cloud strategically used a dominant narrative that typically romanticizes Indigenous peoples and laments their destruction by the forces of European expansion. In so doing, these narratives project ideal images of the past, contrasting them with the current moral-social decline of contemporary industrial society. Cloud's use of this dominant discourse allowed him to use a hegemonic historical perspective for a Native goal: transform the white settlers' frontier pageant into a performance that incorporates Indigenous culture and history.[24] Particularly, his use of the term "evolution" alludes to classic anthropology's assumption that Natives occupy a space on the lower end of a continuum between primitive and civilized. Thus, his

utilization of this term is problematic and could point to a hierarchy created within the Native cultural performances he hoped to organize. It also
shows how he deliberately used dominant discourses whites would understand to reach his own anti–settler-colonial goals. Cloud's doubleness
speech was a Ho-Chunk creative strategy that aided his ongoing efforts.[25]

Elizabeth and the Oregon Trail Women's Club

In 1940, while Henry was working to transform the Pendleton Round-Up,
Elizabeth founded the Oregon Trail Women's Club. This Indigenous wom-
en's organization was the first of its kind on the Umatilla Reservation. It
belonged to the white women's national organization, the General Federation of Women's Clubs (GFWC). Through both this membership and
an affiliation with the Oregon Federation of Women's Clubs, Elizabeth
brought the club in contact with mainstream women's organizations.[26]

Even though Native women are mostly missing from the historical
literature regarding the (largely white) women's clubs' movement around
the turn of the century, they were pivotal and vital players. In these
clubs white women provided help to Indigenous peoples and other disadvantaged groups. In 1921, for example, the GFWC put Indian welfare
on their national agenda. White women's clubs influenced by the GFWC's
call to action provided paternalistic help to Native Americans. They
donated clothing, studied Natives, and wrote to legislators in protest
of the mismanagement of Native affairs. They even taught domestic
practices to traditional Indigenous women—assuming they were inferior
homemakers and caregivers. Indeed, all of these white women's efforts
were done without consulting Natives themselves.[27]

Margaret Jacobs, in *White Mother to a Dark Race*, argues that white
women were intimately tied to settler colonialism through their involvement in federal boarding schools. In these Native federally run schools,
white women reformers assumed traditional Native women were unfit
for motherhood. Instead, white women taught young Indigenous girls'
white notions of domesticity and gender roles.[28] In both federal boarding
schools and mainstream women's clubs, white women imparted white
notions of gender to Native females as part of an assimilationist settler-
colonial program.

Yet Indigenous women did participate in these mainstream women's clubs at an organizational level. Like their white women colleagues, these Native club women were usually middle- or upper-class Christian wives and mothers. They were mostly mixed of Native and white descent and had formal education. These Indigenous women combined their Native and modern identities as they discussed their rights as members of their tribal nations and the U.S. nation-state. For example, by forming the Oregon Trail Women's Club for Umatilla Indigenous women, Elizabeth used these mainstream clubs to support Indigenous women's senses of tribal identity, as well as a place for their empowerment.[29]

Similarly, African American middle-class women used white women's clubs to help "uplift" their race. These African American women taught poor and working-class African American communities white, middle-class values. While these African American club organizers and leaders have been criticized for supporting white culture and not emphasizing enough African American culture or practices, they have also been revered and celebrated for improving their communities and increasing educational opportunities for African Americans.[30] Similarly, Native American club women, who were viewed as "assimilated" and of a higher class than traditional Indigenous women, used these white women's clubs to support a white worldview, encouraging traditional Native women to become more assimilated. At the same time, just like African American women in similar mainstream women's organizations, Elizabeth worked to improve conditions for Native Americans. Elizabeth and other Indigenous women in these mainstream women's clubs occupied a complicated position. They encouraged Native women to mimic white women's norms and roles—thus implicating themselves in settler colonialism—while encouraging the empowerment and maintenance of their tribal identities. Alongside other Indigenous club women, Elizabeth encouraged Native women to combine their tribal and modern identities.

During interviews conducted in 1988 and 2010, Leah Conner, daughter of a women's club member, portrayed Elizabeth as strong, gentle, ladylike, and lighthearted. She described the purpose of the club as for Native women's empowerment. The club developed family and community relationships, helping women take on leadership roles within their tribal community and "improve" their dress and appearance. Conner discussed how Elizabeth encouraged the women to make their own handicrafts— including contemporary buckskin crafts and beadwork—and show these Native arts to others. Elizabeth also encouraged them to have teas and luncheons. Elizabeth encouraged Conner to attend college, which was something she had never considered before. Connor attended Willamette University and the University of New Mexico. She successfully received her bachelor's degree at Eastern Oregon State College at LaGrand, her master's degree in education from Oregon State University, and a BFA from the University of Washington. Conner also described the club as the most positive feminine movement on the reservation, comparing Elizabeth to Eleanor Roosevelt, discussing their similar strengths and work ethic. According to Conner, Elizabeth did not just talk about things but took action and was able to get Native women from the three different tribes on the reservation to work together. The Oregon Trail Women's Club members respected and honored Elizabeth's role as a teacher and a leader and in 1950 supported her nomination as American Mother of the Year.[31]

The Oregon Trail Women's Club was a Native hub under the guise of a settler-colonial name, a subversive trickster strategy of camouflage. Through this subversive naming tactic, Elizabeth secured the support of the GFWC, a settler-colonial women's organization. Elizabeth used this organization to empower Native women and support the development of modern Native identities.

Henry's Heart Attack

On September 3, 1942, while Elizabeth was busy organizing the Oregon Trail Women's Club, and Henry was serving as superintendent, he suffered a major heart attack. I can only imagine how hard Henry worked and how stressful his Indian agent position was. I am certain his busy and taxing job contributed to his heart attack. Elizabeth encouraged their children to return home immediately because they feared Henry might die. My mother, Woesha, for example, traveled from the Jicarilla Apache Reservation, where she was working. She did not leave Pendleton until her father was recovering. Elizabeth wrote Bess Page, Henry's white adoptive cousin, that Henry "suffered terribly for over a week. . . . He must be in bed from six to eight weeks, and cannot return to work until January the first. Marion and Ed came down from Portland. . . . Henry said to tell you he is coming out with a rejuvenated heart, and a boyish figure. He is cut to 1,200 calories a day. He is able to joke a little, so I know he is feeling stronger."[32]

Page responded to Henry that he should starting thinking about some of his priceless Winnebago [Ho-Chunk] material: "You know better than the rest of us how important it is that memories such as yours get onto paper. You know back in your mind you have had the thought of writing up the medicine lodge lore of your uncle and grandfather, and your early pre-school experiences, but you never had time for it. . . . Do try it. You have in Elizabeth an excellent critic right at your elbow."[33]

Henry answered in a letter of September 28, 1942, emphasizing his love and sense of family was all-encompassing, contained both Natives and whites and supported his sense of a Ho-Chunk–centric hub, including family near and far, and his beloved horse, Snippy.

While for the moments, I am concerned to know from my physician as to whether or not I am to give up my riding horse, "Snippy," and very much loved game (golf). (I was stricken while out practicing golf at 7:30 am on Sept. 3rd). I shall make these sacrifices if it is necessary. You have struck a very responsive chord in me when you outline a writing future. I may have been spared to do just such a line of work by which America may get a better understanding of the Indian. . . .

My little Grandson, "Buzz," (nick named by me) left me today for Portland with his parents. He looked so sweet in ribbons and woolens. He is twenty days old today taking his first extended trip. He name is "Edward Roe Cloud Hughes." He is the first to carry on the name "Roe" and "Cloud." My other little grandson waiting in heaven [who passed away] with my little boy and namesake was called "Michael Henry Freed." These dear daughters of mine draw me closer to them by naming their little ones after me.

Ramona [his daughter] left for Vassar Saturday night this week. She looked radiant as a senior at Vassar now and so happy to leave knowing full well that I am now clear out of the woods. . . . I'm only weak from losing 30 pounds. . . . My face for once shows rather high cheekbones. . . . Indians have sent wild flowers from the mountains here. Neighbors have brought eggs, corn and jars of jelly. . . . I had preached six Sundays in succession, and carried on the work of the superintendency at the same time when the blow came. I had hurt my leg, and went on crutches to the pulpit. The load may have been heavy, but the joy was great too.[34]

Henry chose to use "Roe" as his middle name, since the Roes informally adopted him as their son. His daughter Marion passed down the name by giving her son "Buzz" the name Roe as his middle name. Henry relied on the Roes while he was a Yale student, as discussed in chapter 1. Henry and Elizabeth reached out to whites as integral to their work for the betterment of Native Americans. Yet, as discussed in chapter 2, Mary Roe's relationship with Henry as a colonial mother was challenging and difficult. I chose not to continue using the Roe name throughout much of this book manuscript in an effort of decolonization. My choice might be challenging for some, as Henry decided to use Roe as part of his name, and I sincerely believe he did love Mary and Walter Roe. As a Native feminist scholar, however, I argue his decision to become their informally adopted son was influenced by his highly racialized settler-colonial environment, where Native men were seen as nonmen and as children and lower on the evolutionary scale than whites, and he suffered deeply as an orphan after losing his Ho-Chunk mother, father, and grandmother from a horrible flu epidemic. In other words, Henry very likely felt that he had to make a family connection with the Roes to be successful in the white environment of Yale University, including receiving loans. At the same time, I want to honor the positive aspects of Cloud's loving relationship with Bess Page, Cloud's white adoptive cousin, who supported Henry as he was convalescing in the hospital after his heart attack. She also urged him to write about Ho-Chunk culture, respecting him as a Ho-Chunk intellectual. And her encouragement of Henry shows how, to some extent, he had "Nativized" Bess. She emphasized her appreciation for Ho-Chunk culture and took part in Cloud's sense of a Ho-Chunk family or hub. This letter also shows how much he loved and stayed connected to his grandson, who was alive, and his grandson and son, who had passed away.

When Cloud left the hospital, Dr. J. P. Brennan advised that he take at least two months off from living at an altitude of 1,100 feet in Pendleton. This meant he had to leave the reservation and take a break from the terrible strain of his job. Elizabeth and Henry decided to stay with Ed and Marion Hughes, their daughter and her husband in Portland, from mid-November 1942 until the end of the year.[35]

Henry and Ho-Chunk Studies

In 1944, while Elizabeth was busy working with the Umatilla women as part of the Oregon Trail Women's Club, Henry wrote another correspondence to his adopted white cousin, Bessie. They exchanged letters about how to examine history from a Native American perspective. She had sent him her chapter about Indian and white relations in Virginia in the 1600s and requested his feedback.[36] In response, he wrote,

After ten or more points you bring out as to why the Indians attacked the English so violently in 1622 in Va. [Virginia], I think more should be made of the fact of the Indian dispossessed. Show how this process can be so painful to them.

According to the English Diaries the English looked upon the Indians as inferior, fit to be servants to the English and as the Indians occupied the best corn lands, most fertile spots to be found in the country enjoyed the deer and wild fowl, the English longed for these very lands and as shiploads of them came over there was need for more and more of this land. Then too their domesticated animals ran all over the place destroying cornfields causing disturbances not only in Va. but also in other settlements. If there is one thing an Indian resents, it is to be thought of as inferior. As a matter of fact, he thinks or measures himself as superior. . . . Hence pride is one of the most outstanding of Indian nature. Yet was it not [Jonathan] Yardley who took Opechancanough [chief of the Powhatan], by the back of his hair and utterly humiliated him for corn? No man can do that to a chief and not hear from it later. An Indian never forgot such arrogance. He was humiliated by that act [in front of] the whole tribe. . . .

They [English] people prospered on corn, tobacco, cattle, swine and poultry on lands which the Indian considered rightfully his own. They ruthlessly disinterred the bones of the leader of the Powhatan federation, Powhatan in 1621. The resting place to the Indian is terribly sacred. . . . Above all things to alarm the Indians were the English's imported epidemics. . . . In these times, Indians are losing their lands by the loans ostensibly made as a gesture of friendship on the part of the whites, and then find themselves dispossessed of their lands later when unable to repay. . . . If you put these very strong elemental feelings of the Indians which interpreted by the Indians as jeopardizing their existence then the attack assumed economic, racial and rancor from high handed treatment as *casus belli* rather than cruelty per se.[37]

In this quote Cloud makes a convincing analytical case against settler colonialism, discussing how the actions of the English—dispossessing Natives of our land, humiliating our chiefs, digging up of the bones of Powhatan, treating us as inferiors, bringing disease, and jeopardizing Natives' very existence—should be viewed as justification for Natives' acts of war. He discusses how the English's disrespectful behavior would encourage Natives to fight back. His Native-centric view of history attacks the underlying assumptions that work to normalize settlers' behavior to dispossess Natives of our land. Settler-colonial histories describe a heroic fight between good and evil, seeing Native Americans as evil and settlers as good. Cloud undermines this good-versus-evil binary by asserting that Indigenous peoples were justified to wage war against the English, and their behavior was not "cruelty per se." He contests seeing white settlers' behavior toward Natives as based on goodness, friendship, or benevolence by discussing the land loss, when Natives could not pay back the loans provided by the English "ostensibly" as gestures of friendship.[38] He exposes how settlers profited from their occupation of stolen Indigenous land. Moreover, Cloud's intelligent and perceptive consideration of how the English's maneuvers revolved around land dispossession and economic pursuit reveals how colonialism works.

Cloud's analysis of the English's colonial behavior and his highlighting of a Native warrior perspective demonstrates his overall ability to discuss a Native approach to history, and how his Ho-Chunk cultural perspective was vital to his intellectual inquiry. In these ways his intellectual analysis is foundational to the creation of Ho-Chunk studies, which includes later scholars such as Amy Lonetree, Truman Lowe, Tom Jones, David Lee-Smith, Woesha Cloud North (his daughter), George Greendeer, Angel Hinzo, and Allen Walker.[39] Cloud labors to open lines of communication between himself and his white cousin Bessie, urging her to comprehend Natives' rightful retaliation against the English's unfair treatment. By trying to sensitize Bessie to a Native approach to history, culture, and colonialism, Cloud developed a supportive Native hub or network in the midst of his white family, helping him maintain his identity as a Ho-Chunk man and an intellectual.

Elizabeth and Umatilla Native Women Unite in Protest

A few years later, in 1946 or 1947, the Native women at Umatilla joined with Elizabeth Bender Cloud to denounce an article written by a Portland writer, Elsie Dickson, who was the white woman called "The Hat," for her stylish bonnet. The title of her original article is unknown but appeared in the Elks Club's national magazine. It described Dickson's experience at the Pendleton Round-Up. The matter was summed up in a second article by Elsie Dickson that appeared in a local paper, "Indians Heap Provoked Blonde Writer 'The Hat' May Lose Part of Scalp," where she interviewed Elizabeth Bender Cloud. Dickson wrote that the women of the reservation denounced her original article "through Mrs. Henry Roe Cloud . . . herself head of Indian Women's Affairs, Oregon Federation of Women's Clubs," who had found the following excerpt offensive:

> Since the Indians accepted only silver dollars, a man with a sack was posted at the exit to dole out the money. It was also part of the Round-Up tradition to shoot any injured steer and hand it over to the Indians for a barbeque. Squaws used to flock like flies around a carcass until not so much as a grease spot was left on the grounds.
>
> Indians are still hard-money people but they've raised the ante considerably and when a steer is handed to them they delicately cut off the hams and leave the rest where it lies. Like the rest of the rodeo, they've turned it into big business.[40]

In this quote Dickson racializes Native women as squaws and compares them to flies—two dehumanizing and colonial blows. Dickson points to Natives' exploitation as part of "big business." She describes how impoverished Natives would cut off a portion of meat and leave the rest, portraying Natives as wasteful—a common settler-colonial construction.

Elizabeth Bender Cloud told Dickson the following in order to set the record straight:

> In reply to this, the Indian women state: "Meat issued to the Indians at the Round-Up has, for the last 15 years, come from the city butcher shops. Some two years ago, however, one injured steer was killed and from this one Indian man was allowed to cut off two hind quarters and the rest went to the slaughter house.
>
> No carcasses have been left over which the Indians could flock like flies. And Indians, as a group, have long ago abandoned that conduct of life which would cause sickness and infection diseases among them. At the 1946 Round-Up the federal government maintained a man to spread disinfectant to rid the Indian encampment of flies. This was in addition to a supervising nurse and helper.
>
> Indian self-respect and morale are fostered by such measures, and the Indians, themselves, are proud and grateful.
>
> Not an Indian on this reservation would eat until "not so much as a grease spot would be left on the grounds." Hoover may have met such type of eaters in Europe, but it is not so on the Umatilla Reservation.[41]

The Native women, unfortunately, used settler assumptions in their response. When they emphasized Natives no longer left carcasses that drew flies and expressed gratitude for a federal-government employee spreading disinfectant, they portrayed themselves as "good" Indians. As integral to settler colonialism and the elimination of the Native, white settlers viewed us as inferior and in need of civilization to remedy our inherent deficiencies.[42] Elizabeth and the women of the Oregon Trail Women's Club, as modern warrior women, voiced their anger and fought back against racist epithets of Native women and Indigenous people overall. They said Natives were not wasteful and the unused meat was returned to the slaughterhouse. Therefore, the Oregon Trail Women's

Club seemed to be also a training ground for teaching Native women to become warrior women.

The Oregon Trail Women's Club's twenty-five members showcased Native American culture at the GFWC's national convention held in Portland. They made miniature sets of moccasins for table favors and showed a pageant of Indian fashions, named "The New Look in the Long Ago." Elizabeth spoke and Henry attended as an important guest.[43] Elizabeth very well could have named the Native fashion show, and choosing this title was an Indigenous intellectual challenge to dominant assumptions of Natives. Rather than portraying Natives as static relics of the past, whose Native culture and presence were vanishing, the title asserts a creative combination of traditional and modern, emphasizing that Native women were staying Indigenous into the present day. Furthermore, Henry's presence in the audience shows his support of Elizabeth's subversive work with the Native women of Umatilla.

The Indian Agent's Role in Umatilla Reservation's Challenges

In 1939 Natives of the Umatilla Reservation confronted particularly difficult issues. The reservation is a consolidated agency with tribal members of the Umatilla, Cayuse, and Walla Walla tribes. The diversity in membership led to a considerable amount of intertribal tension and factionalism. There was incredibly strong and intense struggle and conflict regarding salmon fishing and land grazing between whites and Natives, and Cloud, as the new superintendent, had to make decisions about the distribution of these resources. Meanwhile, white settlers built dams on the Columbia River, threatening the already dwindling salmon population, which was a crucial resource, supplying greatly needed income and food for Natives. As superintendent, Cloud coordinated the agency's reaction to these various threats, often with a limited budget. And this budget continued to decrease in the late 1930s and early 1940s, as the country turned its focus on the war and away from Indian New Deal's agendas.[44]

On October 10, 1941, early in his ten-year career as an Indian agent, Cloud spoke before the Wildlife Society at the chamber of commerce in Pendleton, Oregon. During this speech Cloud emphasized Ho-Chunk and Indigenous perspectives on "conservation," a settler-colonial term:

My few remarks tonight, I hope, will show something of the Indian attitude on the question of the conservation of game. If the same should be destroyed through uncontrolled, wanton destruction the white hunter cannot hunt for *sport* and the Indian hunter cannot hunt for *subsistence*.

To my mind, conservation of game is justified not so much to supply hunting of opportunity to the white man for sport and to the Indian for subsistence. Conservation rightly viewed is for national self-sufficiency—to preserve the balance existing for ages in nature and for ultimate national defense.

Conservation of game bulked large in the Red Man's philosophy. According to tradition animals were created before man. Priority of existence carried to the Indian mind the endowment of greater powers. The great Creator gave the animals something more than He gave to man. Animals therefore were akin to the beings known as supernaturals. Animals belong to the category of creatures meriting worship and adoration from man. It was believed that the animals also could do the work of supernaturals. These [supernaturals] had power and control over the Red man's most vital interests—over sickness and health, victory or defeat in war, success on the hunt and chase. In the foregoing I have used some big words simply to say that when the Indians' respect for the animal kingdom amounts to a religion, wanton destruction of game can find no room in his thinking. Such practice has never been heard of in Indian experience. From time immemorial game was the means of subsistence for the Indian. Its conservation meant self-preservation of the Indian race itself. . . .

When Indians killed deer, buffalo or any other game they never wasted any portion or part. The hair was made into mattress material. Pads were made of it while it was wet for pack saddles. Ropes were made out of buffalo hair. Indian trunks were made out of buffalo hide. The tail was used for head dress, and in buckskin dresses. The hoof was heated to be cut for ornamental dress purposes. When cut and strung, it had a clear, ringing sound. The Indians ate the inside of the hoof. Tripe was cut, its contents emptied, cleaned thoroughly and cured by smoking for winter food, or boiled for eating immediately.

The lungs were soaked for winter use. The bones were cut into pieces and preserved for soup making in winter. It was cut very thick and hung up. Sometimes it was broken up for tallow by making it into cakes. The meat was sliced very thin and hung to dry in the sun and also inside the tepee. The ear a most valuable dish for the Indian. The skin was peeled and the ear gristle was eaten as a great delicacy. The hide, Indians made into gloves, moccasins and ready to wear clothing. The horns were used for drinking purposes, rings for decoration of the hand, awl handles for scraping hair off the hide. Elk hides were used for robes with hair retained like buffalo robes. When hair is removed, Indians use it for blankets and robes, and for panoply decorations with long fringes on horses. The bearskin being waterproof was used for drum coverings and as throw rugs.[45]

In this speech Cloud as a Ho-Chunk intellectual emphasizes how Natives relate to animals. For Indigenous peoples, Cloud argues, animals are integral to religion and spiritual philosophy and even valued above humans—as opposed to the whites' assumption that humans are superior to animals. In this way Cloud tries to create understanding between whites and Natives about vastly different approaches to conservation. As opposed to white hunters, who killed animals for sport, Natives relied on hunting to feed their families. They used every single part of the animal for multiple purposes, and this approach, Cloud argues, supports "self-sufficiency," "national defense," and the future of the nation. He argues for a Native and environmentally sustainable approach to hunting and conservation that could ultimately contribute to humanity's very survival as human beings. His Ho-Chunk intellectual work recalls his commentary on Bessie's manuscript, when he insisted on a Native perspective. Similarly, he argued to Bessie that choices Native people made were extremely rational. Thus Cloud repeatedly defied the stereotypes that Natives were less intelligent than whites and lower on the socioevolutionary scale. Cloud not only opened up lines of communication between whites and Natives but also validated Indigenous knowledge and perspectives to define conservation and contributed to Ho-Chunk knowledge and studies.

Cloud deeply respected the Ho-Chunk approach to hunting he learned from his relatives, who had a close spiritual connection to animals. For example, Henry cherished the large buffalo hide he used as a blanket. According to his son-in-law, Raleigh Butterfield, Elizabeth would tease him and say, "That thing is so heavy. How can you sleep under that? It's so heavy it will crush you!"[46] Cloud's buffalo blanket not only kept him warm at night but also could remind him of fond memories of his childhood on the Winnebago Reservation surrounded by his Ho-Chunk family. This buffalo blanket symbolized his Ho-Chunk hub that protected him and kept him warm throughout his life. Through this hub he connected to his Ho-Chunk identity and tribe, despite his geographic separation. The blanket also might have elicited beautiful childhood memories of learning to hunt, respecting the animals one killed, offering prayers for the animal, and seeing the sacrifice of one's life for another's survival. Indeed, Henry and Elizabeth, with other family members, would hunt and fish together in the gorgeous mountains and streams surrounding the reservation. These trips must have also supported Ho-Chunk and Ojibwe hubs, both of them possibly connecting to memories from their childhoods with their beloved relatives on their reservations.

Cloud's Support of Native Fishing Rights

Potentially one of the earliest letters ever mailed to Cloud as an Umatilla Indian agent concerned fishing. On August 17, 1939, the Yakima Indian agent, M. A. Johnson, sent him a copy of the correspondence he had already mailed to the commissioner of Indian Affairs. Johnson wrote about the negotiations between the federal government and tribes about restitution for damage to and loss of Native fishing and camping sites caused by the flooding of land behind the Bonneville Dam. The federal government's proposal included the purchase of six replacement sites. Eventually, the tribes and Johnson agreed to the proposal and requested the secretary send additional instructions. Johnson wrote that the settlement should not be viewed as reimbursement "for the loss to the run of the fish which may develop in later years due to the construction of Bonneville Dam."[47]

Whites damming the Columbia River and flooding numerous spiritually vital fishing sites caused much pain and sorrow for Native Americans

Fig. 17. A proud Elizabeth showing off fish caught on a fishing trip with her beloved Henry near Pendleton, Oregon. Photograph courtesy of the Cloud family.

of the Pacific Northwest. Rivers are dammed to provide more water for farming, electrical power, and other uses, but in the process the rushing water kills plants, animals, and many living things. The survival of Natives depended on fishing for thousands of years. The fish were considered a gift from our Creator, so losing access to fishing places marked not only the depletion of an important food source but also a spiritual assault. Natives can no longer walk on our sacred lands, connect to our Creator, or witness the beauty of the amazing river. We can no longer give thanks to the fish for offering their lives for our survival. Throughout the twentieth century the cultural differences between Natives and white settlers played out on the stage of the Columbia River and its surrounding lands, on the lives of animals and fish. Still today Natives believe our people and what white settlers call "nature" are one. Our Creator provides fish—and all life—for sustainable use, not wanton exploitation.[48] This cultural divide and conflict also points to the process of settler colonialism working not only to eliminate Native peoples from our land as integral to building dams but also to control nature for monetary profit.[49]

Natives were the first ones to exchange fish for other goods in the Umatilla Valley. In other words, Native Americans had their own "monetary system" that relied on fish as a unit. In 1944 Cloud asked tribal members from the three Umatilla tribes to compile a list of items their ancestors bartered for in exchange for fish. He learned that they traded fish for drums and cradles, beaver medicine bags, snowshoes, shields, tomahawks, ropes and rawhide thongs, natural dyes, baskets, cooking utensils made of wood burls, mortars and pestles, scrapers for hides, obsidian and flint knives, arrowheads, dressed buckskin, elk and deer meat, buffalo, roots, saddle blankets, buffalo-hide tents and teepees, pipes, bows and arrows, wampum, buckskin clothing, and buffalo robes.[50] This wide range of goods received in exchange for fish shows how valuable fish were to Umatilla Natives. Fish provided them with food and an incredibly long list of needed supplies, cooking utensils, and precious spiritual items. In effect, fish functioned as money, refuting white settlers' assumptions that Natives were "undeveloped" and needed to learn to make "productive" use of animals. Furthermore, when settlers built dams, millions of fish died, Indigenous camping and hunting sites were flooded, and the Indigenous peoples' survival methods greatly decreased. In other words, dams significantly contributed to widespread poverty. Cloud likely collected this information to use it as ammunition in support of tribes' struggles for reparations for losses caused by the flooding caused by dam building.

Natives' legal rights to catch fish were based on 1855 treaties between tribes and Oregon governor Isaac I. Stevens. But, in 1939, when Cloud was superintendent of Umatilla, the interpretation of the treaties had become controversial. One 1855 treaty, article 3, states, "The exclusive right of taking fish in all of the streams, where running through or bordering said reservation, is further secured to said confederated tribes and bands of Indians, as also the right of taking fish at all in the usual and accustomed places, in common with the citizens of the territory, and of erecting temporary building for curing them."[51] Whites could mistakenly view this provision not as protecting Natives' right to fish but as allowing them to fish too.

The treaties of 1855 proclaimed the coming of a new order on the Columbia Plateau. To acquire title to Indigenous lands, while forcibly removing Natives to reservations, the U.S. government had to designate signatory tribes, delineate their differing regions, and determine appropriate "head chiefs" for negotiations. Federal officials partitioned the land into ceded areas, broke up kinship networks, and grouped inhabitants into confederated tribes, which encouraged later strife. Before the treaties it was kinship that structured access to prime fishing sites, not one's status as a "treaty Indian" or not. As soon as Cloud became superintendent, he worked to protect Native fishing rights. As part of his role, he was in charge of the Celilo Falls fishing site. This meant frequent, 225-mile trips to and from Celilo for meetings of the Celilo Fish Committee, which was made up of three members from the reservations as well as representatives of the Indians who lived at Celilo and Rock Creek, to the southeast.[52]

The Columbia River Natives (who were not federally recognized) and members of tribes from the Umatilla, Yakima, and Warm Springs Reservations all had the right to fish at Celilo. But they were in constant disagreement with one another and whites over the fishing sites, partly because Natives had only seven and a half acres on which to camp and fish. Cloud also advised the Celilo Fish Committee, a local intertribal body organized to help govern the activities of the Native fishermen at Celilo Falls. This committee originated in 1934 to negotiate settlements, resolve disagreements, and provide a (somewhat) unified Indigenous voice in debates about the salmon catch on the upper Columbia River.[53] Cloud was a de facto member of the committee. He acted as an adviser. During his first three years as an Indian agent at Umatilla, his involvement with the Fish Committee likely took up most of his time. Cloud balanced and represented various points of view in his role. Dreading losing state cooperation on other matters, the Indian Service took nearly an ambivalent position on Native treaty rights regarding off-reservation fishing. The Fish Committee needed a strong supporter of Indigenous treaty rights, and the Umatilla Natives asked Cloud to advocate for their particular tribal interests too.[54]

There was much distrust between the tribal nations who shared Celilo Falls. By court decision Yakima Natives, for example, were given access to the site a short time ago, and the smaller tribal nations disliked sharing the fishing site with the three-thousand-member tribe. The smaller tribal groups also resisted the Natives of the Warm Springs Agency from being allowed to fish and have access to Celilo Falls. Cloud often was compelled to act as both mediator and manager among the various groups. For example, Cloud was a leader, who persuaded the superintendents of the reservations who fished at Celilo Falls to agree to the Fish Committee's strategy to give identification cards to authorized Natives so that the police could identify trespassers at Celilo Falls.[55]

Cloud discussed his involvement in the Celilo situation in an interview after he left his post as superintendent of Umatilla. He remembered working with other superintendents to improve the difficult living and fishing conditions at Celilo by trying to gain funds from the federal government:

> Fortunately, I have ten-year experience with the Celilo situation. Chief Tommy Thompson and his small band belong to the Warm Springs Agency, Warm Springs, Oregon. . . . This small band at once surrendered all their rights under the 1855 treaty and became thereafter

virtual squatters on the Celilo fishing location. The treaty Indians, on the other hand, namely the Umatilla and Yakima tribes, did not oust this small band of Indians but permitted them to continue this occupation of the Celilo fishing site. Reasons of humanity, moral considerations, beside [sic] Indian generosity have been exercised in Tommy Thompson's favor. The Federal Government on its part have [sic] not pressed the technical requirements of law under the treaties but have proceeded to remedy the untoward situation at Celilo.[56]

Cloud calls Tommy Thompson and his people "virtual squatters," because they were not treaty Indians and from a colonial perspective had legally lost their "right" to live and fish at Celilo and were therefore legally trespassers and unlawful tenants. He then discusses that it was "humanity, moral considerations," and "Indian generosity" that stopped Umatilla and Yakima Natives from ousting them from living and fishing there, and that the federal government also did not follow the technical requirements of the law. Cloud's discussion demonstrates how Natives challenged the naturalizing of settler-colonial constructions based on treaty-related legal definitions regarding who could live and fish at Celilo. His statement also shows how the federal government did not rely on these settler-colonial constructions either, not forcing Tommy Thompson and his people from leaving Celilo. Further, choosing not to oust Tommy Thompson and his people was a way to honor Native kinship.

Natives and non-Natives had overwhelmed the Celilo fishing area. Starting in the mid-1860s the use of industrial processing and canning techniques transformed the salmon runs of the Columbia River into a profitable commodity. Specifically, Seufert Brothers Company, the biggest packing operation, deteriorated the problems at Celilo. In 1930 the company made several cableways that connected the Oregon shore to various islands. The company would rent the cables to Natives, and they could climb into a fish box and use a zip line to ride above the roaring waters to stands built on the opposite shore, where they could fish. This cable system drew an increasing number of newcomers to Celilo. Most were Natives from reservations, who wanted to make money from selling fish, because the damming of streams, including the Yakima and

Umatilla, had pushed many Indigenous peoples away from traditional fishing sites. Local Indigenous peoples and others from as far away as Alaska joined the crowds of whites in search of seasonal work and economic relief from the Great Depression.[57]

While Cloud was Indian agent, he used his settler-colonial position to gain additional monies from the federal government for the Natives at Celilo. He continued in the same interview after he left his post: "For ten years as Superintendent of Umatilla Indian Agency, I with the superintendents of Yakima and Warm Springs struggled to bring about Congressional appropriations for Celilo. We worked for $250,000.00 and finally got only $125,000.00. This amount was adequate for only the major improvements, namely housing, drying sheds, water system, electrical utilities and sewage disposal. The crying need for an underpass and road to the fishing locations will have to come from the railroads involved and the State of Oregon. The State Highway Commission should get busy with their improvements."[58]

Sampson Tulee Court Case

The Sampson Tulee court case presented Cloud an additional opportunity to act as mediator. A Yakima Native, Tulee fished at Celilo Falls. He, along with other Natives who fished there, struggled with Washington State laws developed to regulate and control Indigenous people's right to fish. The state had never been very welcoming of the Indigenous fishermen. By 1937 Washington enforced license fees on them. Natives immediately protested, arguing that these fees violated the 1854–55 Stevens Treaties that protected their right to fish without state interference in the "usual and accustomed places." Washington State and Indian Service officials anticipated that Tulee's case would resolve this treaty-related conflict and issue. After Tulee's arrest his case began its journey through the court system.[59]

Cloud and Celilo fishermen monitored this case closely. Like most treaty-related cases, it was not decided quickly. The Fish Committee regularly gave Tulee's family fish since he was in jail for close to a full year—an instance of them taking care of community members. Because state officials avoided working with the Fish Committee, Cloud became the negotiator, who argued for Natives to continue to fish at the site while the case moved through the courts. In the beginning Natives were allowed to fish if they had fishing licenses. Eventually Cloud and others persuaded Washington State not to charge Natives the fees for fishing licenses until after the ruling.[60]

In late 1942 the Tulee case was resolved, even though obscurely. The Supreme Court decided that the state could not collect license fees if the objective was to limit Natives' right to use traditional fishing sites. In this aspect Natives won, as the court determined that requiring Natives to have fishing licenses was illegal. The court, however, also ruled that the state could still control the Natives' catch and fishing seasons for conservation purposes. This judgment gave the state wide-ranging powers over Natives. Around eighteen months later, in the fall of 1944, the Northwest superintendents' council was still uncertain about what the decision meant for their reservations and jurisdictions. They delegated Cloud the job to examine the Tulee decision and present his findings at their December meeting.[61]

Cloud gave a speech at the December 8 and 9, 1944, Northwest superintendents' meeting. He discussed the distressing purpose of reservations:

> The reservation so-called in our American history came into being for the first time in this particular Northwest area in the process of this treaty making. . . . The creation of a reservation at that time was as everyone knows, for the purpose of keeping Indians in subjection by confinement in limited areas and particularly to protect and encourage settlement of the country by whites.[62]

Cloud's analysis of settler colonialism as based in land dispossession and the removal of Natives to reservations reveals how Indigenous intellectuals were discussing the reality of colonialism almost eighty years ago. And this early analysis laid powerful groundwork for present-day discussions of colonialism and struggles for Native rights in Indigenous studies. Settler-colonial discourse, according to Penelope Edmonds, imagines Natives and their relationship to land as an earlier stage of human development, prior to private property. This evolutionary logic legitimized the violent and "legal" dispossession of lands without Native consent.[63]

Cloud emphasizes, from an Indigenous perspective, Natives' right to fish in locations both on and off the reservation—in the "usual and accustomed places," according to the 1855 Umatilla, or Yakima, Treaty. In his talk Cloud makes it clear he was not a lawyer, which explains his qualifying assertions with "my personal opinion" and "the purposes of discussion":

> [For] the purposes of discussion today on this important question, I will state as my personal opinion that the legal status of "usual and accustomed places" outside Indian reservations in the light of the Yakima or Umatilla Treaty of 1855 is the same as the status of the reservation proper. I think you will grant me the contention that there were Tribal domains clearly recognized by all tribes as affording Indian tribes more than sufficient wildlife resources to maintain that standard of living to which they were accustomed. Inter-tribal wars came about when tribes invaded these respective domains at the time when the treaty was made. These very domains were clearly comprehended as economic units in terms of hunting and fishing by Governor Stevens and the United States Commissioners who spoke on behalf of the United States. The Indians no less comprehended for no one knew their environment as they did. A glance at the original exterior boundaries of these domains set apart at that time is proof sufficient of this fact governing the situation.[64]

Cloud uses the dominant logic of economics to enlarge fishing rights to include hunting rights, a Native-centric objective. This shows how Cloud utilizes the colonizer's language for Native goals, as he did previously, when he fought for Geronimo's freedom and support of the Fort Sill Apaches' struggle over land with the federal government. Once again Cloud's mixture of Native and dominant rhetoric is a form of doubleness speech, using colonial language for Native objectives.

Again linking hunting and fishing, Cloud argues that the "domain" where Indians fish and hunt are protected under the treaty. In the same speech to other superintendents, Cloud said,

> As a matter for discussion only, I will say that the activity known as hunting and fishing denoted an Indian economic activity. This activity

was the outgrowth of the problem of self-preservation. While "fishing" as such might be termed as an enterprise by itself of our coast tribes, Indians in the Northwest area carried forward this means of making a livelihood along with hunting as an inseparable unit of activity. Game and wildlife abounded along the wooded areas of streams as well as fish in the rivers. The domain reserved under the Treaty was an economic unit which could not be torn apart and parts or portions thereof defined as having certain specific activities and rights as distinct from certain other parts or portions with activities along with excusive rights or privileges. There is no denying the fact that the Supreme Court considers a fishing case as the defendant Sampson Tulee was taken in the act of fishing. The place involved may have also been an exclusive fishing area.[65]

Cloud continues to expand fishing rights to include hunting by arguing that Natives' perspectives of their treaty includes both hunting and fishing and that whites' perceptions of the law does not influence Natives' own legal conceptions of their treaty. In this way Cloud emphasizes an Indigenous perspective of the treaty, stressing that white perspectives are irrelevant and Natives deserve rights, because they gave up huge expanses of land in exchange:

It is well to state that Indians believed their treaty was one law and hence to them it meant that one law governed their hunting and the same one law governed their fishing. What legal decisions the whites came to about their fishing as such did not alter one iota their conceptions as to the inherent meaning of the treaty agreement to them. The courts have been wont to declare that this treaty must be interpreted in the light of the understanding the Indians had of its intrinsic meaning. The Indian understood the Treaty that he was protected in his hunting rights in consideration of the vast territory be relinquished to the whites. This meant that he had the utmost freedom to hunt and fish within the boundaries of his reservation, as well as along streams bordering his reservation and also in the "usual and accustomed places." One phrase of the treaty has apparently been allowed to go by default as the "usual and accustomed places" were guaranteed to them along with the guarantee of the reservation itself. Everyone knows their guaranteed usual accustomed places outside the reservation boundaries have been allowed to be occupied one after the other until now hardly any usual and accustomed places remain notwithstanding the fact that a hundred or more such places have been surveyed and claimed as such by delegations of Indians of the many such locations have been allowed to be claimed—dams have destroyed many and civilization's water pollutions have destroyed many others.[66]

While Natives as part of their treaty had been guaranteed to hunt and fish both on the reservation and in their "usual and accustomed places," Cloud astutely emphasizes, white settlers had overrun many of these Indigenous sites. Places had been lost to flooding caused by dams and water pollution created by settler-colonial industry. In other words, Cloud strongly implicates white-settler society and civilization as the cause of Natives' loss of their treaty-guaranteed hunting and fishing sites. As such, Cloud ultimately challenges the impact of settler colonialism, again showing his Ho-Chunk–centric intellectual lens.

Cloud ends this speech with a discussion how the state of Washington was already ignoring the Supreme Court ruling: the state closed the Klickitat River to Native fishing. Cloud argued that this prohibition goes against the Tulee Sampson decision:

The bold claim has been made here by me that the state is now at liberty to enforce conservation measures inside an Indian reservation by restrictions as to hunting of a regulatory nature. Our Department attorneys have taken the stand that this move for conservation of game by the state must confine itself to regulation and most important of all it must be reasonable regulation. It is my understanding that the present Klickitat fishing case takes the aspect of absolute prohibition as opposed to regulation on the part of the state. The state has not imposed seasons, limits, or kind of catch but simply has closed an area of certain dimensions. This is an instance of unreasonable regulation for the purpose of conservation as a locality protected by treaty.[67]

Through the example of the Klickitat fishing site, Cloud reveals the federal government's conversation measures as merely a way to control treaty rights. He also contrasts the state and federal definitions of the ruling here, as both are concerned with regulating Native fishing. The word "conservation" is imbedded in settler-colonial environmental discourse that juxtaposes dominant society against Natives' treaty rights to fish. Settlers believe they have a right to control the waterways to protect fish as an exploitable resource, ultimately interfering with Natives' treaty rights to fish in the "usual and accustomed places." But, using a Ho-Chunk–centric lens, Cloud argues that the government's action is an "unreasonable regulation" that goes against Natives' fishing rights.

Cloud's Ho-Chunk intellectual stance, in support of Natives' treaty rights, foreshadows the powerful 1960s Indigenous activism. This movement, based on treaty rights, resulted in huge political, social, and educational gains. During the 1960s and later, returning to the treaties was a favored tactic for Natives to struggle for tribal sovereignty, self-determination, and power. Thus, Cloud's appeal to the treaties in his fight for Indigenous rights was a harbinger of activism to come, breaking crucial intellectual ground in Native studies.[68] Cloud's analysis of the treaties could also point to a larger intellectual conversation among Natives that predated the 1960s and the Red Power movement, which anthropologists, historians, and Native-studies scholars need to explore today. Similarly, Cloud's astute intellectual insight and development of a Native-studies curriculum at the American Indian Institute precede the formation of Native Studies programs on university campuses largely as a result of Indigenous activism of the 1960s.[69] His daughter and my mother, Woesha Cloud North, took part in the powerful 1960s Indigenous political movement. She taught at Red Rock School on Alcatraz during the Native occupation of the island, and she fought for Native rights. She must have heard about Henry's struggle in support of tribes' hunting and fishing rights, and perhaps his fight encouraged her role in the occupation of Alcatraz Island. She also could have listened to her mother discuss her support of Native women joining male-dominated tribal councils as part of her involvement in the National Congress of American Indians, as discussed in the next chapter. Her parents' labor as Native activists and intellectuals could have influenced her decision to live on Alcatraz Island during the Native occupation. Her parents' work as Native intellectuals also must have motivated her to teach in Native studies at colleges, such as San Francisco State University; California State University, Fresno; and University of Nebraska, Lincoln, where she ultimately received her doctorate in 1978.

Cloud's Vexed Role as an Indian agent

At the beginning of Cloud's tenure as an Indian agent, Umatilla Natives welcomed him as a Native superintendent, which was unusual in the Indian Service at that time. Omar L. Babcock, the superintendent who preceded Cloud, had served one of the longest terms in the Indian Service. He had been the superintendent when Cloud was growing up on the Winnebago Reservation close to forty years before. This fact was emphasized in the press. Babcock controlled the agency strictly and was the kind of Indian agent Cloud frequently condemned. Under Babcock there was little participatory democracy for Natives. In contrast, the tribal council preferred Cloud's comparatively open and informative manner.[70]

As superintendent, Cloud was immediately thrust into the conflict-laden Umatilla Reservation politics. There were tensions between "mixed-blood" and "full-blood" Natives among the three tribes under his jurisdiction, regarding lumber sales, fishing rights, and land leases. For the first few years Cloud was appreciated for his openness about his goals and objectives. "I want to open it [tribal business] up and put it before the people so they know what we are doing," Cloud said. "We will not put anything under the blanket or in the dark," and he reiterated this message often in the early meetings of his tenure, working hard to distinguish himself from the previous white superintendent.[71]

At first, Cloud chaired the tribal council meetings, but this later got him into trouble. By presiding over the meetings, he opened himself up to being viewed as paternalistic like other white reservation superintendents. To reach his goals as the superintendent, he emphasized that he was Native too, which was something most superintendents could not claim. Cloud influenced general reservation council decisions, which other superintendents did at that time. But by being open about his perspective, he stressed that he was different from his predecessors. Overall, during his first few years as superintendent, the general reservation council respected Cloud, but the Business Committee was more likely to challenge him.[72]

As time passed, Cloud slowly let go of control and turned more and more of the actions over to the tribal council. He talked less often, and he behaved in a manner similar to his actions on the Celilo Fish Committee. He offered explanations, information, and, when the conversation was going off topic, guidance. By 1942 Cloud used a revised type of *Robert's Rules of Order*, and the council rapidly started to run most of their meetings with little involvement or advice from Cloud. The reservation had twice voted against the Indian Reorganization Act. This disheartened Cloud, but he agreed early in his term that he would not encourage following the IRA. During meetings, however, he would discuss the benefits of the IRA, including rules about the use of a quorum and who could vote. Cloud's remarks about the advantages of the IRA potentially alienated Umatilla Natives, who may have viewed the IRA as a settler-colonial imposition from outside their community.[73]

As discussed in the previous chapter, Cloud claimed coauthorship of the IRA. However, integral to the IRA was self-government, a settler-colonial concept in which a tribal government became in a sense a corporate body under the paternalistic power of the federal government. Cloud's role as a superintendent of Umatilla was under the auspice of the Indian Service and thus inextricably linked to paternalism. Even though Cloud tried to disentangle himself from the paternalism inherent in his role by, for example, not speaking much at meetings, he still seemed to struggle with the inherent paternalism of his position.

Cloud's position as superintendent was complicated, since he was Indigenous *and* an agent. On the one hand, he was able to speak from a Native position in regard to fishing and hunting rights, which diverged from the Indian Service's own ambivalent position. On the other hand, he had to answer to his superiors and carry out their goals, including encouraging Natives to farm their own land. Cloud supported Natives at Umatilla to become farmers so that they could reap huge profits rather than lease their land to white farmers and lose potential income. Many were reluctant, because, unlike fishing, farming was not a traditional activity among these tribes. At the November 24, 1941, tribal meeting,

Cloud asked tribal members to approve the appointment of an agricultural extension agent for the reservation. The government-funded agent would help mitigate soil erosion, suppress weeds, and encourage young farmers. Council members Lillie Corbert, James Kash Kash, and Andrew Barnhart approved the idea, but all the other members opposed it. At the next meeting, December 18, 1941, Cloud's request was voted down, forty-two to three. Two and a half years later, on April 28, 1944, the tribal council agreed to the federal government's request to practice weed control and soil conservation.[74]

On the Umatilla Reservation, timber was now worth twice as much, and some Natives on the reservation wanted more money right away. Cloud advised them to wait for the highest offer and argued that selective cutting bids protected the forests. The Natives of the Umatilla Reservation realized the land leases were worth far more, and they wanted more money. Partly because of multiyear land-lease rates signed before the war, rents had remained low. But now the farmers' profits were increasing, so the Native landowners wanted to boost land-lease rent as well. The white farmers who benefited from the low rates of land leases reacted with hostility. In some cases, rents rose before the leases expired, and Cloud was on the committee that bargained for lots of these increases. He also lobbied for the end of multiple-year leases, to reduce future conflict. At the same time, the end of multiple-year leases would protect the farmers in case wheat and pea prices fell considerably.[75]

White leasing of Native lands was a contentious issue, which caused Natives to distrust Cloud. Since the 1800s whites have profited dramatically from leasing Native American land—and this settler-colonial practice continues today. Charles Luce, a young, white lawyer hired by the tribal council to investigate Cloud, argued that Cloud did not require competitive bidding for new leases and that Native landowners were at the mercy of white ranchers who held the previous leases.[76] At the same time, Doris Bounds, chair of Inland Empire Bank in Hermiston, Oregon, argued that Cloud was forceful in his dealings with the leasing problems. She said he arrived at the bank, Native leases in hand, and strongly complained that Natives were not getting fair market value. Cloud, according to Bounds, told bank employees that Natives did not have the proper equipment—or the money to buy the needed equipment—to farm their own land, so they leased the land instead to non-Natives.[77]

Cloud's work boosted local self-government and helped the reservation share in the increased fortune of World War II. His labor, however, to lessen his power in tribal politics soon had remarkable impacts. By 1941 Natives' appreciation of his relatively open approach toward tribal governance concluded, and he became the recipient of more and more grievances. Some of these complaints revolved around tensions between "mixed-blood" and "full-blood" Natives. Jim Kanine, the Business Committee leader and chief of the Walla Walla, condemned him for marginalizing the older "full-blood" Natives, while Andrew Barnhart, on the general tribal council and a leader of "mixed-blood" Natives, indicted him for backing the "full-blood" Natives. As a modern, "full-blood" Native, Cloud's own identity did not perfectly align with either group, and his complicated identity seemed to alienate him from both factions. Now both groups accused Cloud of wielding too much influence, a fascinating turn of events, given their previous compliments of his open approach. Frequently, his Indian Service superiors heard their grievances, and he felt forced to defend himself to his supervisors.[78]

Some challenged Cloud about continuing to chair the general council meetings, which was a frequent criticism and pointed to his paternalism. In response, Cloud requested tribal members to elect someone else to become chair. But since no chair was selected, he told them they could not complain about his role of chair. Even so, a year later Cloud still chaired the meetings and received even stronger complaints about his control over meeting agendas. Cloud dealt with this issue at the next council meeting. He refused to act as chair beyond that meeting, compelling the council to elect its own chair. It required only one ballot to elect a new chair.[79]

To put tribal members' complaints into historical context, after 1934 there was a growing trend for Natives, in general, and tribal councils, in particular, to challenge the power of their Indian agents. In *Return of the Native*, Stephen Cornell argues that after the 1930s and the IRA, there were suddenly centers of power on Native reservations other than BIA superintendents. The development of tribal councils and other tribal organizations encouraged conflict.[80] Even though the Umatilla Reservation did not adopt the IRA, this challenging of Cloud could point to this over-all transfer of power on reservations, and any Indian agent very likely would have experienced attacks.[81]

Cloud's conflicts with the tribal council became even more grave. The most difficult and challenging was tribal members' decision to hire a tribal attorney, Charles Luce, as mentioned earlier. During this time it was common for tribes to hire a tribal lawyer. The Umatilla Natives hired Luce to represent them regarding damages created by the Columbia River dams and to investigate Cloud, their superintendent. Cloud, in response, wrote a long letter to the commissioner of Indian Affairs, arguing that hiring this attorney was a response to merely five men's personal complaints against him. Cloud argued that Luce was not trained in Indian law and therefore not an appropriate choice. The five men, including Kanine and Barnhart, were longtime opponents of Cloud and charged him with stealing cattle. It was determined that the cattle had been stolen by one of Cloud's employees.[82]

Cloud's immediate superior, E. Morgan Pryse, had known Cloud for a decade and supported him during this conflict. In his report to the commissioner of Indian Affairs on this disagreement, he emphasized that Cloud did not oppose the hiring of a tribal attorney but rather specifically opposed Luce, because of his relative lack of experience in Indian law. While Pryse agreed with Cloud's reasoning, he emphasized that hiring an attorney was up to the tribal council. Cloud promised to cooperate with Luce and the tribal council if the regional office approved Luce's contract.[83]

Because Pryse realized that the disagreement regarding hiring Luce caused conflict and tension between Cloud and the Umatilla Native community, he decided it was time for Cloud to leave his post. He offered Cloud the position of superintendent of the Grand Ronde–Siletz Agency, a small Native agency on the Oregon Coast. In the fall of 1948, Cloud accepted this new post, where he had developed a preliminary roll of tribal members early in his tenure at Umatilla.

Henry's Work for the Siletz and Grande Ronde

In Oregon the Grand Ronde area is around twenty miles from the Pacific Ocean. It is a valley with hills around its perimeter. The workplace of the

Confederated Tribes of the Grande Ronde is north of the city of Grande Ronde. Located in a valley also surrounded by hills, Siletz is around fifteen miles northeast of Newport, Oregon.[84] Cloud represented the government for about five hundred members of the Confederated Tribes of Siletz and more than seven hundred members of the Confederated Tribes of the Grand Ronde.[85]

Two months after Cloud was hired, the Grand Ronde–Siletz Agency was eliminated, and Cloud was reassigned as a regional representative. In 1949 the newly founded Indian Claims Commission heard the cases of the Grand Ronde and Siletz tribes. The commission decided in the tribes' favor and granted them $16 million.[86] The Supreme Court had determined that the tribes had a valid claim regarding the federal government robbing land from these tribes in 1855, and the money from the settlement would be given to their descendants.[87] Cloud's job as regional representative to the Grand Ronde–Siletz Agency Natives was partially to decide who was entitled to a portion of the money. His administrative job was painstaking and would impact every descendant of the displaced tribes to this day.

Cloud described his work for the Siletz Native community in an undated interview in our Cloud family archive: "I have administered the affairs of these Indians for a little over a year. Undoubtedly, the TB [tuberculosis] situation has been bad and is needing serious attention. The teeth of the children were in a deplorable state. Since my incumbency I have secured a contract physician for the Siletz Tribes. He should give his major thinking and time on the TB situation." He, furthermore, discussed how he drove Siletz children to the dentist to have their teeth fixed. He then emphasized how the recent per capita payment of a hundred dollars to the Siletz from the accumulated tribal timber sales and the coming distribution of $16 million would improve tribal members' health, education, and social progress.[88] After receiving the over $16 million from the federal government, the Siletz needed an accurate roll of the tribe, and Cloud diligently worked on this project until his death on February 9, 1950.

The judicial system had been involved in this matter since 1935, when Congress referred it to the courts.[89] Since 1940 this case had been in active litigation.[90] The Supreme Court's decision of November 25, 1946, determined that the tribes had the right to recover damages from the federal government for 2,775,000 acres of land in western Oregon stolen from Native Americans in 1855. The government had forcibly moved Natives in 1855 to the new Siletz Reservation, but the Senate failed to ratify the treaty, which should have provided them with money, buildings, and trust lands. In 1946 the Supreme Court ruled that four coast Native tribes were affected: the Chetco, Tillamook, Too-too-toNey, and Coquille. And in the fall of 1947, the U.S. Court of Claims was given the job of deciding the amount due each tribe, which would then be divided among each living descendant.[91]

After the Supreme Court's decision, Colonel Pryse, the regional director of the Bureau of Indian Affairs, discussed the need to hire a person to compile tribal lists, and that job was given to Cloud.[92] Cloud decided what fraction of each tribe's settlement each member should receive. It was a complicated task, as some members were descended from all four tribes and would receive portions from each tribe's settlement. His new assignment was challenging and painstaking and required the utmost diligence.

Cloud began his new assignment on October 11, 1948. The Grand Ronde–Siletz Agency office was located at Chemawa Indian School, north of Salem. The school's officials were no longer willing to provide the agency office space, and Colonel Pryse, with Cloud's agreement, moved the office to the Bureau of Indian Affairs office at Swan Island, on the Willamette River on the north side of Portland.[93] Consequently, when Cloud had to work at the regional office, he commuted across Portland from his home in West Linn and to miss rush-hour traffic he woke up at five in the morning.[94] Moving the Grand Ronde–Siletz office to Portland meant Cloud had to travel often to provide services to the tribes. According to my cousin, Gretchen, Cloud found a place to stay during his visits with the tribes in a house in Siletz. Elizabeth often accompanied her beloved Henry on these visits, and sometimes their grandchildren came along. They stayed in a two-story house in a building the people at Siletz called "The Old Courthouse."[95]

On October 17, 1949, Cloud guided Francis LaFrances, his employee, to put in alphabetical order the names of enrolled Siletz tribal members, compare it to the office files to check if anyone was missing, and place these names on voucher forms. Cloud stressed that, as required by the commissioner of Indian Affairs, it would become the final roll of members as of July 15, 1949. He required that LaFrances double-check everything to make sure all the names on the list were successfully moved to the voucher forms. Cloud explained it would be the final, binding roll: "This I require because there are chances of error even with great care in this job."[96] This letter shows how meticulous Henry was while compiling this roll for the Siletz tribe. Cloud wanted to do right by Native people, so he took great care compiling this essential tribal roll.

Henry drove to Siletz on February 6, 1950, for a two-day stay. Elizabeth had been concerned about Henry's health and didn't want him to stay in Siletz alone, but Henry was more worried about the water system at home and wanted Elizabeth to stay home to make sure the pipes didn't freeze. During the night on February 9, an intense chest pain came. According to our cousin Gretchen [Freed-Rowland], Henry reached for the bottle of nitroglycerine pills, but the bottle fell over. The tablets spilled across the bedside table, and our beloved Henry died.

The next day Natives observed that Henry's car was parked at "The Old Courthouse" when he would not usually be home. Finally, someone went looking for Henry, went inside, and found him. A friend of the Clouds called Elizabeth and told her Henry had passed away. He was sixty-six years old and died while still working hard for Natives' benefit. His daughter Marion and her husband, Ed, drove with Henry's beloved wife, Elizabeth, to Siletz, and our Cloud family's grieving began.

The final chapter of Henry's life on the Umatilla Reservation as an Indian agent was filled with challenges and struggles over fishing and hunting rights, ultimately supporting tribes' fight for tribal self-determination and sovereignty. Cloud was different from his white predecessor Babcock and tried to transform a government position through a Native lens, fighting against racism by working to change colonial cultural performances of the Pendleton Round-Up, Happy Canyon, and Wild West Show, while creatively combining dominant and Indigenous perspectives in his writing and speeches to battle for Native rights. All of his intellectual work and efforts were certainly foundational to Ho-Chunk and Native studies, as he analyzed Indigenous "conservation," settler colonialism, Native history, and treaties to support hunting and fishing rights while working to open lines of communication between whites and Natives. Henry's middle-class position, Yale education, and job as an Indian agent may have contributed to some Umatilla Natives possibly viewing him as untrustworthy and leading to his transfer to the Grand Ronde–Siletz Agency, where he died in service to Native people, compiling important tribal rolls. As his granddaughter, I am deeply proud of my grandfather's lifelong service to Native people. In contrast, Umatilla women professed their love and devotion to Elizabeth, his wife. She garnered much respect and was remembered fondly as contributing to a strong Umatilla women's movement of empowerment. Elizabeth continually encouraged Umatilla women to attend college and become leaders. In fact, Umatilla women nominated Elizabeth to become American Mother of the Year, which is discussed in the next chapter.

CHAPTER 5

Elizabeth Bender Cloud's Intellectual Work and Activism

While Henry left the national stage, transferred to work as an Indian agent on the Umatilla Reservation, his wife, Elizabeth, began her impressive rise to national prominence as a Native leader. At first, she worked at the local level. She co-directed the American Indian Institute with her husband, Henry, and started the Oregon Trail Women's Club. Later, as she grieved the loss of her much-loved and cherished Henry, she was named Oregon Mother of the Year and eventually American Mother of the Year. As Elizabeth's reputation grew, so did her activist and intellectual commitments. Initially, Cloud seemed to see tribal termination—the abrogation of Natives' treaty rights and end to Natives' special status with the federal government—as an inevitability, but later, as Indian Affairs chair of the General Federation of Women's Clubs (GFWC) and treasurer and field secretary of the National Congress of American Indians (NCAI), she fought against the settler-colonial goal of tribal termination.

As a modern-day Ojibwe warrior woman, Cloud struggled to protect tribes' rights and interests. She fought for tribal self-determination and sovereignty, linking issues of gender and tribal nations. She supported Native women's membership of tribal councils during a time when our councils were usually composed of men only, laying the groundwork for later discussions of Native feminisms. At the same time, she supported Indigenous cultural citizenship—the right to be different and belong to the nation-state and our tribal nations. In her role as a "good" Christian Native woman, Cloud challenged settler colonialism. She wore professional dresses and fashionable hats, while she spoke fiercely against racism and settler colonialism. Cloud employed an Ojibwe trickster methodology and could shape-shift, transforming herself into a "good" Indian among white reformers and a "bad" Indian in Native environments. She followed similar rhetorical strategies as other Society of American Indians (SAI) Native intellectuals of her generation, mixing white and Native-centric rhetoric in her struggle for Native rights.[1] Her involvement in the pantribal hub of NCAI placed her among other warrior women, encouraging her to fight for tribal nations. At a pivotal moment in history, Native women leaders of NCAI banded together to fight termination and build tribal nations. Elizabeth Bender Cloud was a complicated woman: an Ojibwe and a Christian, a citizen and a warrior, a supporter of tribal self-determination and absorption into the U.S. nation-state.

Indian Affairs Committee of GFWC

As part of their involvement with white women's organizations, Native American women regularly participated in Native policy reform. Elizabeth Bender Cloud and Zitkala-Sa (Gertrude Bonnin), a Yankton Dakota, were both actively involved in SAI and the Indian Welfare Committee (later the Indian Affairs Committee) of the GFWC. Native women's involvement in the GFWC provided them with philanthropic support and a platform for their Native rights struggles. In 1921 Zitkala-Sa founded the GFWC's National Indian Welfare Committee, an Indigenous hub, and from 1923 to 1924 she acted as a GFWC research agent in Oklahoma. In the early 1920s the GFWC sponsored research agents, who were also creating their own Native reform organizations. In fact, the former commissioner of Indian Affairs, John Collier, was a GFWC research agent in New Mexico and formed the American Indian Defense Association (AIDA) in 1923. The AIDA was a reform group of non-Natives with several SAI Native intellectuals on its advisory board, including Zitkala-Sa. She was involved in the investigation of Osage Natives in Oklahoma. The ensuing AIDA report was titled *Oklahoma's Poor Rich Indians: An Orgy of Graft and Exploitation of the Five Civilized Tribes; Legalized Robbery*

(1924). It revealed how Lecie Stechi had been murdered by poison and many other cruelties. This work inspired a full Senate investigation.[2] Thus, Native women working with and gaining support from GFWC, a mainstream women's organization, were instrumental in their struggle for Native concerns, interests, and rights.

White women's clubs provided Elizabeth Bender Cloud, like her predecessor Zitkala-Sa, the ability to gain national distinction and to discuss Native American affairs, helping her move from local to state leadership.[3] In 1948 she became Indian welfare chair for the Oregon GFWC, and in 1950 she became the chair for the Indian Affairs Division of the GFWC, established to assist Native women to assimilate into mainstream U.S. society. Mainstream women's clubs were similar to federal boarding schools. These clubs encouraged Native women to modernize and assimilate, making the modern, good Indigenous woman the ideal. These clubs were paternalistic, assuming Native women needed guidance from white women and others. They supported a gendered settler colonialism, encouraging Native women to follow white, middle-class notions of gender.

At the same time, Native American women involved in women's clubs often combined Native and modern identities and struggled for their rights as members of sovereign tribal nations and citizens of the United States. Elizabeth Bender Cloud, Roberta Campbell Lawson, Louie LeFlore, and Ida Collins Goodale all belonged to Native clubs, and their stories are relatively unknown.[4] Cloud was also a member of NCAI, a strong pantribal group that fought hard against termination.

NCAI and Termination

NCAI was founded in 1944 in an atmosphere of termination and assimilation policies, which worked to abrogate tribes' treaty rights. The NCAI began in Denver, Colorado, when around eighty delegates from fifty different tribes gathered together to fight the emerging and growing threat of termination. Thomas Cowger, a historian, argues that NCAI is one of the most important pantribal organizations of the modern era. It provided, Cowger says, an important space to encourage political activism and awareness regarding issues facing Native tribes and communities.[5]

Members of this Native hub advocated for a greater emphasis on Native education and accreditation of Native schools. They campaigned fervently against termination, supported tribes, and backed pro-Native legislation to protect voting rights and welfare, among other issues. In terms of citizenship, the group supported dual citizenship, membership in our tribal nations and the U.S. nation-state.[6]

Most scholars who have examined the termination era agree that it began during the Truman administration.[7] In 1947 the Senate Civil Service Committee assigned the acting commissioner of Indian Affairs, William Zimmerman, the task of categorizing and identifying tribes in regard to their "readiness" for termination. Unfortunately, Zimmerman created the lists without approval or awareness of the tribes themselves. Zimmerman later realized his error, even saying his plan was a policy of "extermination" and not "staged termination." But it was too late. The "Zimmerman Plan" laid down the foundation for the termination policies of the Truman and Eisenhower administrations.[8] While termination policy is usually linked to the 1940s and 1950s, the taking away of federal services was not a novel idea. Federal officials, conservative reformers, and policy makers had constantly pressured the U.S. government to assimilate Natives into the American mainstream. Adversaries of John Collier's philosophy of cultural pluralism emphasized problems of the Indian New Deal and advocated for termination.[9]

By 1949 the federal government was establishing the political groundwork for getting out of Native American affairs. That same year the Commission on Organization of the Executive Branch of the Government (the Hoover Commission) advised the gradual transfer to state governments of the administration of social programs for Natives. In addition, tribal property would be shifted to Native-owned corporations, and Native American lands would no longer have tax-exempt status. In the meantime, until additional Native taxes were collected, the federal government would transfer monies to state governments.[10] By the 1950s the federal government abandoned its previous focus on economic development on Native reservations and pushed the rapid assimilation of Native Americans into U.S. society. Federal-government officials fought politically to end tribes' federal-trustee status. From

1953 to 1964, 199 tribes were terminated, and federal responsibility and jurisdiction was turned over to state governments. A total of 1,365,801 acres of Native trust land was removed from protected status, and 13,263 Native Americans lost their tribal rights.[11] Soon, through her involvement with GFWC and NCAI, Elizabeth Cloud would be in the heat of the Native battle against termination.

Oregon and American Mother of the Year

Along with Cloud's involvement with NCAI and GFWC, the motherhood award was a powerful way for Cloud to acquire public attention, fame, and power. These Mother of the Year honors generated speaking and writing invitations, which provided her opportunities to discuss Native American affairs across the United States. Cloud's honors offered her a national platform and an Indigenous, gendered hub to support and publicize Native concerns.

Feminist writers argue that motherhood is a site of empowerment as well as a place of oppression. As a tactic of cultural genocide, the U.S. settler-colonial project continually denied Native women the right to motherhood. The federal government sanctioned widespread sterilization and reproductive abuse as well as the forced separation of children from their mothers. It is in this context that Native women continually fought for the right to be mothers.[12] Native women elders have argued that motherhood is not a site of oppression but instead supports female Native power. Historian Kim Anderson's research on Native women and motherhood suggests that, in many Native cultures, traditional female roles have been celebrated—not viewed as beneath male roles.[13] Cloud's socialization and training by her own Ojibwe mother, Mary Razier, must have taught her to revere motherhood and see it as a site of power, not oppression.

On April 4, 1950, Oregon governor Douglas McKay announced Cloud's selection as Mother of the Year for Oregon. Henry's illness had prevented Cloud from winning the state honor the year before, even though Native women of the Oregon Trail Women's Club had submitted her name for consideration. The Oswego Women's Club and their fellow workers at the Oregon City Presbyterian Church also backed her nomination. She was a member of the Grange, the National Conference of Social Workers, and NCAI. In 1940 President Franklin D. Roosevelt had even appointed her as a delegate to the White House Conference for Youth and Children. Governor McKay awarded Cloud a certificate for Oregon Mother of the Year at the General Federation's banquet on April 20, 1950.[14]

The Clouds' youngest child, Lillian Freed, nominated Elizabeth as American Mother of the Year—a process starting at local women's club and state levels. Lillian asked Henry's white adoptive cousin, Bess Page, to write a letter of support to strengthen the backing from the Umatilla women's Oregon Trail Women's Club and other white women's clubs. Lillian wrote that the chair of the state-selection committee was an official for the Oregon Federation of Women's Clubs. This representative would know of Cloud's involvement with the clubs, likely improving her odds in the selection process. Lillian also wrote how winning the award of American Mother of the Year would support her mother while she processed her profound grief over the loss of her husband: "We are still much saddened by the loss of our cherished and well-loved father. . . . It is human that there seem [sic] now to be a tremendous void in our lives, but his was such a fine life of integrity and service that we cannot but feel fortunate in our rare privilege of having had him. Mother has been magnificent—wonderfully brave, although her immediate loss is greatest of all. It is fitting that we seek such an honor for her as a tribute to her valiant spirit."[15]

Even after Henry's death, Bess Page continued to support our Cloud family. She contacted the Mother of the Year Selection Committee on April 12, 1950, in support of Cloud's nomination:

Although she is a member of a minority group and as such has been subjected to the humiliations and obstacles which beset such people, she has never allowed this to embitter her or warp her clear judgment. She brought to her chosen profession of teaching a fine mind which she was willing to discipline and a warm breath of sympathy which found an equal challenge in the quick response of the bright child and the bewildered groping of the least gifted. She carried both the clarity of mind and the warmth of heart combined with a very rare common sense into her marriage, and the remarkable achievement of her husband, gifted as he was would have been far more limited without her understanding and discriminating partnership. To have seen her with her children when they were tiny and growing up was an exciting experience. . . . Her work with her husband and for her race has brought her into the highest governmental circles where her contribution has been sound and wise. To have been able to create the balance between the need of her family and her community as she has done with outstanding success is to me her greatest claim to this honor.[16]

When she writes that Cloud did not become "embittered," Page positions Elizabeth as a "good" Indian who supported whites despite "humiliations and obstacles," not a "bad" Indian who fought back. In testament to Cloud's ability to bridge private and public spheres, Bess comments on Cloud's facility with multitasking. During this time women lived in the midst of much sexism and were viewed as "good women" only if they married a man, behaved dutifully and subserviently, and remained in the domestic sphere. In fact, their involvement in the public sphere was acceptable only if they properly attended to their domestic duties first. Finally, Page emphasizes how Cloud's work with her husband and her race brought her into the "highest governmental circles." In this way Elizabeth's partnership with Henry followed Native notions of gender roles, which called for complementary and equitable distribution of labor across the sexes.

Cloud was the sixteenth American Mother of the Year ever selected. She was picked out of fifty-two finalists, including Clara Ford. She was honored and revered across the nation. The Saint Augustine mission school in Winnebago, Nebraska named her honorary Indian princess. The Minnesota Chippewa Tribe honored her—which included all the Ojibwe reservations except for Red Lake—with a unanimous congratulatory resolution.[17] Elizabeth and our family rejoiced after receiving the news of her winning the Mother of the Year award.

The *Christian Science Monitor* acknowledged Cloud as the "first of her race to be selected." The selection committee chose her because of her own religious faith, honesty, and character, as well as the achievements of her children. Cloud's identities as a Native Christian and modern

Fig. 18. Elizabeth Bender Cloud in the foreground, examining newspaper clippings of herself winning the Mother of the Year award. Photograph courtesy of the Cloud family.

Native woman who encouraged her children to graduate from college were certainly contributing factors. Her oldest daughter, Marion Hughes, was the first Native to graduate from Wellesley College; her second oldest daughter, my mother, Woesha Cloud North, was the first Native to graduate from Vassar College; Ramona Butterfield, her third eldest daughter, also graduated from Vassar College; and Lillian, her youngest daughter, completed her freshman year at the University of Kansas.[18] During this time Native women attending and graduating from college was certainly rare. The Clouds encouraging their daughters to attend college points to their belief that girls and young women should attend college, not believing in the sexist notion of the early twentieth century that college is for men only (see chapter 2).

The first American Mother of the Year was chosen in 1935. It was created as a public acknowledgment of mothers who contributed to the national U.S. community. In 1950 the award's notion of community expanded, and the selection committee distributed awards to mothers from other countries for the first time. The *International Mothers' Digest* argues that "an invisible chain draws women around the world together; for regardless of nationality, race, or creed, the mothers of the earth have a common bond in their aspirations and dreams for their children's welfare."[19] When Cloud received the American Mother of the Year award, a newspaper reporter stressed her Ojibwe identity by describing her as wearing "a pair of orchids, a quiet smile, and a yard-long silver necklace hammered with symbols of her Chippewa (Ojibwe) Indian parentage." While accepting this honor, Cloud said, "My being made the American Mother of 1950 will do a tremendous amount of good for Indians in both North and South America. It means that there is to be something of a square deal for the Indian—finally." Cloud argued that her selection as American Mother of the Year could also help Natives gain equal rights. By claiming that Natives did not have a "square deal" yet, Cloud emphasizes her incredibly powerful and independent point of view. She directly challenges Henry's own argument in an earlier radio

Fig. 19. Anne Woesha Cloud standing next to her proud father, Henry, on her graduation day at Vassar College. Photograph courtesy of the Cloud family.

address that Natives already had a "square deal."[20] She goes on to cross nation-state boundaries, borders that often separate Natives today. By stressing her desire to support Indigenous peoples' struggles throughout the Western Hemisphere, in other words, she had developed a "Western Hemispheric consciousness." An Indigenous concept coined by Muscogee scholar Victoria Bomberry, a Western Hemispheric consciousness is the ability to see connections between Natives across national boundaries. Cloud's words, far ahead of her time, forged a transnational Native hub consciousness and encouraged relatedness between Native peoples throughout the Americas.[21]

When Cloud officially accepted her honor as American Mother of the Year, she discussed it with humility. She recognized all the mothers throughout the United States who were fulfilling their roles beautifully. She viewed motherhood not as a site of oppression, as some feminist writers have argued, but as a place of responsibility and privilege. She talked about the importance of both mothers and fathers providing compassionate love and encouraged Native children to be resilient—a perspective especially poignant in contrast to her own childhood in a federal boarding school. Federal-government policy stripped her of her right to live with her parents and of her parents' right to care for her. As discussed in chapter 2, Elizabeth's sister, Anna, was away in a federal Indian boarding for so long she no longer remembered our family when she returned home. The horrific agony our Native ancestors suffered while separated from our mothers and fathers is profound. Cloud's honor of American Mother of the Year could have represented a healing for her but also might have triggered difficult memories of her childhood filled with the painful separation from her parents. Cloud gestured to the racist environment by discussing her appreciation for her selection as not influenced by race or color.[22] Cloud stressed how strong her sense of spirituality was, arguing that spiritual faith needs to guide parents in raising their children.

In an interview about her accolade, Cloud told the St. Louis *Post Dispatch* that her Ojibwe childhood on the White Earth Reservation motivated her to put religion at the center of her life: "The Indian lives in the vast outdoors; he searches for the mystical, for an answer to the mountains and forests and plains. Long before the first missionaries, Indians spoke humbly of 'The Great Mystery.' . . . Religion has given the Indians an anchor, a moorage. Today it is more important to him than ever, for he needs some sanctuary from the bustle and clamor of civilization. This is provided by the church, especially by a church which shows interest also in the Indian's social and economic problem."[23] In this quote Cloud uses storytelling to make a connection to her Ojibwe land, her sense of spirituality, and the importance of the divine. Cloud makes sense of the tremendous wonder of nature, creates a virtual Ojibwe hub, and supports her Ojibwe identity. Her words don't encourage the domestication of the land—like settler-colonial narratives do—but they call for a relationship with the land that educates and answers spiritual questions.[24] At the same time, Cloud argues that a combination of Ojibwe spirituality with Christianity provides a sense of rootedness and connection in the midst of civilization. Thus, as she espouses anti–settler-colonial values, she embraces her Native Christianity identity, arguing that the Christian Church helps Natives better their social and economic situation.

Fighting Racism and Settler Colonialism

Through Ojibwe storytelling in newspapers, Cloud transformed her Mother of the Year title into a modern, gendered, and Ojibwe-centric hub and a platform to fight for Native civil rights. She fought against racism and for civil rights laws. She supported policies in the Western states that would forbid discrimination against Natives and other racial minorities in hotels, theaters, and restaurants. The reporter Richard Neuberger wrote, "The brown-skinned grandmother set her jaw stubbornly when she discussed Hollywood's version of the Indian. 'Our western movies show the Apache as a fierce and primitive savage,' she remarked bitingly. 'Yet he loved his home and family and he had strong spiritual feelings. He was trying to defend his native soil from traders who plied him with whiskey and from land grabbers who stole the only valleys fit for agriculture.'"[25] In this quote the reporter emphasizes her dark skin color and her tense jawbone, racializing her as an angry Native woman. Cloud fights to protect Native Americans from whites' racism and settler-colonial behavior. She argues for the passage of civil rights laws, and she sharply criticizes Hollywood's racist portrayals of Indians as "primitive." She even challenges settler colonialism when she underscores that Apaches fought to protect our lands, and whites used alcohol as a tactic in support of Native land dispossession. Thus, Cloud emphasizes Ojibwe-centric ideas in her role as American Mother of the Year. Once more we see the complexity of her layered identities: Native, Christian, and a modern warrior woman.

Cloud kept in close contact with her siblings and Ojibwe mother throughout her life. She maintained a virtual and geographic Ojibwe gendered hub with frequent letters, trips, and visits to the White Earth Reservation. My mother, Woesha, wrote, "Elizabeth [her mother] kept in touch with her natal family all her life. . . . Later, Mary Razier came to help my mother taking over the household and [took] care of my sister, Marion and me when we were two and four years old, and she was there other times for lengthy visits."[26] Cloud's close and continual connection with her mother, Mary Razier, meant she could speak her Ojibwe language, hear her tribe's stories, and receive her mother's encouragements to be a strong woman leader and warrior. Some Ojibwe women had been leaders of their tribes and met with government officials (see chapter 2). As late as the nineteenth century, U.S. government sources named three Ojibwe women as chiefs of their bands. Indeed, some Ojibwe women became honored warriors, including Hanging Cloud Woman of the Lac Courte Oreilles band of the Ojibwe, who, in the 1850s after Dakotas killed her father, grabbed her father's gun and pursued them. Afterward various Ojibwe lodges from the surrounding territory honored Hanging Cloud Woman.[27] Mary Razier, Cloud's Ojibwe mother, taught Cloud to be strong and independent and to speak her mind. Mary was a medicine woman who hunted and skinned her kill. She lived independently in a log cabin near the Canadian border until she died.[28] During an informal interview Cloud told my mother, Woesha Cloud North, that she could do any job as good as any man. Cloud was a modern-day warrior woman whose weapons were words, not a gun, like Hanging Cloud Woman.

On May 12, 1950, Cloud was presented a specially designed gold-leaf motherhood medal and a scroll citation at an awards breakfast ceremony held at the Waldorf-Astoria in New York City.[29] Two days later, on May

14, Cloud was honored as American Mother of the Year at the Salvation Army's Mother's Day celebration at Central Park Mall in New York City. Afterward she journeyed to attend a NCAI meeting in Washington DC. There Cloud met with Dillon S. Myer, the new commissioner of Indian Affairs, who developed the federal termination and relocation policy, an attempt to terminate treaty rights and force assimilation. The federal relocation program was integral to the government's goal of the termination of treaty rights. It moved Natives from reservations to cities for vocational training and employment, and it was part of the federal government's goal to assimilate Natives and move us from our tribal land bases.[30] They were both Native policies supporting settler colonialism, attempting to dispossess Indigenous peoples of our lands and eliminate us culturally as Native yet again.

In response Cloud once more used a newspaper to create a virtual Native hub, discussing both white and Native ideas. According to the Washington Merry-Go-Round newspaper column, Cloud told Myer—who was also the mastermind behind the Japanese internment camps during World War II—"Indians don't want to be treated like museum pieces, but as Americans. They need, above all, good schools and a chance to earn a decent living. All we want is half a chance." She continued, "Indian children should go to public, rather than segregated schools. We are Americans first and Indians second." She said, "Let the tribal councils take a greater part in running Indian affairs. It is far, far better for them to make a few mistakes at first than for Washington to say, 'You are no good. White men must run your lives.'"[31]

In these quotes Cloud defends Natives, while challenging settler colonialism, sharply criticizing Myer for treating Natives as static relics of the past. Static notions of culture based in classic anthropology support the notion of the vanishing Native, which is another way to make Natives disappear—an act of elimination and, therefore, settler colonialism. She also emphasizes that Natives deserve to be treated as equal American citizens both economically and educationally. She privileges Natives' identity as American citizens over our identity as members of tribal nations, alluding to her strong support for Natives becoming apart of the U.S. nation state, a move that arguably weakens tribal sovereignty and supports settler colonialism. At the same time, she challenges the federal government's paternalism of Natives and instead supports our right for self-determination and tribal sovereignty, relying on tribal councils to run our own affairs. In this way Cloud fought for Natives' right to Indigenous cultural citizenship, becoming full members of the U.S. nation-state and active governing members of their tribal nations, ultimately a kind of dual citizenship.

At the same time, Cloud supported a modern motherhood that "traditional" Native women needed to aspire to, a problematic and painful settler-colonial assumption. In June 1950 Cloud visited Wichita, her old home, where she helped run the American Indian Institute. She told a reporter for the *Wichita Eagle* that "modern mothers . . . have more leisure to devote to welfare of their children. They no longer have to be household drudges. They can organize a better home life, and have time to help build a better community. . . . The home has to be organized much in the same manner as a good business. . . . It has to be run wisely and have good management. That's what I did as a young mother, and my children show the results possible with such a program." She also discussed the work of the NCAI, which she said was fast improving the status of Indians. "Through the work of such agencies," she said, "Indians are starting to run their own affairs. Soon, rigid supervision by government agents will be a thing of the past."[32] In this quote Cloud supports NCAI's efforts to help fight for tribal self-determination and sovereignty, promoting NCAI, an Indigenous hub. Indeed, Cloud often performed the role of a spokesperson for NCAI. She also emphasizes the importance of efficiency so women can contribute to the world outside the home, bridging the private and public spheres. Her discussion of efficiency is a white idea that fits within progressive, white, modern ideals of motherhood. During the late 1800s and early 1900s, "scientific mothering" became popular. Women were expected to rely on parenting experts to mother children appropriately. Children were assumed to need rigid control and scheduling to help them master their natural "drives" and impulses.[33]

Thus, Cloud encouraged Native women to develop a modern mother identity, tribal nationhood, and sovereignty. This points to her complicated

Ojibwe *and* modern identity, supporting both settler-colonial notions of motherhood and tribal nations' fight for self-determination. It is unlikely white reformers would have given Cloud a platform to speak as American Mother of the Year or Indian Affairs chair of the GFWC unless she was a "modern," Native Christian woman. She certainly did not occupy a pure category of Ojibwe warrior woman—like Hanging Cloud Woman might have—but her identity was much more complex. Elizabeth Cloud occupied many categories all at once. Her complicated identity, similar to other SAI intellectuals, means her warrior stance seems to have been missed, especially by historian Hazel Hertzberg in her famous book, *The Search for an American Indian Identity*, and by Lisa Tetzloff in her article, "Elizabeth Bender Cloud: Working for and with Our Indian People."

Cloud talked to a reporter for the *Oregonian* on October 1, 1950, about her hope for the improvement of Natives' lives: "Though the General Federation has done much in bringing about beneficial legislation, given scholarships, [and] has been mindful of starving groups in a land of plenty, we must be more determined and more enlightened in our efforts to inform ourselves and act upon the problems involved. . . . Like tribes and nations across the sea, like all peoples everywhere, Indian tribes in our midst are struggling to survive, and it is our goal to make possible adjustment which will assure this survival."[34] Here Cloud compares Natives in the United States to tribes and nations in other countries, alluding to Natives' status as sovereign nations, like other nations. She also gives the GFWC credit for its support of disadvantaged groups, while suggesting the importance of Natives' independence, as opposed to the paternalism of the GFWC. She encourages Natives to assert our own tribal autonomy and sovereignty. Her involvement in NCAI, an important pantribal Native hub, could have influenced her Native intellectual ideas, strengthening her resolve to support tribes' struggles.

The month before, in September 1950, Cloud was one of forty representatives of the General Federation of Women's Clubs who traveled to Europe to learn about Marshall Plan aid and European perspectives. Cloud's trip to Europe could have influenced her conversation in October of same year with the reporter for the *Oregonian* about people in other parts of the world. Indeed, Cloud met with Queen Juliana of

Holland, who had also been given the Mother of the Year award. Cloud discussed feeling depressed about the plight of displaced people in refugee camps in Europe. She was especially saddened to learn about the struggles of elderly refugees.[35] Cloud's traveling to Europe must have expanded her intellectual insights to include peoples' experiences across national borders. Other Natives had traveled to Europe, including the famous Pocahontas, who died in England and never made it back home.[36]

Cloud's discussion of Natives' citizenship and belonging ranged from spirituality and family values to the U.S. Constitution. She argued against racism and for Native cultural citizenship—our right to both be different and belong to the U.S. nation-state and our tribal nations. In an article Cloud wrote for the Associate Press, she related family values to the character of society: "We shall have little fear if we provide the spiritual guidance for our children which alone gives unwavering strength, the steadiness of vision, the clarity of perspective so needed by a world in its values."[37] In an address to the sixtieth convention of the GFWC in May 1951 in Houston, Texas, she evoked the language of the U.S. Constitution to promote the values parents should teach to their children: "Spiritually motivated . . . [It] is the foundation stone of our democratic way of life—the enunciation of our fundamental belief in the infinite worth and dignity of each individual, in the basic truth that all men are created equal with certain inalienable rights. . . . How splendid would be the growing up years of our children and young people if from their earliest years they knew and felt the enrichment of life that comes from our differences from one another, rather than seeing our differences as bitter divisive forces in daily living."[38]

Cloud traveled to New York City for the GFWC's national board meeting and to Chicago to accept the Indian Council Fire's 1950 Achievement Award—an award that Henry received in 1935. In 1923 Indians and non-Indians founded the Indian Council Fire. It provided education, legislative, and social services to reservation and urban Indians. The Indian Council Fire Achievement Award emphasized that Native self-development is rooted in traditional values and not merely a result of federal programming.[39] According to the Indian Council Fire, Cloud "has rendered distinctive service in educational work for Indian young people; in advancing the cause of Indian welfare; and in religious work. She is outstanding as a lecturer on the interests of Indian people, and in great demand as a speaker before prominent women's and missionary organizations."[40]

American Indian Development Project

In 1951 Cloud exchanged her honorary role of American Mother of the Year for the paid position of assistant director of the American Indian Development (AID) project. NCAI and the Field Foundation backed this Native self-assistance effort. Cloud's friend Ruth Muskrat Bronson was executive director of NCAI, and Cloud was field secretary. These two Indigenous women in NCAI leadership positions worked together to support and build tribal nations. The purpose of AID was Native community development and revitalization. D'Arcy McNickle, a Cree, who was enrolled on the Flathead Reservation and a founder of NCAI, was one of the initiators of this project, and it was funded by the tax-exempt Arrow company. McNickle hoped that summer workshops would encourage tribal leaders to transform Native communities and make them more economically self-sufficient. As participants discussed and communicated similar ideas and experiences, the workshops helped to bring the community together. Cloud was a fundamental part of this project—which encouraged Native independence and discouraged BIA paternalism—and certainly shows her support of self-determination and sovereignty.[41]

Cloud supported the development of tribal self-determination and sovereignty and encouraged Natives to solve our own problems. In July 1951 she participated in NCAI's summer workshop held at the Intermountain Indian School in Brigham City, Utah. The purpose of the workshop was to reach out to Natives from reservations and rural areas and identify their needs. Around fifty to seventy-five Natives attended, including a student group, representing leaders from the Navajo, Blackfoot, Pueblo, Apache, Nez Perce, Sioux, and other tribes. Cloud discussed the workshop's emphasis of self-help and democratic participation to the student group.[42] Along with the growth of AID were summer workshops for Native youth in 1955, organized by the Anthropology Department at the University of Chicago.

In 1959 AID began facilitating these summer workshops for Native youth, giving them a Native pantribal hub to discuss Native American affairs, ultimately inspiring the creation of the Native youth movements of the 1960s. Eventually these summer workshops influenced Clyde Warrior, a Ponca leader of the National Indian Youth Council, and he decided to become an activist. He ultimately coined the term "Red Power." Thus, by organizing these summer workshops for NCAI, Cloud supported community organizing that laid the groundwork for mobilizations in the 1960s, in which Natives fought for tribal self-determination and sovereignty.[43] With the support of NCAI leadership, including Ruth Bronson, Cloud was instrumental in strengthening and building tribal nations.

In late October 1951, as part of their NCAI duties, Cloud and Bronson joined a delegation of three leaders of the Pyramid Lake Paiutes of Nevada to Washington DC. Their trip as representatives of NCAI showed this Native organization's support of tribal nations' struggles and concerns, including fighting to retrieve stolen land, challenging settler colonialism, and strengthening the creation of a pantribal hub. While talking to Bronson and Paiute leaders, Cloud could let down her protective mask and speak openly about tribal rights and concerns. For ninety years the Paiutes had been fighting for the return of three hundred acres that white squatters had stolen and occupied. The Paiutes sent a delegation of six to seek the BIA commissioner Myer's approval for the tribe's contract with Washington attorney James E. Curry. Myer, however, said the tribe could send only two delegates because the Indians had only $6,700 in their budget, according to an article in the *New York Times*.[44] This article describes Myer as a Hitler-like dictator and the tool of a senator who did not actively support Natives, showing how incredibly difficult and challenging Myer was for Cloud and other Native leaders to deal with.

While advocating for tribes' interests, Cloud discussed her "Point Four Program." This program was in her report for the chair of the Indian Affairs Division of the GFWC, assuming the inevitability of termination. It discussed Natives' absorption into the U.S. nation-state—a change that would lead to second-class Native citizenship and loss of tribal rights. Cloud was aware of the federal government's plan for termination and her program prepared Natives for the government's withdrawal. The most painful aspect of the program for me was training Native leadership for the end of self-government—including adult education regarding social, political, economic, and citizenship responsibilities—to anticipate the gradual withdrawal of supervision of Indian affairs. Reading this part of the report was especially difficult for me, because her husband, Henry, had worked so hard supporting self-government and ending assimilation. According to Elizabeth, Natives should attend public schools, thereby reducing the "segregation" of Natives while promoting integration. At the same time, she encouraged Natives' practice of our arts and crafts, which contribute to the richness of U.S. culture, suggesting the importance of maintaining tribal identities. Cloud's ideas were consistent with the mainstream women's clubs' goal of assimilating Native Americans.[45]

Reading about Cloud's "Point Four Program" was incredibly distressing and challenging for me. It stimulated memories of the terrible assimilation campaign of the federal boarding schools that indoctrinated Native children to abandon our tribal nations, land, and sovereign rights. Cloud's report was a plan for Natives' dispossession of our tribal rights. Reading this report recalled in my mind the "thicket of white ideas" my mother, Woesha Cloud North, discussed in her memoir notes (see introduction). In this instance Elizabeth's warrior identity seemed mostly masked or camouflaged by settler-colonial rhetoric. Cloud, however, did not support Natives' assimilation or erasure of our tribal identities like Richard Pratt, the founder of the federal boarding schools. Therefore, historians Tetzloff and Hertzberg calling her an "assimilationist" is incorrect and does not honor her struggle to support tribes' interests. This "Four Point Program," however, does show a contradiction between her work anticipating tribal termination and developing and supporting Native autonomy, self-determination, and sovereignty.

At the same time, in her report as chair of the Indian Affairs Division of the GFWC, Cloud included AID's "Charter of Indian Rights" that was adopted at NCAI's October 1952 Phoenix Workshop. The charter revolves around Natives' citizenship and belonging to "exert active citizenship within his Tribe, State, and Nation." The charter includes, for example,

1) ... training for business management of tribal enterprises and for the practice of the professions in Indian communities;

2) ... development of natural resources to the end that our Indian people will benefit fully from the lands and waters left in their care by their forefathers;

3) ... opportunity to participate in tribal and inter-tribal meetings, which train leadership;

4) ... a health plan which will provide adequate and safe water, sanitation, control of conditions leading to disease, health education, suitable housing, adequate diet, medical care and hospitalization;

5) ... removal of discrimination in the application of social legislation, such as social security benefits intended for all of the people; and

6) ... the dissemination of news through newspapers, radio, and television, to the end that Indian leadership be informed and win recognition in state and national affairs.[46]

Indeed, Cloud's incorporation of the Charter of Indian Rights suggests her support of Natives' fight for dual citizenship and Native cultural citizenship, tribal belonging, and U.S. citizenship.

Cloud's ambivalent rhetoric points to her doubleness, being both a "good" and a "bad" Native woman simultaneously. Cloud employed dominant rhetoric with white women reformers, reinforcing assimilation. At the same time, she worked for the NCAI in strong and passionate support of tribes' self-determination and sovereignty. Both Elizabeth and Henry may have learned doubleness speech from listening to Ho-Chunk and Ojibwe trickster stories while living in the midst of settler colonialism. I argue it was a tribal trickster methodology that taught shape-shifting and the ability to move in multiple contexts, including both Native and settler-colonial environments. Cloud could be seen as a "good" Indian among white women reformers and then shape-shift into a "bad" Indian among Natives. This way she could fight to support Native rights, including tribal sovereignty and self-determination. In newspaper articles she is both a "good" and a "bad" Indian, employing Native-centric rhetoric about tribal independence and dominant discourses that frame Natives' identity as secondary to our identity as U.S. citizens. Cloud was complicated and subversive. She cannot be pigeonholed into static categories. She was Ojibwe, Christian, warrior, citizen, "good," and "bad." And this flexibility was necessary to gain the support of white women reformers—support that could eventually be used for Native goals and objectives. Indeed, SAI intellectuals of Elizabeth's generation had to work with white reformers to gain power in the public sphere and fight for Native rights; consequently, playing the role of a "good" Indian was necessary.

Cloud described the NCAI's American Indian Development project in a guest editorial for the newsletter, the *Amerindian*.[47] Although still in the developmental stage, she said, the project responded to the expressed wishes of Natives of many tribes for improved conditions under which to raise their children, which included cheaper and better housing; improved health facilities and care; superior home industries, education, and scholarship aid for Indian youth; and robust recreational and community programs. She argued that the project strived to secure, for every Indian community, the opportunity for every person to be educated and healthy, to have an adequate standard of living, and to receive moral and spiritual training. Again, Cloud, as the director of AID, supported Natives' efforts to claim their right for full citizenship in Native communities *and* the nation-state, which was a move toward Native cultural citizenship.

In 1953 participants of the American Indian Development project summarized their experience with it in one statement: "The community grows when the people get together. . . . We have lost much, but we can gain this back with renewed vigor in the right direction, each doing his best in solving the problem at hand. Each mother making a good home for her children. Each father living a good, exemplary life for his sons. It is in group cooperation and activity that the needs within a neighborhood can be met. It is in the stimulation of group cooperation and activity that Indian leadership will make its real contribution."[48] In this quote AID participants discuss the energizing experience of gathering together to solve their own problems, meet their own needs, and claim leadership of their own destiny—all actions necessary for working toward Native autonomy and tribal sovereignty. Participants also emphasize Native women as "making a good home for her children," honoring their role as mothers.

On June 22, 1953, while vising the Navajo Reservation in Window Rock, Arizona, Cloud discussed her involvement in NCAI's American Indian Development project in a letter to her daughter Marion and her family:

I have just been swamped with engagements, interviews, planning the Ft. Defiance workshop, and short trips to Indian communities— Sawmill, Hunters Point, St. Michaels, Mexican Springs, Ganado, and Crystal and all within a radius of sixty miles. We had the most successful workshop that we have ever had and we held it at Fort Defiance from June 15th to June 20th. Our morning sessions averaged around 40, afternoon 35 and evening meetings twenty to thirty. The day sessions we had to use an interpreter and he was excellent, a college man and formerly a teacher. The more time I spend among the Navajos, the more knowledge I gain as to their way of life, philosophy, ethics and humor. They are a kind, friendly people and will share with one their last morsel of food, as Daddy would say, "Not steengy." . . .

We shall be here until the sixth or seventh of July. Then I shall go to Mescalero for two or three days, where we shall plan our Aid project. Two very intelligent Apache women drove all the way from Mescalero (southern part of N.M.) to give us the invitation. The older woman knew Daddy. . . .

We shall be in Oklahoma again about the 17th of July for two weeks, then back here again in August.

We are stressing *housing* here and you would be surprised how the Navajos are really wanting better homes. One dear Navajo woman said to me, "I am not young. I am old, about 66. I see only in one eye. I would like to get a pension. I live with the same man all my life. He is not young. He is old. I think 78. He is too old to work. My well is dried up and full of dirt, so I haul water two miles. I need a new well and a new house, just a small one. I am tired of the old, old Hogan. My name is Yonci Nez."

She was such a sweet old lady. When she got up to leave she said, "Thank you sister, because you listen to my story."[49]

Cloud's letter describes how busy she was working on this project for NCAI. She supported Natives' goals for better housing, education, health, and leadership trainings, and she organized well-attended workshops focused on these issues. She listened to Natives' goals and objectives rather than pressing an outside agenda. In other words, she supported tribal sovereignty. Cloud stresses her respect for Navajo culture and describes participants feeling heard by her and appreciating her community-development work. Participants even invited her to provide these services elsewhere, showing her ability to be respectful and to connect with Navajo women and with Natives' goals and objectives.

Cloud's work to help provide Natives with scholarship aid fit with NCAI's goals and objectives. It helped Indigenous people become educated. As part of her involvement in AID, Cloud visited Sophie Van S. Thies in New York to discuss the need for scholarship money for Phil Dixon, a Navajo, to attend school to become a qualified hospital technician and for Stella Tsotsie, who needed scholarship aid to get a master's degree in education.[50] According to a letter Cloud sent to Helen Peterson on May 26, 1954, this visit was successful in receiving scholarship aid from Sophie Van S. Thies.[51]

For NCAI Cloud traveled around Indian Country and conducted field visits of Native communities in California and Arizona, evaluating schools and socioeconomic and health conditions on reservations. She visited Sherman Institute, a federal Native boarding school in Riverside, California, and Cook Indian Training School in Phoenix, Arizona. She spent three days on the San Carlos Reservation, and one day she attended the tribal council meeting. In her NCAI report, she wrote, "Their council was made up only of men, that these days we say that this is also a woman's world. Later on as I talked to some of the council men, they told me that they would welcome the participation of their women as members of the council but the women were timid and too bashful."[52]

In this NCAI report Cloud claims a gendered, Ojibwe virtual hub. She writes about her experience challenging sexism within tribal councils composed of only men and alludes to the right for women to become tribal council members. In this way Cloud links gender, tribal nation, and sovereignty together. She emphasizes that it is a "woman's world," pointing to women's right to be in leadership positions and on tribal councils. This linkage of gender, tribal nation, and sovereignty foreshadows Native feminist discussions today, which emphasize Native women's right to become full members of our tribal nations.[53] Finding Cloud's NCAI field report made me realize that I learned my passion for Native feminism from my Ojibwe female ancestors, who passed down the importance of the struggle for Native women's rights. As discussed in the last chapter, my mother occupied Alcatraz Island and taught for Red Rock School in 1969. My mother also was a founding member of the Native Women's Action Council, formed around the same time. Contemporary Native women's struggles and my Ojibwe lineage have influenced my Native feminist ideas.

When Dwight D. Eisenhower started his presidency of the United States in 1952, he picked Governor McKay of Oregon to become his secretary of the interior. On November 21, 1952, Cloud wrote McKay to wish him well and to advocate for Natives to occupy leadership positions in the Bureau of Indian Affairs. This letter shows her role as a vital and significant Native leader involved in national politics and concerns. She discussed necessary qualifications for commissioner, and she spoke on behalf of herself: "For myself and for those whom I know to be the most sincere, able and reliable of the Indian leaders . . . we feel the time has come when we should look to qualified Indian leaders to assist in leading Indian people out of the dilemma of the present Indian Bureau administration with its high-handed, dictatorial, misunderstood, mass 'withdrawal' program," under commissioner of Indian affairs Dillon S. Myer.[54] Here Cloud sharply critiques federal termination. She uses strong language, including "high-handed, dictatorial, [and] misunderstood," suggesting that the leadership of the BIA is paternalistic and unsympathetic to Native concerns and issues.

Cloud also wrote in her letter to McKay that, even though she was not of the same party (a Democrat) like John Collier, the former commissioner of Indian Affairs was usually seen as compassionate of Natives. She incorporated Collier's statement of policy, which Native leaders chiefly supported. Cloud wrote, "I am fervently hopeful that you will guide this nation into more responsible discharge of its trusteeship obligations towards Indians rather than give support to the idea of mass, premature withdrawal of essential federal services."[55] In this quote she argues that Natives had to be consulted in the transfer of federal services, that Natives would cooperate when the transfer occurred without damage and with efficiency, and that the federal government must consider each reservation as a separate case. Cloud emphasizes the importance of tribal consent, and she argues against the federal government forcibly terminating tribes. In other words, she fights back against the government's paternalism by arguing that Natives should be consulted. NCAI had been grappling with the federal government's enforcement of termination, and Cloud's discussion supported NCAI's political goal: consent of the governed, not government by force.[56] She also wrote that the qualifications of the new commissioner should include the ability to collaborate with Congress, good administration skills, real knowledge of Indians, humanitarian instincts, specialized knowledge in one or more technical fields, and the desire to plan and execute programs in cooperation with tribal leadership.

Cloud proposed two possible Native candidates for the position of commissioner of Indian Affairs: William Keeler, principal chief of the Cherokees and an executive of Phillips Petroleum; and Benjamin Reifel, a Sioux, who had a Harvard doctorate in public administration and was superintendent of the Fort Berthold Reservation in North Dakota. She recommended candidates for assistant commissioner, including Reginald Curry, a Brigham Young University graduate and tribal chair of the Uintah and Ouray Utes; and Francis McKinley, a George Washington University graduate and business manager for the Uintah and Ouray Utes. Thus, Cloud emphasized the importance of Natives rising to the position of commissioner of Indian Affairs.

In this same letter Cloud revealed that Native politics impacted the timing of her correspondence. NCAI had assembled in Denver the week prior, developing a "conditional endorsement of Alvin Simpson of New Mexico, for the post of Commissioner of Indian Affairs. . . . The involved resolution, which contained at the very end the conditional endorsement referred to, was brought before the convention after a very lengthy, delayed and bitter session of the National Congress, at about three o'clock in the morning, after at least half of the delegates had left. . . . It was introduced and pushed through with the use of objectionable, confusing methods."[57] Sixty-five thousand Navajos and many other tribal groups, she wrote, had strongly challenged the NCAI's backing of Simpson.

Commissioner of Indian Affairs

Cloud's national prominence extended beyond her national Native leadership positions. Her name was put forward as a candidate for commissioner of Indian Affairs. Woody Crumbo, a Potawatomi, an alumnus of the American Indian Institute, and a famous artist, suggested Cloud as the next commissioner of Indian Affairs. Crumbo wrote McKay in January 1953 that Elizabeth Bender Cloud was the most capable and logical candidate for the job. He said he encouraged Cloud to pursue the position, and she answered, "If I were offered the position I would not turn it down, because I do feel that I have an understanding of the Indian problem and could do much to alleviate the bottle necks which have stymied the growth and development of Indian progress." Crumbo wrote that Cloud was one of the greatest living Americans:

> [Cloud is] greater by far than the celebrated Sacajawea (spoken with all due respect) who merely guided Lewis and Clark on a river expedition. . . . She has never intimated to me as a student or as an adult that we should expect the government to look after our affairs, but that we should prepare ourselves to handle our own interests and take our place in society just as any other people are obligated to do. Mrs. Cloud probably knows more about the needs and working possibilities of the American Indian, as well as how to deal with their problems, than any living person.[58]

Crumbo's high praise shows how much Cloud was respected as an Ojibwe activist, intellectual, and administrator in her own right—not just as the widow of her late husband, Henry. Crumbo alludes to Cloud's support of Native citizenship and inclusion in the U.S. nation-state, emphasizing that she urged him and the other students at the American Indian Institute to "handle our own interests and take our place in society," like everyone else. Crumbo's statement that Cloud was greater than Sacagawea—who led the Lewis and Clark expedition—recalls her position as a helper of whites and as a "good" Indian.

After her two favorite candidates, Keeler and Reifel, both Natives, removed themselves from consideration, Cloud supported Glenn Emmons, a New Mexico banker, for the position of commissioner of Indian Affairs. During a workshop in Fort Defiance, New Mexico, in June 1953, Cloud shared with a reporter that "since my favorite sons are out of the picture it doesn't matter to me whether the new appointee is Indian or non-Indian, provided he has a comprehension of the Indian needs and sees to it that the withdrawal program does not injure the Indians of the southwest." In a telegram Cloud endorsed Emmons succinctly, arguing that appointment of a new commissioner was essential. "Morale of Indians and Indian Service is at low ebb. Many valuable employees resigning. Indians disturbed over propaganda hasty withdrawal services."[59] She discussed that Emmons was a great businessman and knows about tribes of the Southwest, and she was impressed with his honest approach to the Indian situation.

Emmons took office on August 10, 1953. He was commissioner of Indian Affairs for eight years under the Eisenhower administration. Unfortunately, Emmons, similar to Myer, supported the federal government's attempts to abrogate the federal government's treaty relationship with Native Americans and dispossess us of our lands and tribal rights—whether we chose to be terminated or not. Emmons followed in the footsteps of Myer and continued to implement the government's plan of termination.

At the same time, in 1953 another warrior woman, Helen Peterson, a Northern Cheyenne but enrolled Oglala Sioux, took the important job of the new executive director of NCAI. Cloud traveled to Washington DC to help Peterson in the transition. She and Peterson visited reservations throughout Indian Country in Cloud's late-model Chevy to listen to Native needs and create tribal contacts. Peterson got much support from Ruth Bronson, whom she called almost daily. Bronson shared her experience, talents, and time with the new executive director of NCAI. Peterson was the right leader of NCAI. Her grandmother had always taught her to be a role model for the Native community and to respect and deeply value land. She had been active in NCAI since 1948.[60]

Cloud's trip with Helen Peterson was a mobile, gendered, and Native hub experience. Strong warrior women had trained these two Native women leaders. Mary Razier had educated Cloud to be an independent and powerful Ojibwe warrior woman who spoke her mind and fought back. And Peterson's grandmother taught her to respect and value Native land. Driving together provided alone time to discuss tribal concerns, needs, and issues.

While Elizabeth was busily involved in NCAI and GFWC, she learned of wonderful news about her brother Charles. During September 1953 Charles Albert Bender was inducted into the Baseball Hall of Fame in Coopertown, New York. Bender had a lifelong career in baseball. He regularly experienced racism, and he was usually called "Chief." Fans repeatedly greeted him with war whoops, and he would challenge them, calling them "foreigners." He pitched for Connie Mack and the Philadelphia Athletics from 1903 to 1943. Mack referred to Bender as the best money pitcher the game has ever known.[61] Charles's induction into the Baseball Hall of Fame was a happy occasion for Elizabeth and our Cloud family.

Federal termination was made into a reality when House Concurrent Resolution 108 (HCR 108) was approved on August 1, 1953. It proclaimed that Natives "should be subject to the same laws and entitled to the same privileges, rights, and responsibilities" as all American citizens.[62] It recommended the immediate removal of federal guardianship and supervision over certain tribes. Congress proposed the immediate termination of the Flatheads of Montana, Klamaths in Oregon, Menominees of Wisconsin, Potawatomis of Kansas and Nebraska, and the Chippewas of North Dakota. The resolution called for the secretary of interior to recommend legislation to end federal responsibility by January 1, 1954.

Congress began a series of deliberations about the termination bills for various tribes on February 15, 1954. Both the Senate and House Subcommittees on Indian Affairs began joint hearings. Representatives were pressured by the unreasonable deadline of January 1, 1954, and draft termination bills were discussed before Congress, state officials, or Indian tribes had the opportunity to evaluate their consequences.[63]

Emergency Conference

While Cloud was working hard to support Native leadership training and back tribal self-determination and sovereignty, Congress pushed for the termination of tribes. Consequently, NCAI called an Emergency Conference of American Indians on Legislation in Washington DC from February 25 to 28, 1954. Tribal members gathered together to fight back against termination. This emergency session was a strong and intense expression of pantribal agreement and a powerful intertribal hub. Tribal members from the across the country gathered to challenge the federal government's attempt to eliminate them as tribal peoples with treaty rights to land, education, and other rights, a governmental act of settler colonialism. According to Cowger, the NCAI's Emergency Conference encouraged an incredibly potent Native protest that was comparable in strength and size only by the Red Power protest ten years later. Refusing the enforced nature of termination policy and asserting Natives' right to control our own destinies, NCAI had been fighting in the postwar years to beat or change the coercive termination policy. As the chair of Indian Affairs of the GFWC, Cloud wrote a "Policy Statement on American Indian Legislation," in support of the tribes' fight against termination. She presented it at NCAI's Emergency Session:

The present bills now before Congress to terminate federal super-vision of American Indian property and the trustee responsibilities assumed by the nation for our American Indian citizens are being pushed through Congress in the face of Indian opposition, and with-out Indian consent, and without Indian participation at the tribal community level. Our democratic system of government is founded on the basic principle, government by the consent of the governed. The General Federation of Women's Clubs must insist that Indians should be given the respect due all citizens under such a system of government—that of self-determination and consent. Because these bills violate this principle basic to our democratic way of life they must be opposed vigorously. Indians believe that the above legislation is aimed at destroying tribal existence and that while the above bills now before Congress may affect only certain named tribes that such bills are introduced singly as trial balloons to test public reaction and because it is easier to destroy one tribe at a time before attacking the whole Indian concept of cultural identity and freedom of Indian choice in the ownership of their property under the trustee status of the federal government. The Indian tribes are unanimous in their desire to keep their trustee status, and the General Federation of Women's Clubs supports them in this. The motives behind these bills as the Indians see it, is to destroy not only their cultural existence as a distinct group within our nation, but also their basic economy, which is land and the natural resources accruing from the land. The American Indian has had too harsh treatment in the past at the hands of the exploiters within our nation. The General Federation of Women's Cubs cannot accept legislation affecting them which will break the Nation's treaty commitments to this group of loyal and useful citizens, nor do we wish to see our nation embark upon a second "Century of Dishonor" in or relations with these people whose country we conquered.[64]

In this quote Cloud fights against the settler-colonial goal of tribal termination and for tribal sovereignty and self-determination. Ultimately, Cloud supports Natives' treaty rights. She links her argument for tribal sovereignty to the American democratic goal of consent of the governed. She exposes the federal government's insidious use of tribal termination as a barometer of public reaction and as the first step toward the erasure of the tribes' existence overall. She emphasizes an Indigenous analytical perspective when she frames tribal termination as trying to erase not only tribes' cultural existence as distinct groups but also our separate economies tied to our tribal land bases. Cloud underscores the history of Natives' oppression by the colonizer, using the word "exploiters." She even alludes to Helen Hunt Jackson's book, *A Century of Dishonor*, when she argues that the federal government should not make the same colonial mistake twice. Finally, she asserts the power of the General Federation of Women's Clubs as political leverage to support tribes' continued cultural and tribal existence and sovereignty. In this way she strategically uses her leadership role in white women's clubs for Native goals and objectives.

In the letter of March 30, 1954, to Helen Peterson, executive director of NCAI, Cloud discusses the Emergency Conference: "I am wondering if the 'big blow' is over and as you view the 'Emergency Conference,' . . . you discover some very real accomplishments. You and your staff worked practically twenty-four hours during the conference and we who attended marveled as to your organizational ability and the excellent meetings. Some of the California delegates were on the same plane as far as Kansas City, and we discussed the conference quite at length. They . . . were in high praise over NCAI's aid and help."[65] This letter is evidence of Cloud's encouraging spirit, as she recognizes the fierce efforts of Helen Peterson as the executive director and her staff and evidence of the strength of NCAI as a pantribal hub. These two warrior women seemed to have a supportive, strong relationship as part of a Native and gendered hub.

Cloud resigned as assistant director of the NCAI's American Indian Development project on February 1, 1954: "I have given thoughtful planning, time and service in connection with the work of American Indian Development. And since I have spent forty years as educator and welfare worker and religious work director among the Indian people at the American Indian Institute and at Haskell Institute as well as field worker on several reservations, I feel that I have earned a goodly rest and can carry on some of the hobbies I have had in mind for a long time."[66] Cloud fought back against the federal government's efforts to abrogate Native treaty rights and terminate federal responsibility to tribes. She would go on to observe the culmination of the termination era in the 1960s and the exciting mobilization of Native activism. Philleo Nash followed Emmons as commissioner of Indian Affairs, and Robert La Follette Bennett replaced Nash in 1966, becoming the first American Indian commissioner since Ely Parker in 1869.

That same year Cloud traveled to Wichita, Kansas, for the naming ceremony of the newest school in the Wichita School District: Henry Roe Cloud School. Zelma Zimmerman, principal of the school, invited her. "I had so hoped to have a real dedicatory service at the school, Oct. 10, but due to shortness of time (We have been open only three weeks), and the lack of an auditorium, this was not advisable. The newly organized P.T.A has therefore planned an Open House to which we will be most honored to have you present."[67]

Cloud's final years revolved around family. She lived with her daughter Marion. She regularly traveled to visit each of her daughters and would stay with them for a few months at a time. When she came to visit our childhood home, my siblings and I were very happy to have her with us for a few months each year. Marion Hughes followed in her mother's footsteps and was busy with community work. She was president of the Portland League of Women Voters from 1955 to 1957. In the early 1960s Cloud suffered a series of strokes. Unfortunately, my aunt Marion was no longer able to care for her, and she moved into a nursing home. Her daughters and grandchildren visited her there. I remember my mother telling me that the strokes had impacted her recent memory. She lived in the past, as though the events of her childhood had occurred yesterday.

Lyndon Johnson's presidential inauguration in 1965 provided an opportunity for honoring Henry Cloud's memory. On January 20 the inaugural parade included a float called "Great Achievements," including people who dressed as Sequoyah, the author of the Cherokee alphabet; the artist Ace Blue Eagle; and Henry Cloud. The parade honored Henry Roe Cloud, along with Jim Thorpe, Charles Curtis, Chief Joseph, Will Rogers, Dr. Charles Eastman, and Sacagawea.[68]

On September 16, 1965, at the age of seventy-seven, Elizabeth Georgian Bender Cloud died. She was buried adjacent to her cherished husband, Henry, in the Crescent Grove Cemetery in Tigard, Oregon.[69] Elizabeth Bender Cloud was an important warrior and a Christian woman, an intellectual and an activist, who fought back against termination and struggled for tribal sovereignty and self-determination as the Indian welfare chair of the GFWC and NCAI. Cloud worked closely with other warrior women, including Helen Peterson and Ruth Bronson, to build tribal nations and struggle against termination. Cloud's attire included stunning dresses and stylish hats that concealed her subversive Ojibwe warrior woman identity. With this camouflage and with the help of virtual and geographic hubs, Elizabeth kept her Ojibwe gender and identity strong. Cloud was an inherent contradiction: she supported Natives' absorption into the nation-state, while aligning herself with tribal interests and fighting against settler colonialism. By supporting Natives' struggle for equal belonging in the United States and fighting for tribal sovereignty, Cloud asserted Native cultural citizenship. She also linked gender, tribal nation, and sovereignty together by advocating for women to serve on tribal councils, supporting later discussions of Native feminisms. She emphasized the importance of connections between Natives throughout the Western Hemisphere, demonstrating a Western Hemispheric consciousness. She was an articulate and smart and a loving grandmother. As her granddaughter and a professor of Native studies and anthropology, I am deeply proud of her and her efforts to make the world a better place for Native peoples at the local, community, tribal, national, and international levels.

Conclusion

The couple of dusty cardboard boxes filled with my mother's collection of Cloud family archival material that sat underneath my office desk for years was the beginning of an incredibly long journey of visiting many archives, Ho-Chunk Nation headquarters, my Winnebago Reservation, and relatives' homes and discussions with Ho-Chunk and Ojibwe historians, UCSC graduate students, anthropology and history colleagues, and Cloud family members. The main inspiration for this book is my precious and beloved mother, Woesha Cloud North, Ho-Chunk and Ojibwe artist, poet, activist, and scholar, whose footsteps I decided to follow to become a professor of anthropology and Native studies.

When I first conceptualized this book, I planned to write about the activism and work of my mother, Woesha, as a Ho-Chunk and Ojibwe intellectual, but then I decided to save this discussion for future writing, where I can incorporate pictures of her beautiful artwork, her poetry, an analysis of her Ho-Chunk–centric PhD dissertation, and her activism when Natives occupied Alcatraz Island in the San Francisco Bay Area. After writing this book, I now realize that she was following her parents' example by joining a Native hub on Alcatraz Island and fighting for Native American rights. I learned that both her parents supported and fought for tribal sovereignty. Henry, for example, used treaties to struggle for Indigenous hunting and fishing rights, and Elizabeth, as part of NCAI's

American Indian Development project, organized community gatherings—which eventually led to the Red Power movement— to support tribal "revitalization," while supporting Native women to be on tribal councils, an early precursor to later discussions of Native feminisms. The Clouds fighting for tribal sovereignty encourages historians, anthropologists, and Native-studies scholars not to divide so sharply the early twentieth century and the Progressive Era from later struggles against termination, relocation, and the formation of the Red Power movement of the 1960s. Indeed, more work examining the activist and intellectual work of Society of American Indian intellectuals is needed as a possible way to find these connections between their efforts and later Native activist movements, including the Red Power movement.

My mother, Woesha, decided to join the many Native activists when our people chose to occupy Alcatraz Island in 1969, to protest and make public the horrible socioeconomic conditions of Native peoples, settler-colonial policies of termination and relocation, the high suicide rates of Natives, their low life-expectancy rates, and many other important issues. This pivotal Native hub was a place for my mother to connect and reconnect with many other urban Native Americans and join together to support Indigenous culture, identity, gender, and belonging, while becoming empowered and struggling for social change. She had grown up surrounded by Native people at the American Indian Institute and traveled around Indian Country with her parents and siblings, including annual summer visits to see her Ojibwe grandmother, Mary Razier, on the White Earth Reservation and to visit Ho-Chunk relatives on the Winnebago Reservation, including Alice Mallory Porter, whose loving family had taken Henry in when his parents and grandmother died. My mother had lived a Native-hub existence, and she continued living in a Native hub, taking her children and my siblings on annual trips to the Winnebago Reservation to visit Alice Mallory Porter, the LaRose family, and our close Ho-Chunk relatives, the Hunter family in Wichita, Kansas—the site of the American Indian Institute.

I use the Paiute activist Laverne Roberts's notion of the hub to show how Elizabeth and Henry maintained their Ho-Chunk and Ojibwe gender, culture, identity, and belonging, living away from their tribal land bases of the Winnebago Reservation and White Earth Reservation.[1] The hub challenges previous literature in history and classic anthropology that assume that Native culture is incarcerated in the land, and movement away from tribal land bases means a distinct break from one's tribal culture, gender, and identity.[2] Henry and Elizabeth relied on flexible and fluid notions of gender, identity, culture, community, and belonging that they carried with them as they traveled around Indian Country and within white environments, such as federal boarding schools, white schools, and government jobs. The hub challenges older scholarship that assumes that traditional Natives lived on reservations, fight settler colonialism, and are "bad" Indians, whereas assimilated and progressive Natives were "apples" and "sell-outs" and fought to become full U.S. citizens. These static notions contribute to conflicts between "good" and "bad" Indians, "traditional" and "modern" Natives. This book challenges static notions of identity, where scholars and Native community members placed Elizabeth and Henry Cloud into fixed boxes as "assimilationists," "apples," "sell-outs," and a "white bull with a red face," and instead emphasizes their complexity—Ho-Chunk, Ojibwe, Christian, citizen, warrior, and "good" and "bad" Indian.[3]

I argue that the Clouds combined their Native modern and warrior identities to fight settler colonialism and struggle for tribal sovereignty and Native cultural citizenship. I also argue that Elizabeth and Henry used their modern identities and ability to perform, wearing professional-looking clothes, shiny shoes, and great-looking hats as a camouflage to cover their Ho-Chunk and Ojibwe warrior identities, helping them in their struggles to fight in support of Native rights. Thus, both Elizabeth and Henry Cloud were "good" and "bad" Indians simultaneously, and their ability to morph between the two identities enabled them to become involved in high-governmental circles and fight for Native peoples. Their outer appearance and behavior made them look and be perceived as "good" Indians who helped whites, while, underneath, their Ho-Chunk and Ojibwe warrior identities were continually simmering just below the surface, and their "bad" Indian self would emerge at any moment and struggle for Native causes and rights. I argue that Henry and Elizabeth learned how to shapeshift and use masks from listening as children to Ho-Chunk and Ojibwe trickster stories. These stories also taught them how to use doubleness

speech—speaking in language that the colonizer would not find objectionable, while underneath were powerful moments of resistance that often
happened under the colonizers' radar, while mixing dominant and Native
discourses. Henry and Elizabeth Cloud as Native intellectuals used these
tribal trickster strategies to challenge settler colonialism.

This family-tribal history revolves around the work and activism of
my grandparents, Henry Cloud (1884–1950), a Ho-Chunk, and Elizabeth
Bender Cloud (1887–1965), an Ojibwe. Their activism and intellectual
work occurred during the twentieth century, including involvement in
the Society of American Indians, the National Congress of American
Indians, and the General Federation of Women's Clubs. Even though
Henry has been recognized as the most important Native policy maker
of the early twentieth century, only two books and four articles have
been written about him.[4] While Elizabeth fought against termination
as part of her role in NCAI and GFWC, only one article has been written
about her. Indeed, this is the first Ojibwe-centric and Ho-Chunk–centric
analysis of Henry and Elizabeth Cloud.

Henry and Elizabeth grew up in the midst of settler colonialism and
had to confront living in an extremely racist society that saw them as
less than full human, as "savages" lower on the social-evolutionary scale
and less intelligent than whites. They lived in the midst of dominant
civilizing discourses that attempted to break their connection to Native
land, treaty rights, and tribal identities. They were seized and taken to
federal boarding schools—a cultural genocidal and abusive environment
that attempted to erase their tribal identities and socialize them to follow
white gender norms, become submissive, and follow white notions of
the nuclear family. They both faced settler-colonial policies, including
the reservation system, removals, and the Allotment Act, and Elizabeth
confronted termination—all governmental efforts of land dispossession
and the elimination of the Native. The Clouds fought these policies in
varied ways. Henry documented the horrible abuse of the federal boarding
schools, co-wrote the Meriam Report of 1928, and, according to available
evidence, coauthored the Indian Reorganization Act of 1934.[5] Elizabeth
and Henry worked together, running a college-preparatory Christian
high school to educate Native young boys to become educated warriors

for their tribes, who could then also fight settler-colonial policies. (They wished to include Native girls too, and school officials did eventually decide to admit girls, starting in 1932.)

The Clouds lived with, and struggled against, the impact of the dominant discourse of classic anthropology that incarcerates Natives in the land, supporting static notions of culture and identity and contributing to the notion of the vanishing Native—a story told over and over in Wild West shows, Hollywood films, museums, and popular culture overall. Henry struggled to change the colonial nature of the Pendleton Round-Up and Wild West show, and Elizabeth confronted Dillon Myer, the strong supporter of termination and relocation, to stop seeing Natives as "museum pieces."[6] This book also revolves around gender and settler colonialism, including how relationships in the intimate realm influence oppression along the lines of race, class, and gender. It examines how Mary Roe attempted to destroy Cloud's Ho-Chunk kinship bonds in our Cloud family and replace them with white notions of the nuclear family and how Henry chose to marry Elizabeth, a strong Ojibwe warrior woman, and strengthen his Native kinship ties.

Standing Up to Colonial Power is a Native feminist approach to family-tribal history, arguing that Native archival materials are not always available for public consumption, and archival researchers should work with Native families, communities, and tribal nations in a collaborative manner, while relying on intersectional analysis to analyze government documents, letters, interviews, newspapers, and other materials. Rather than viewing Natives, and by extension our letters and archival materials, as "data" divorced from Native families, archival information is precious and should be respected and carefully used in conjunction with Native families' permission, collaboration, and involvement. This book uses the Native feminist approach of intersectional analysis, not privileging one oppression, such as race, class, and gender, over another, and places colonialism at the center of my analysis. My methodology also incorporates my perspectives as an "insider," as my beloved ancestors are Henry and Elizabeth Cloud, and an "outsider," as a scholar, writing from these two social positions. The book is part of my work to decolonize our family-tribal history. Consequently, I usually call my grandparents the Clouds rather than the Roe Clouds, since Henry's relationship with the Roes had a colonial element.

Drafting the book my mother, Woesha Cloud North, hoped to write (but, unfortunately, died before achieving her goal) took eight years from start to finish, while I, along with family members, including my sons, Lucio and Gilbert, and my daughter, Mirasol; and Ned Blackhawk and Reynaldo Morales, also made a film about Henry Cloud, primarily funded by the Ho-Chunk nation, in the midst of trying to write this book. I am following in the footsteps of not only my mother, Woesha, but also my aunt Marion and grandmother, Elizabeth, who also wanted a book written about the Cloud family. These female relatives started compiling archival documents and interviews and saving important pieces of family information. I must honor the efforts of these Cloud family women. Without their work at collecting material, this family-tribal history would not have been written.

I began this family-tribal history by staring at a couple of boxes underneath my desk and contemplated the idea of working on a book that discusses the activism and intellectual work of Henry and Elizabeth Cloud with my sisters, Mary McNeil and Woesha Hampson; my brother, Robert Cloud North; my cousins Robin and Mark Butterfield, Gretchen Freed-Rowland, and Susan Freed Held; my brother-in-law Chris McNeil; my Ho-Chunk colleague Amy Lonetree; my husband, Gil; my children, Lucio, Mirasol, and Gilbert; my niece Tasha Adams; and other family members. When I traveled with my son, Gilbert, to conduct archival research in the Yale Sterling Library during the summer of 2008, I had no idea how long of a journey this book would take from start to finish. As I sat next to my son in the Yale library, I felt the spirit of my mother, Woesha, sitting next to me and remembered her tearful phone calls, discussing the colonial aspect of the letters I was reading. As I write the final words of this book, I can feel my mom's spiritual presence, and I am now shedding tears of joy that I have fulfilled the promise I made to her to write the book she wanted to draft but died before accomplishing her objective. I love our Cloud family, and this book is for all of my Ho-Chunk and Ojibwe relatives, colleagues, and friends and everyone whose lives were touched by Henry and Elizabeth Cloud.

NOTES

INTRODUCTION

1. L. Tetzloff, "Elizabeth Bender Cloud."

2. Messer, *Henry Roe Cloud*; Pfister, *Yale Indian*; Crum, "Henry Roe Cloud"; Ramirez, "From Henry Roe Cloud"; Ramirez, "Henry Roe Cloud"; Ramirez, "Ho-Chunk Warrior." See also PhD dissertations about Henry Roe Cloud: J. Tetzloff, "To Do Some Good," and Goodwin, "Without Destroying Ourselves."

3. "Script," *Northwest Neighbors* radio program, April 11, 1945, Portland OR, CFPC.

4. Ramirez, *Native Hubs.*

5. Rosaldo, "Cultural Citizenship," in Flores and Benmayor, *Latino Cultural Citizenship*, 27–39.

6. Ramirez, "Henry Roe Cloud."

7. Maddox, *Citizen Indians.*

8. Pfister, *Yale Indian.*

9. See, for example, Maddox, *Citizen Indians*; P. Deloria, *Indians in Unexpected Places*; Vigil, *Indigenous Intellectuals*; and Ackley and Stanciu, *Laura Cornelius Kellogg.*

10. Bhabha, *Location of Culture.* See Bhabha for a discussion on mimic men.

11. See, for example, Denetdale, *Reclaiming Diné History*; Miles, *Ties That Bind*; P. Deloria, "Of the Body," in P. Deloria, *Indians in Unexpected Places*, 109–35; and Miranda, *Bad Indians.*

12. Radin and Densmore were classic anthropologists who followed static notions of culture and identity while assuming that Natives were "primitives" and their intellectual, cultural, and philosophical ideas were lower on the socioevolutionary scale. See, for example, Radin, *Winnebago Tribe*; Densmore, *Chippewa Customs*;

and Moon, "Quest for Music's Origin." See also Arjun Appadurai, "Hierarchy in Its Place," for a discussion of the "incarceration" of Natives in the land.

13. Pfister, *Yale Indian*; Messer, *Henry Roe Cloud*; J. Tetzloff, "To Do Some Good"; L. Tetzloff, "Elizabeth Bender Cloud."

14. Hoxie, *Talking Back to Civilization*; Iverson, *Carlos Montezuma*; Cahill, *Federal Fathers and Mothers*; Ackley and Stanciu, *Laura Cornelius Kellogg*; Porter, *To Be an Indian*; Martinez, *Dakota Philosopher*.

15. See Hall, "Introduction," in Hall and Gay, *Questions of Cultural Identity, 1–17*. He discusses identity as flexible and fluid rather than static.

16. See Ramirez, *Native Hubs*, for a discussion of Roberts's notion of the hub.

17. Sinclair, "Trickster Reflections," in Reder and Morra, *Troubling Tricksters*, 21–59; Reder and Morra, *Troubling Tricksters*.

18. North, "Informal Education"; Reder and Morra, *Troubling Tricksters*.

19. Blaeser, *Stories Migrating Home*.

20. Ballinger, *Living Sideways*; Madsen, *Understanding Gerald Vizenor*.

21. Radin, *Winnebago Tribe*.

22. Sinclair, "Trickster Reflections," in Reder and Morra, *Troubling Tricksters*, 21–59; Reder and Morra, *Troubling Tricksters*.

23. Radin, *Trickster*, 22, 39, 53; Sinclair, "Trickster Reflections," in Reder and Morra, *Troubling Tricksters*, 21–59; Reder and Morra, *Troubling Tricksters*.

24. Sinclair, "Trickster Reflections," in Reder and Morra, *Troubling Tricksters*, 21–59; Reder and Morra, *Troubling Tricksters*.

25. Sinclair, "Trickster Reflections," in Reder and Morra, *Troubling Tricksters*, 21–59; Reder and Morra, *Troubling Tricksters*.

26. Martin, *Dancing the Colorline*; Gates, *Signifying Monkey*; Scott, *Domination and the Arts*.

27. M. Pratt, *Imperial Eyes*; Scott, *Domination and the Arts*.

28. M. Pratt, "Contact Zone."

29. Green, "Pocahontas Perplex," in Lobo and Talbot, *Native American Voices*, 203–11.

30. See Maddox, *Citizen Indians*.

31. North, "Informal Education"; Radin, *Trickster*; Blaeser, *Gerald Vizenor*; Vizenor, "Trickster Discourse," in Vizenor, *Narrative Chance*, 187–213; Ballinger, *Living Sideways*; Hinzo, "Dialoging with Ho-Chunk Tricksters."

32. Vizenor, "Trickster Discourse," in Vizenor, *Narrative Chance*, 187–213.

33. Berkhofer, *White Man's Indian*.

34. Miranda, *Bad Indians*. Miranda argues that her ancestors were "bad Indians," giving me an insight about my ancestors, who were both "good" and "bad" Indians.

35. See Reder and Morra, *Troubling Tricksters*. This collection of essays is a revisioning of trickster criticism in light of recent critique against it. See also Blaeser,

Gerald Vizenor. Blaeser analyzes Vizenor's ("Trickster Discourse," in Vizenor, *Narrative Chance*, 187–213) use of the trickster.

36. See Bhabha, "Foreword to the 1986 Edition"; and Fanon, *Black Skin, White Masks*, xxi–xxxviii.

37. Scott, *Domination and the Arts*, Scott, an anthropologist and political theorist, argues that the oppressed often rely on subtle forms of resistance to oppose the abuse of power, such as disguises, folktales, linguistic tricks, ritual gestures, anonymity, metaphors, and euphemisms. These approaches are especially useful in moments where violence and abuse are used to control the oppressed, allowing for a veiled discourse of dignity and self. See also Martin, *Dancing the Colorline*.

38. See, for example, Child, *My Grandfather's Knocking Sticks*; Child, *Holding Our World Together*; North, "Informal Education"; Jones et al., *Big Voice*; Vizenor and Doerfler, *White Earth Nation*; Hinzo, "Voicing across Space"; Harper, "French Africans"; D. Smith, *Folklore*; and Buffalohead, "Farmers, Warriors, Traders."

39. Miranda, *Bad Indians*.

40. For a discussion of Native American history, see, for example, Mihesuah, *Native and Academics*; P. Deloria, "Historiography," in Deloria and Salisbury, *Companion*, 6–24; L. Smith, *Decolonizing Methodologies*; and Denetdale, *Reclaiming Diné History*.

41. For new imperial histories, see, for example, Burton, *Colonial Modernities*; Burton, *Heart of Empire*; Briggs, *Reproducing Empire*; Chaudhuri and Strobel, *Western Women and Imperialism*; and Clancy-Smith and Gouda, *Domesticating the Empire*.

42. Articles in the journal, *Settler Colonial Studies*, include, for example, Morgensen, "Theorizing Gender"; and Erai, "Responding." Other settler-colonial scholarly efforts include, for example, Snelgrove, Dhamoon, and Corntassel, "Unsettling Settler Colonialism"; Veracini, *Settler Colonialism*; Coombes, *Rethinking Settler Colonialism*; Driskill et al., *Queer Indigenous Studies*; Tuck, Arvin, and Morrill, "Decolonizing Feminism."

43. Wolfe, "Elimination of the Native"; Wolfe, *Settler Colonialism*, 2–22.

44. Wolfe, "Elimination of the Native"; Wolfe, *Settler Colonialism*, 2–22; Jacobs, *White Mother*; Glenn, "Settler Colonialism as Structure."

45. Hoelscher, *Picturing Indians*; Jones et al., *Big Voice*.

46. See Appadurai, "Hierarchy in Its Place," for a discussion of "incarceration" of Natives in the land. See also Ramirez, *Native Hubs*.

47. Kat Anderson, *Tending the Wild*.

48. May et al., *Salmon Is Everything*.

49. V. Anderson, *Creatures of Empire*; Hernandez, "Agents of Pollination."

50. See, for example, the special issue, Salamanca et al., "Past Is Present," in *Settler Colonial Studies*.

51. While some scholars may disagree with putting the words "settler" and "colonialism" together, as they could fear that readers of their scholarly work might feel attacked or threatened if they are settlers or descendants of settlers. This fear of facing our ancestors' role in settler colonialism or our own involvement in colonialism is certainly problematic and is a way to live in denial.

52. Stoler, *Carnal Knowledge*.

53. Morgensen, *Spaces between Us*; Avalos et al., "Standing with Standing Rock"; Dhillon and Estes, "Standing Rock"; Tallbear, "Badass (Indigenous) Women."

54. Snelgrove, Dhamoon, and Corntassel, "Unsettling Settler Colonialism."

55. Foucault, *Discipline and Punish*; Foucault, *Order of Discourse*.

56. Stromberg, "Rhetoric of Irony," in Stromberg, *American Indian Rhetorics*, 95–110.

57. See Bobroff, "Retelling Allotment"; for allotment's specific impact on women, see Dussias, "Squaw Drudges."

58. Glenn, "Settler Colonialism as Structure."

59. Jacobs, "Maternal Colonialism," 462; Estelle Reel, "Her Work for the Indians," n.d., folder: "Articles," box 1, WSA.

60. Glenn, "Settler Colonialism as Structure."

61. R. Pratt, "Advantages," in Prucha, *Americanizing the American Indians*, 260–71.

62. Palmer and Rundstrom, "Internal Colonialism."

63. Cahill, *Federal Fathers and Mothers*, 9.

64. Miner, *Corporation and the Indian*, 26–27.

65. Stromberg, "Rhetoric of Irony," in Stromberg, *American Indian Rhetorics*, 95–110.

66. Hertzberg, *American Indian Identity*.

67. Maddox, *Citizen Indians*.

68. Simpson, *Mohawk Interruptus*; Cattelino, *High Stakes*; Bruyneel, *Third Space of Sovereignty*; Deloria and Lytle, *Nations Within*; Barker, *Native Acts*; Fixico, *Treaties with American Indians*.

69. Maddox, *Citizen Indians*.

70. P. Deloria, *Indians in Unexpected Places*; Hoxie, *Talking Back to Civilization*; Ackley and Stanciu, *Laura Cornelius Kellogg*; Cahill, *Federal Fathers and Mothers*.

71. Warrior, *Tribal Secrets*; Goeman, *Mark My Words*.

72. See, for example, Maracle, *I Am Woman*; Shanley, "Thoughts on Indian Feminism," in Brant, *Gathering of Spirit*, 214–16; Ramirez, "Tribal Nation"; Goeman and Denetdale, "Native Feminisms"; A. Smith, "Native American Feminism"; and Suzack et al., *Indigenous Women*.

73. After reading Pfister's book, *The Yale Indian*, I began my research and writing journey that culminated in this family-tribal history. The title *The Yale Indian* elucidates the central problem of the book, and that is to view Cloud as an individual, the Indian removed from his Ho-Chunk people. Pfister portrays him as mainly a product of white cultural and institutional education, especially with

Yale and his white adoptive family, the Roes. Pfister, therefore, removes Cloud from his tribe and Native people. As Pfister himself admits, his book is primarily based on Cloud's personal writings and his letters to the Roes. Many of these letters, however, very likely discuss what Cloud strategically chose to write in the context of colonial dynamics related to race, class, and gender. Indeed, these power dynamics can make subordinated people feel uncomfortable to express their true feelings or perspectives. Even so, there is correspondence in the Yale archive in the Sterling Library that emphasizes Ho-Chunk viewpoints missed by Pfister entirely. Pfister makes a mistake about Cloud's clan, calling him a member of the Bear Clan. This error shows his lack of care regarding a pivotal Ho-Chunk cultural attribute and his lack of knowledge about the powerful importance of clan membership in Ho-Chunk educational training and upbringing. He also makes a mistake about Elizabeth's tribal affiliation. She grew up on the White Earth Ojibwe (Chippewa) Reservation in Minnesota and was not a Bad River Chippewa. Pfister chose not to conduct research in many archives but rather to focus only on Yale's Sterling Library. He also did not conduct interviews of Ho-Chunks or get permission from our tribe or Clouds' descendants. Furthermore, Pfister uses my grandfather, Henry Roe Cloud, as a case study to support his argument about individuality and Native Americans. The main goal of *The Yale Indian*, according to Pfister, is to use Cloud to discuss "interconnected reproductive processes of emotion making, race making, class making, and incentive making" (xiv). Therefore, it seems that Pfister uses Henry as a theoretical point rather than as a human being with complications and contradictions as well as family relations outside of his involvement with a white missionary couple, the Roes. See also Ramirez, "From Henry Roe Cloud."

74. A Native-led nonprofit organization, the Association of Tribal Archives, Libraries, and Museums provides culturally relevant instruction to our nation's 519 tribal archives, libraries, and museums. Researchers should contact this organization for further information and training; see Speed et. al, "Remapping Gender"; L. Smith, *Decolonizing Methodologies*.

75. Ramirez, "Henry Roe Cloud."

76. P. Deloria, *Indians in Unexpected Places*; Lyons, *X-marks*.

1. HENRY CLOUD'S CHILDHOOD

1. Marion Cloud Hughes, interview, April 27, 1987, CFPC.

2. Hinzo, *Voicing across Space*.

3. Lonetree, "Visualizing Native Survivance."

4. Henry Roe Cloud to Mary Roe, July 18, 1907, folder 1078, box 67, SL.

5. North, "Informal Education."

6. H. Cloud to M. Roe, July 18, 1907, SL.

7. "Son Fulfills Prophecy Made by Old Indian," unidentified newspaper article, n.d., CFPC; Ramirez, "From Henry Roe Cloud."

8. North, "Informal Education."

9. It is difficult to read Hard-to-See's Ho-Chunk name in the genealogy. It could be "Na-gees-na-pingah."

10. Francis Cassiman and Alice Mallory Porter, with Robin Butterfield, "Genealogy," CFPC.

11. H. E. Bruce to Sidney Nyhus, August 9, 1950, CFPC. Bruce, superintendent of the Winnebago Reservation, enclosed a certificate that showed Henry was enrolled and born in 1883. See also Sheridan Fahnestock and Thomas Sorci, "Roe Cloud" (unpublished book manuscript, 1991) chs. 1–11, CFPC.

12. Cloud, "From Wigwam to Pulpit"; Ramirez, "Henry Roe Cloud."

13. Cloud, "Graduation Speech to Mount Edgecumbe High School Students," May 1949, Sitka, Alaska, CFPC.

14. Jacobs, *White Mother*.

15. North, "Informal Education"; Radin, *Trickster*.

16. Minnie Littlebear, interview by Woesha Cloud North, June, 17, 1976, CFPC; North, "Informal Education."

17. Felix White Sr., interview by W. Cloud North, May 15, 1976, CFPC; North, "Informal Education."

18. Cloud, "From Wigwam to Pulpit."

19. H. Cloud, "Graduation Speech," CFPC.

20. Felix White Sr., interview by W. Cloud North, May 15, 1976, CFPC; North, "Informal Education."

21. Cloud, "From Wigwam to Pulpit."

22. Lomawaima, *Prairie Light*.

23. See DeCoteau, *2017 Annual Report*. This group documents the abuses against Native children in Indian boarding schools for healing and reparation.

24. H. Cloud, "Graduation Speech," CFPC.

25. H. Cloud, "An Anthropologist's View of Reservation Life," address delivered at the Northwest, Inter-mountain, and Montana Superintendents' Conference, Pendleton OR, September 11–13, 1941, CFPC, 5–6,.

26. Cloud, "From Wigwam to Pulpit."

27. Steinmetz, "New Missiology," in Holler, *Black Elk Reader*, 262–82. Steinmetz argues that Black Elk was able to accommodate Christianity into his strong belief of the Lakota religion. Rather than arguing this, I am arguing that Henry Cloud kept his Ho-Chunk identity intact while accommodating Christianity.

28. Cloud, "From Wigwam to Pulpit."

29. Cloud, "From Wigwam to Pulpit."

30. Guenther, "Santee Normal Training School."

31. J. Tetzloff, "To Do Some Good," 15.

32. Lillian Alberta Cloud Freed (unpublished manuscript, n.d.), CFPC; Fahnestock and Sorci, "Roe Cloud," CFPC, ch. 2, p. 28.

33. Fahnestock and Sorci, "Roe Cloud," CFPC, ch. 2, p. 27.

34. Sinnema, introd. to Smiles, *Self-Help*, vii–xxix.

35. Oskison, "Making an Individual."

36. J. Tetzloff, "To Do Some Good," 17.

37. H. Cloud, application, Cloud, student file, NMHSA; Fahnestock and Sorci, "Roe Cloud," CFPC, ch. 2, pp. 29, 30.

38. A. L. Riggs to Henry F. Cutler, June 7, 1901, Cloud, student file, NMHSA; Fahnestock and Sorci, "Roe Cloud," CFPC, ch. 2, p. 30.

39. William T. Findley to Henry F. Cutler, June 15, 1901, Cloud, student file, NMHSA; Fahnestock and Sorci, "Roe Cloud," CFPC, ch. 2, p. 30.

40. Morgan, *Ancient Society*, xxix–xxx; Maddox, *Citizen Indians*, 60.

41. Wolfe, "Elimination of the Native"; Jacobs, *White Mother*.

42. Cloud, "From Wigwam to Pulpit."

43. Cloud's academic record, Records of the Office of the Registrar, NMHSA; J. Tetzloff, "To Do Some Good," 19.

44. H. Cloud, "Graduation Speech," CFPC.

45. J. Tetzloff, "To Do Some Good," 19.

46. Carrol, *American Masculinities*, 206; Ramirez, "From Henry Roe Cloud."

47. L. McCall, introd. to Basso, McCall, and Garceau, *Across the Great Divide*, 1–25.

48. Ellinghaus, *Taking Assimilation to Heart*, 65.

49. Ellinghaus, *Taking Assimilation to Heart*, 65.

50. H. Cloud's yearbook, Cloud, student file, NMHSA; Fahnestock and Sorci, "Roe Cloud," CFPC, ch. 2, pp. 35–36.

51. Ellinghaus, *Taking Assimilation to Heart*.

52. Culin, *Games*; Fletcher, *Indian Games*.

53. H. Cloud's yearbook, Cloud, student file, NMHSA; Fahnestock and Sorci, "Roe Cloud," CFPC, ch. 2, p. 36.

54. Cloud, "Salutatory."

55. Hughes, interview, April 27, 1987, CFPC, 1, 2; Fahnestock and Sorci, "Roe Cloud," CFPC, ch. 2, p. 8.

56. Hughes, interview, 9–10.

57. Hughes, interview, 4–5.

58. Hughes, interview, 4–5.

59. H. Cloud, "Graduation Speech," CFPC.

60. Denetdale, *Reclaiming Diné History*.

61. H. Cloud to M. Roe, January 7, 1908, folder 1082, box 67, SL.

62. Cloud, "From Wigwam to Pulpit."

63. Ramirez, "From Henry Roe Cloud"; for Native masculinities, see Hokowhitu, "Maori Masculinity"; Tengan, *Native Men Remade*; and Anthony, Clark, and Nagle, "White Men, Red Masks," in Basso, McCall, and Garceau, *Across the Great Divide*, 109–30.

64. J. Tetzloff, "To Do Some Good," 23.

65. Ramirez, "From Henry Roe Cloud."

66. M. Roe to H. Cloud, November 12, 1909, folder 1097, box 67, SL.

67. Jacobs, *White Mother.*

68. M. Roe to H. Cloud, September 1911, folder 1137, box 67, SL.

69. Ramirez, "From Henry Roe Cloud."

70. M. Roe to H. Cloud, March 21, 1909, folder 1090, box 67, SL.

71. See, for example, M. Roe to H. Cloud, November 5, 1912, folder 1149, box 70, SL.

72. M. Roe to H. Cloud, [August?] 1911, folder 1134, box 69, SL; see also Pfister, *Yale Indian.*

73. M. Roe to H. Cloud, September 3, 1911, folder 1135, box 69, SL; see also Pfister, *Yale Indian.*

74. H. Cloud to M. Roe, November 1909, folder 1098, box 67, SL.

75. H. Cloud to M. Roe, July 18, 1907, SL.

76. H. Cloud to M. Roe, September 29, 1907, folder 1079, box 67, SL.

77. Elizabeth Bender Cloud to Mary Roe, November 22, 1915, folder 1166, box 71, SL; Pfister, *Yale Indian.*

78. After Henry Cloud's marriage to Elizabeth Bender, the frequency of his letters to Mary Roe greatly decreased.

79. H. Cloud to Walter Roe, April 4, 1910, folder 1108, box 68, SL.

80. Silko, *Gardens in the Dunes.*

81. Garland, "Red Man's Present Needs."

82. P. Deloria, *Playing Indian.*

83. H. Cloud to W. Roe, January 30, 1912, folder 1142, box 70, SL.

84. H. Cloud to M. Roe, September 29, 1907, SL.

85. H. Cloud to Elizabeth Page, October 6, 1907, folder 1980, box 67, SL.

86. H. Cloud to Page, October 6, 1907, SL.

87. E. Cloud to Page, September 15, 1950, CFPC.

88. H. Cloud to M. Roe, April 13, 1910, folder 1109, box 68, SL.

89. J. Tetzloff, "To Do Some Good," 26, 22–23.

90. Cloud, "Missions," 520.

91. Jacobs, *White Mother*; Ramirez, "From Henry Roe Cloud."

92. H. Cloud to W. Roe, January 30, 1912, SL.

93. Hughes, interview, April 27, 1987, CFPC.

94. Hughes, interview, April 27, 1987, CFPC.

95. J. Tetzloff, "To Do Some Good," 29.

96. H. Cloud, "Anthropologist's View," CFPC.

97. *Sixteenth Annual Meeting*, 14–16.

98. Maddox, *Citizen Indians*.

99. H. Cloud, untitled, August 13, 1931, CFPC, 1–4.

100. Rosaldo, *Culture and Truth*.

101. Cloud, "Education," 15.

102. Cloud, "Social and Economic Aspects," 155.

103. H. Cloud, untitled, n.d., CFPC, 1–5.

104. Radin, *Winnebago Tribe*; Cloud, "Winnebago Medicine Lodge"; H. Cloud, "Among the Winnebago," folder 1188, box 72, SL; J. Tetzloff, "To Do Some Good," 52–53.

105. "Statement by the Winnebago Delegation on Behalf of the Nebraska Branch," frame 0807-16, series A: Indian Delegations to Washington, Central Classified Files, 1907–39, BIA-W; H. Cloud to Robert Valentine, July 5, 1912, file 74294-12, Classified Files 34-013, RG 75, Tomah Agency, BIA-W; H. Cloud to Walter Roe, September 2, 1912, folder 1148, box 70, SL; J. Tetzloff, "To Do Some Good," 54–55.

106. H. Cloud to M. Roe, February 9, 1915, SL.

107. Ramirez, "From Henry Roe Cloud."

2. SOCIETY OF AMERICAN INDIANS

1. Wishart, "Roe Cloud, Henry," in Wishart, *Encyclopedia*, 176; Turcheneske, *Chiricahua Apache Prisoners*.

2. Ramirez, "Ho-Chunk Warrior."

3. Maddox, *Citizen Indians*, 11. Maddox argues that Cloud's Society of American Indian contemporaries were strategic about what they spoke and wrote about because of power dynamics.

4. Maddox, *Citizen Indians*, 11–12.

5. J. Tetzloff, "To Do Some Good," 40; Larner, *Papers*, 1–9.

6. H. Cloud to Arthur Parker, August 4, 1914, folder 1157, box 70, SL.

7. Watermulder, "Injustice to the Apaches"; J. Tetzloff, "To Do Some Good," 31–32.

8. "New Haskell Head Came from Wigwam to Lead His People," *Kansas City Star*, August 6, 1933; J. Tetzloff, "To Do Some Good," 32.

9. Hillaire and Fields, *Rights Remembered*.

10. See Coppersmith, "Cultural Survival"; Turcheneske, *Chiricahua Apache Prisoners*; and Stockel, *Apache Nation*.

11. H. Cloud to Cato Sells, November 3, 1912; December 13, 1913, file 18700/13, Kiowa Agency, RG 75, Central Classified Files, 1907–39, BIA-W; Larner, *Papers*; H. Cloud, "The Case of the Fort Sill Apaches, Again," October 25, 1913, frame 0447-52, reel 10, SAIA.

12. H. Cloud to M. Roe, October 7, 1913; October 16, 1913, folder 1156, box 70, SL.

13. Wolfe, *Settler Colonialism*. The Allotment Act revolved around settler colonialism and taking land away from Natives.
14. H. Cloud to M. Roe, October 21, 1913, folder 1156, box 70, SL.
15. H. Cloud, "Fort Sill Apaches," SAIA.
16. H. Cloud to M. Roe, October 7, 1913, SL.
17. H. Cloud, "Fort Sill Apaches," SAIA.
18. E. Bender to Society of American Indians, July 27, 1914, SAIA.
19. Molin, "Training the Hand."
20. Hughes, interview, September 15, 1987, CFPC.
21. "School Registration Form," E. Bender, student file, HUA; Hughes, interview, December 14, 1989, CFPC.
22. Hughes, interview, September 15, 1987, CFPC.
23. Molin, "Training the Hand," 94.
24. Woesha Cloud North, untitled, n.d., memoir notes, CFPC.
25. Buffalohead, "Farmers, Warriors, Traders."
26. Buffalohead, "Farmers, Warriors, Traders," 242–43, 240–41.
27. W. North, memoir notes, untitled, n.d., CFPC.
28. E. Bender to Friend, 1905, E. Bender, student file, HUA.
29. E. Bender to Miss Jay, January 1906, E. Bender, student file, HUA.
30. E. Bender to Friend, March 15, 1904, E. Bender, student file, HUA.
31. W. North, memoir notes, n.d., CFPC.
32. E. Bender to Friend, March 15, 1904, E. Bender, student file, HUA.
33. E. Bender to Friend, 1905, E. Bender, student file, HUA.
34. E. Bender to Dr. Hollis Frissel, October 2, 1900, E. Bender, student file, HUA.
35. E. Bender to Friend, February 1905, E. Bender, student file, HUA.
36. Silko, "Language and Literature," in Silko, *Yellow Woman*, 58.
37. E. Bender to Jay, January 1906, E. Bender, student file, HUA.
38. E. Bender to Jay, January 1906, E. Bender, student file, HUA.
39. Anna Bender to Scholarship Benefactor, February 1905, Anna Bender, student file, HUA; Molin, "Training the Hand," 95.
40. A. Bender to Scholarship Benefactor, February 1905, A. Bender, student file, HUA; Molin, "Training the Hand," 95.
41. A. Bender to Mrs. Pierce, May 4, 1903, A. Bender, student file, HUA; Molin, "Training the Hand," 95.
42. Molin, "Training the Hand"; Spack, "English, Pedagogy, and Ideology."
43. Molin, "Training the Hand."
44. Emery, "Writing against Erasure."
45. E. Bender, "From Hampton to New York," *Talks and Thoughts*, February 1905, HUA, 3.
46. Molin, "Training the Hand."

47. For more on Natives working for the Indian Service, see Cahill, *Federal Fathers and Mothers*.
48. Molin, "Training the Hand," 98.
49. E. Bender to Hampton Endeavors, January 6, 1913, CFPC.
50. E. Bender to Caroline Andrus, October 22, 1914, CFPC.
51. Bender, "Hampton Graduate's Experience," CFPC, 112, 109.
52. Bender, "Hampton Graduate's Experience," CFPC, 112.
53. L. Tetzloff, "Elizabeth Bender Cloud," 85.
54. E. Bender to Caroline Andrus, E. Bender, student file, June 2, 1915, HUA.
55. DeCora, "Angel DeCora."
56. E. Bender, "Training Indian Girls."
57. Maddox, *Citizen Indians*; Batker, *Reforming Fictions*.
58. E. Bender, "Training Indian Girls," 155.
59. Hale, "Acceptance and Rejection."
60. Harold Buchannan, interview by Robin Butterfield, n.d., CFPC.
61. H. Cloud to M. Roe, August 6, 1916, CFPC; Ramirez, "From Henry Roe Cloud."
62. Madigan, "Education of Girls."
63. "Girls to Join Indian School," *Wichita Beacon*, July 22, 1932, CFPC.
64. Hughes, interview April 22, 1987, CFPC; Fahnestock and Sorci, "Roe Cloud," CFPC, ch. 3, p. 6.
65. Hughes, interview, September 15, 1987, CFPC.
66. Hughes, interview, September 15, 1987, CFPC; Fahnestock and Sorci, "Roe Cloud," CFPC, ch. 3, p. 21.
67. Pawnee council meeting minutes, untitled, April 22, 1927, CFPC.
68. Pawnee council meeting minutes, untitled, April 22, 1927, CFPC.
69. Robertson, *Power of Land*.
70. Freire, *Pedagogy of the Oppressed*.
71. H. Cloud, "Graduation Speech," CFPC.
72. Deloria and Lytle, *Nations Within*.
73. H. Cloud, "Graduation Speech," CFPC.
74. Helene Lincoln, informal interview by Renya Ramirez, July 15, 2001, CFPC.
75. Fahnestock and Sorci, "Roe Cloud," CFPC, ch. 3, p. 24.
76. Cuban, *How Teachers Taught*.
77. Woesha Cloud North, "Autobiography of a Winnebago-Ojibwa Family," n.d., CFPC; Crum, "Henry Roe Cloud"; for a discussion of Ho-Chunk powwows, see Arndt, *Ho-Chunk Powwows*.
78. See H. Cloud, "Winnebago Story," n.d., CFPC.
79. For a discussion of Indigenous philosophy, see, for example, Martinez, *Dakota Philosopher*; see also North, "Informal Education," and North's discussion of

Ho-Chunk stories as traditional Ho-Chunk education that encourages Ho-Chunk children to behave appropriately.

80. Hughes, interview, April 27, 1987, CFPC; Fahnestock and Sorci, "Roe Cloud," CFPC, ch. 3, p. 21.

81. H. Cloud, untitled, August 13, 1931, CFPC, 1–4.

82. Rosaldo, *Culture and Truth.*

83. For more discussions on Native-studies programs and curriculum, see, for example, Champagne and Stauss, *Native American Studies*; and Forbes et. al, "Hemispheric Approach," in Champagne and Stauss, *Native American Studies*, 97–123. The authors argue that traditional Native American–studies scholars before colonization searched for knowledge and wisdom that could be relied on to live in balance with one another and all living things. With the coming of the Europeans, Native studies changed to deal with the onslaught of colonialism. An early Indigenous-studies scholar is Felipe Huaman Poma de Ayala, an Incan Quechua-speaking scholar who wrote about the Spanish invasion before and after 1600; see North, "Informal Education." Henry Cloud's daughter, Woesha Cloud North, discusses how Ho-Chunk stories were fundamental to Ho-Chunk traditional education.

84. See Bailey, "UC Davis Scholar." Forbes helped develop Native-studies programs after Indigenous activism in the 1960s. See also Goodwin, "Without Destroying Ourselves." Goodwin argues that Henry Cloud's Native leadership training was an early example of Native-studies pedagogy. Forbes et. al, "A Hemispheric Approach," in Champagne and Stauss, *Native American Studies*, 97–123.

85. E. Bender to Andrus, May 12, 1919; February 28, 1917; April, 19, 1923, CFPC.

86. Robert North, interview, March 25, 1988, CFPC.

87. E. Bender to Mother Townsend, E. Bender, student file, January 14, 1920, HUA.

88. E. Bender to H. Cloud, March 12, 1920, CFPC; Ramirez, "From Henry Roe Cloud.".

89. E. Bender to H. Cloud, March 23, 1920, CFPC; Ramirez, "From Henry Roe Cloud."

90. E. Bender to H. Cloud, March 23, 1920, CFPC.

91. M. Roe to H. Cloud, December 21, 1919, CFPC.

92. Hughes, interview by Thomas Sorci, n.d., CFPC.

93. Cloud North, interview, August 15, 1987, CFPC.

94. *Wichita Eagle*, untitled, June 6, 1933, CFPC.

95. H. Cloud to Edna R. Voss, May 15, 1934, folder: "American Indian Institute," PHSA; J. Tetzloff, "To Do Some Good," 207.

96. "Script," *Northwest Neighbors* radio program, April 11, 1945, Portland OR, CFPC.

3. HENRY CLOUD'S ROLE

1. "Script," *Northwest Neighbors* radio program, April 11, 1945, Portland OR, CFPC.

2. Edward E. Dale to Lewis Meriam, folder 11, box 45, October 9, 1928, WHC.

3. J. Tetzloff "To Do Some Good."

4. Meriam, *Problem of Indian Administration*, 81, 72.

5. Parman, "Lewis Meriam's Letters."

6. J. Tetzloff, "To Do Some Good."

7. H. Cloud, "Rosebud Boarding School Report," n.d., CFPC.

8. H. Cloud, "Yankton Indian School Report," n.d., CFPC.

9. See books and films on Indian boarding schools, for example, Lomawaima, *Prairie Light*; Child, *Boarding School Seasons*; Adams, *Education for Extinction*; and Gibbons and Thomas, *Residential School Experience*. See Jacobs, *White Mother*, for a discussion of the linkage between settler colonialism and federal boarding schools.

10. Wolfe, "Elimination of the Native."

11. Meriam to Dale, September 25, 1928, WHC; Fahnestock and Sorci, "Roe Cloud," CFPC, ch. 5, p. 6.

12. Young, *Politics of Difference*.

13. Dale to Meriam, October 9, 1928, WHC; Fahnestock and Sorci, "Roe Cloud," CFPC, ch. 5, p. 7.

14. See Meriam to Dale, October 29, 1928, WHC. In this letter to Dale, Meriam discusses correspondence he had received from Cloud asking for the endorsement from the survey staff to become commissioner of Indian affairs.

15. Meriam to H. Cloud, October 26, 1928; copy sent to Dale, WHC; Fahnestock and Sorci, "Roe Cloud," CFPC, ch. 5, pp. 7–8.

16. Dale to Meriam, November 1, 1928, WHC; Fahnestock and Sorci, "Roe Cloud," CFPC, ch. 5, p. 8.

17. Dale to Meriam, February 21, 1929, WHC.

18. Meriam to Dale, February 18, 1929, WHC.

19. Dale to Meriam, October 9, 1928; February 21, 1929, WHC.

20. W. North, interview, August 15, 1987, CFPC.

21. Critchlow, "Lewis Meriam."

22. Parman, "Lewis Meriam's Letters"; J. Tetzloff, "To Do Some Good," 66–67.

23. "Roe Cloud Endorsed by Navajos," *Gallup Independent* 44, no. 29 (1933), CFPC.

24. Crum, "Henry Roe Cloud,"

25. Hughes, interview by Sorci and Fahnestock, n.d., CFPC.

26. Hughes, interview by Sorci and Fahnestock, n.d., CFPC.

27. Hughes, interview by Sorci and Fahnestock, n.d., CFPC; Fahnestock and Sorci, "Roe Cloud," CFPC, chs. 9–10. The engraving is a line from "Work," a poem by Henry Van Dyke.

28. J. Tetzloff, "To Do Some Good," 75; Ramirez, "Henry Roe Cloud."

29. R. North, interview, March 25, 1988, CFPC.

30. Philp, *John Collier's Crusade*; Kelly, *Assault on Assimilation*.

31. Hughes, interview, April 27, 1987, CFPC.

32. Samuel Anderson to H. Cloud, September 12, 1933, August–November 1933, box 135, RG 75, BIA-K.

33. Warren, *Quest for Citizenship.*

34. Jacobs, *White Mother.*

35. Stoler, "Tense and Tender Ties," 830; Stoler, *Carnal Knowledge*, 10; Hurtado, *Intimate Frontiers*, xxix. Hurtado refers to "intimate frontiers" as "frontiers of the mind, frontiers of the heart, frontiers of difference."

36. Warren, *Quest for Citizenship.*

37. H. Cloud, "Her New Frontiers," 14, 16, 15.

38. J. Tetzloff, "To Do Some Good," 126–27.

39. H. Cloud to E. C. Little, September 12, 1933, file: "Henry Roe Cloud Correspondence," BIA-K.

40. H. Cloud to Commissioner of Indian Affairs, November 24, 1933, file: "Henry Roe Cloud Correspondence," BIA-K.

41. Albert Hensley to H. Cloud, November 11, 1933, file: "Henry Roe Cloud Correspondence," BIA-K.

42. H. Cloud to A. Hensley, November 23, 1933, file: "Henry Roe Cloud Correspondence," BIA-K.

43. H. Cloud, "The Wheeler-Howard Bill," speech, April 10, 1934, Pine Ridge Indian Reservation, South Dakota, folder 45: "Addresses and Speeches," box 160, RG 75, BIA-K; Carlson, *Indians, Bureaucrats, and Land*; Otis, *Dawes Act.*

44. H. Cloud, "Wheeler-Howard Bill."

45. As white settlers greedily snatched up more and more land, the earth, our mother, could no longer care for us by providing animals to hunt, plants to eat, or botanical medicine to heal us. Our loss of connection to our mother and our lands also broke our spirit, and this combined emotional and physical illness made us sick, causing us to die too soon.

46. Minutes, meeting held by H. Cloud, April 9, 1934, Wanblee, South Dakota, folder 45: "Addresses and Speeches," box 160, RG 75, BIA-K.

47. McDonnell, *Dispossession.*

48. For more discussion regarding economic culture, see Champagne, "Economic Culture," in T. Anderson, *Property Rights*, 195–213.

49. H. Cloud, "Wheeler-Howard Bill," BIA-K; H. Cloud, speech, April 10, 1934, ECW Camp, Allen, South Dakota, folder 45: "Addresses and Speeches," box 160, RG 75, BIA-K.

50. "Script," *Northwest Neighbors* radio program, April 11, 1945, Portland OR, CFPC.

51. Deloria and Lytle, *Nations Within*, 66–80.

52. "Script," *Northwest Neighbors* radio program, April 11, 1945, Portland OR, CFPC.

53. H. Cloud, "Anthropologist's View," CFPC.

54. Deloria and Lytle, *Nations Within.*

55. John Collier to William O. Roberts, April 17, 1934, Central Classified Rosebud Decimal 066-File 56439-33, RG 75, BIA-W; Clow, Indian Reorganization Act"; Kalt and Singer, "Myths and Realities."
56. Kalt and Singer, "Myths and Realities."
57. Deloria and Lytle, *Nations Within*.
58. Prucha, *Great Father*, 324–25.
59. "Script," *Northwest Neighbors* radio program, April 11, 1945, Portland OR, CFPC.
60. "Dr. Roe Cloud Wins Achievement Award," *Indian Leader*, October 11, 1935, CFPC.
61. Buchannan, interview by R. Butterfield, August, 1988, CFPC.
62. Buchannan, interview by R. Butterfield, August, 1988, CFPC.
63. "Script," *Northwest Neighbors* radio program, April 11, 1945, Portland OR, CFPC.

4. THE CLOUDS AT UMATILLA

1. Antone Minthorn; Viola Wocatse; Sonny Picard; Margarite Red Elk; Elizie Farrow, interviews, July 14–27, 1988, CFPC.
2. Hughes, interview, May 14, 1987, CFPC.
3. Luce and Johnson, "Modern Tribal Governance," in Karson, *As Days Go By*, 151–71.
4. Wolfe, "Elimination of the Native"; Palmer and Rundstrom, "Internal Colonialism."
5. Luce and Johnson, "Modern Tribal Governance," in Karson, *As Days Go By*, 151–71.
6. Hughes, interview, May 14, 1987, CFPC.
7. H. Cloud to Commissioner of Indian Affairs, attention E. J. Skidmore, March 12, 1940, CFPC; Fahnestock and Sorci, "Roe Cloud," CFPC, ch. 7, p. 16.
8. Cahill, *Federal Fathers and Mothers*, 137.
9. R. North, interview, March 25, 1988, CFPC.
10. John Blackhawk, interview by Renya Ramirez, August 20, 2011, CFPC.
11. Jon Greendeer, interview by Ramirez, August 15, 2011, CFPC.
12. Hughes, interview, May 14, 1987, CFPC.
13. Leah Conner, interview, July 25, 1988, CFPC.
14. Hughes, interview, May 14, 1987, CFPC.
15. H. Cloud, handwritten sermon, n.d., reference to war indicates it was given sometime from 1942 to 1945, CFPC.
16. Wolfe, "Elimination of the Native"; Jacobs, *White Mother*; Glenn, "Settler Colonialism as Structure."
17. Jacobs, *White Mother*; Arvin, Tuck, and Morrill, "Decolonizing Feminism"; Morgensen, *Spaces between Us*.
18. H. Cloud to Commissioner of Indian Affairs, draft letter, February 2, 1940, CFPC; Fahnestock and Sorci, "Roe Cloud," CFPC, ch. 7, pp. 18–19.

19. Moses, *Wild West Shows.*
20. Furlong, *Let 'er Buck*; Fahnestock and Sorci, "Roe Cloud," CFPC, ch. 7, p. 17.
21. D. McCall, *Ranch under the Rimrock*, 58–59.
22. Waggoner, *Happy Canyon.*
23. H. Cloud to Commissioner of Indian Affairs, draft letter, February 2, 1940, CFPC; Fahnestock and Sorci, "Roe Cloud," CFPC, ch. 7, pp. 19–20.
24. Foucault, *Discipline and Punish.*
25. Goeman, "Introduction to Indigenous Performances."
26. L. Tetzloff, "Elizabeth Bender Cloud"; L. Tetzloff, "Indian Remain Indian."
27. L. Tetzloff, "Elizabeth Bender Cloud"; L. Tetzloff, "Indian Remain Indian."
28. Jacobs, *White Mother.*
29. Conner, interview, July 25, 1988; Conner, interview by Ramirez, July 1, 2010, CFPC.
30. Kinser, *Motherhood and Feminism*, 61.
31. Conner, interview, July 25, 1988; July 1, 2010, CFPC.
32. E. Bender to "Dear Bee," September 15, 1942, CFPC; Fahnestock and Sorci, "Roe Cloud," CFPC, ch. 7, pp. 69–70.
33. Page to H. and E. Cloud, 1942, CFPC.
34. H. Cloud to Page, September 28, 1942, CFPC; Fahnestock and Sorci, "Roe Cloud," CFPC, ch. 7, pp. 70–71.
35. Fahnestock and Sorci, "Roe Cloud," CFPC, ch. 7, p. 73.
36. Ramirez, "From Henry Roe Cloud."
37. H. Cloud to Page, September 24, 1944, CFPC.
38. Furness, "Challenging the Myth," in Coombes, *Rethinking Settler Colonialism*, 172–92.
39. Jones et al., *Big Voice*; Walker, *Every Warrior*; D. Smith, *Folklore*; North, "Informal Education"; Hinzo, Voicing across Space."
40. Elsie Dickson, "Indians Heap Provoked Blonde Writer 'The Hat' May Lose Part of Scalp," [late 1946 or early 1947?], unidentified newspaper clipping, probably *East Oregonian* or *Oregon Journal*, CFPC.
41. Fahnestock and Sorci, "Roe Cloud," CFPC, ch. 7, pp. 23–24.
42. Wolfe, "Elimination of the Native"; Jacobs, *White Mother.*
43. L. Tetzloff, "Elizabeth Bender Cloud."
44. J. Tetzloff, "To Do Some Good," 172; Fisher, *Tangled Nets.*
45. H. Cloud, "Remarks," speech to Wildlife Society, Pendleton OR, October 10, 1941, CFPC.
46. Raleigh Butterfield, interview, March 24, 1988, CFPC.
47. M. A. Johnson to Commissioner of Indian Affairs, with copy to Cloud, August 17, 1939, CFPC; Fahnestock and Sorci, "Roe Cloud," CFPC, ch. 7, p. 61.
48. May et al., *Salmon Is Everything.*

49. Hernandez, "Agents of Pollination"; Silko, *Gardens in the Dunes.*
50. H. Cloud memo, January 5, 1944, CFPC; Fahnestock and Sorci, "Roe Cloud," CFPC, ch. 7, p. 63.
51. Wilkins and Lomawaima, *Uneven Ground,* 125.
52. Fisher, "Tangled Nets."
53. Fisher, "Tangled Nets."
54. J. Tetzloff, "To Do Some Good," 175.
55. J. Tetzloff, "To Do Some Good," 175–76; Donald L. Parman, "The Tulee Decision," paper delivered at the 1994 Pacific Northwest History Conference, March 22, 1994, Bellingham WA, 5; Walter Woehlke to M. A. Johnson, October 21, 1940, folder: "Celilo Fishing," box 4, RG 75, Umatilla Agency Records, BIA-S.
56. H. Cloud, interview, ca. late 1949–early 1950, CFPC.
57. Fisher, "Tangled Nets."
58. H. Cloud, interview, ca. late 1949–early 1950, CFPC.
59. J. Tetzloff, "To Do Some Good," 176; Fisher, "Tangled Nets."
60. C. R. Whitlock and others to the Commissioner of Indian Affairs, John Collier, August 18, 1934, folder: "Hunting and Fishing as Pertains to Celilo, 1932–36," box 4, RG 75, Umatilla Agency Records, BIA-S; J. Tetzloff, "To Do Some Good," 177.
61. J. Tetzloff, "To Do Some Good," 177.
62. H. Cloud, "Sampson Tulee Supreme Court Decision and It's Implication on Conservation of Wildlife on Indian Reservations" (paper presented at Superintendents' Conference, December 8–9, 1944, Portland OR), CFPC.
63. Edmonds, "Urban Strategies."
64. H. Cloud, "Sampson Tulee," CFPC.
65. H. Cloud, "Sampson Tulee," CFPC.
66. H. Cloud, "Sampson Tulee," CFPC.
67. H. Cloud, "Sampson Tulee," CFPC.
68. Wilkins and Lomawaima, *Uneven Ground*; V. Deloria, *Behind the Trail*; Deloria and Wilkins, *Constitutional Tribulations.*
69. J. Tetzloff, "To Do Some Good," 172; "Winnebago Graduate of Yale Named Dr. Henry Roe Cloud, Nebraska Boy under Babcock, His Successor," *Eastern Oregonian,* July 29, 1939.
70. Jack Forbes, for example, helped to found Deganawidah-Quetzacoatl University (DQ University), a two-year Indigenous university, in 1971 and was a co-founder of Native American Studies at UC Davis. See Bailey, "UC Davis Scholar."
71. Tribal Council meeting, minutes, December 22, 1939, folder 064: "Councils, Tribal Misc. 1935–41," box 9, RG 75, Umatilla Agency Records, BIA-S; J. Tetzloff, "To Do Some Good," 184.
72. J. Tetzloff, "To Do Some Good."

73. Coordination Council of Northwest Superintendents, quarterly meeting, minutes, March 8, 1940, Chemawa Tribal Councils, 1940, box 1541, RG 75, Tribal Operations Branch General Subject Files, Portland Area Office, BIA-S; J. Tetzloff, "To Do Some Good," 185–86.

74. Tribal Council meeting, minutes, November 24, 1941, cover letter, H. Cloud to J. Collier, January 7, 1942, CFPC; Fahnestock and Sorci, "Roe Cloud," CFPC, ch. 7, pp. 38–39, 44.

75. Regular Tribal Council meeting, minutes, December 15, 1944; May 26, 1944, folder 064: "Tribal Council Meetings, 1944," box 12, RG 75, Umatilla Agency Records, BIA-S; J. Tetzloff, "To Do Some Good," 186–87.

76. Luce and Johnson, "Modern Tribal Governance," Karson, As Days Go By, 151–71.

77. Doris Bounds, interview, July 24–27, 1988, CFPC.

78. For Jim Kanine's complaints against Cloud, see Kanine to President Roosevelt, April 18, 1941, file 25692-41-155, box 274, Umatilla Records, Central Classified Files, 1940–43, RG 75, BIA-W. For one example of Barnhart's complaints, see Cloud to William Zimmerman, March 31, 1942, file 3-42-155, box 274, BIA-W; J. Tetzloff, "To Do Some Good," 187.

79. Tribal Council meeting, minutes, February 1, 1946; March 5, 1946, folder: "Tribal Council Minutes, 1946 (Part 1)," box 12, RG 75, Umatilla Agency Records, BIA-S; J. Tetzloff, "To Do Some Good," 188–89.

80. Cornell, Return of the Native, 156

81. J. Tetzloff, "To Do Some Good," 188.

82. H. Cloud, "Confidential Report and Recommendations on the Candidacy of Charles Luce, Attorney, for Tribal Attorney for the Confederated Tribes of the Umatilla Reservation," March 1948, file 37222-47-174, box 130, Umatilla Agency, Central Classified Files, BIA-W; J. Tetzloff, "To Do Some Good," 189.

83. E. Morgan Pryse to John H. Provinse, Assistant to the Commissioner of Indian Affairs, March 12, 1948; J. Tetzloff, "To Do Some Good," 190–91.

84. Sheridan Z. Fahnestock, notes, July 11, 1988, CFPC.

85. "Tribal Bill Covers Land," Oregonian, January 29, 1951, CFPC; Fahnestock and Sorci, "Roe Cloud," CFPC, ch. 9, p. 3.

86. H. Cloud to L. P. Towle, July 1, 1949, folder 051: "Reports, Annual Progress Grand-Ronde-Siletz Administration, 1949," box 52, Grand Ronde Siletz Agency Records, RG 75, BIA-S; J. Tetzloff, "To Do Some Good," 192.

87. R. C. Butterfield, interview, March 24, 1988, CFPC.

88. H. Cloud, interview, n.d., CFPC.

89. "Oregon Indians Win Land Claim of $16,515,604," Oregonian, January 4, 1950, CFPC.

90. "Gold Rush, 1950 Style, Is On! Coast Indians Speaking Up for Share of $16 Million Award," Oregon Sunday Journal, January 8, 1950, CFPC.

91. "Four Oregon Tribes Ask U.S. for $65,000,000 for Lands Illegally Claimed by Settlers," *Oregonian*, October 21, 1947, CFPC.

92. J. Tetzloff, "To Do Some Good," 191.

93. Pryse to Acting Commissioner of Indian Affairs, telegram, October 28, 1948, CFPC; Fahnestock and Sorci, "Roe Cloud," CFPC, ch. 9, p. 6.

94. W. North, interview, August 15, 1987, CFPC.

95. Gretchen Freed-Rowland, interview, May 10, 1988, CFPC.

96. H. Cloud to Francis LaFrances, October 17, 1949, CFPC; Fahnestock and Sorci, "Roe Cloud," CFPC, ch. 9, pp. 25–26.

5. ELIZABETH BENDER CLOUD

1. Maddox, *Citizen Indians*.

2. Ness, *Encyclopedia*, 703.

3. L. Tetzloff, "Elizabeth Bender Cloud."

4. L. Tetzloff, "Elizabeth Bender Cloud."

5. Cowger, *National Congress*.

6. Beaulieu, "Place among Nations," in Clark, *Minnesota*, 397–433.

7. See Fixico, *Termination and Relocation*; and Burt, *Tribalism in Crisis*.

8. Cowger, *National Congress*, 100.

9. Philp, "Termination."

10. Beaulieu, "Place among Nations," in Clark, *Minnesota*, 397–433.

11. Prucha, *Great Father*.

12. Kinser, *Motherhood and Feminism*.

13. Kim Anderson, *Life Stages*.

14. "Mrs. Henry Roe Cloud Oregon Mother of '50," *Oregon Journal*, April 5, 1950, CFPC; Fahnestock and Sorci, "Roe Cloud," CFPC, ch. 10, pp. 2–3.

15. Lillian Alberta Cloud Freed to Page, March 20, 1950, CFPC; Fahnestock and Sorci, "Roe Cloud," CFPC, ch. 10, p. 2.

16. Page to Golden Rule Foundation, April 12, 1950, CFPC; Fahnestock and Sorci, "Roe Cloud," CFPC, ch. 10, p. 4.

17. "Mrs. Roe Cloud 'Princess' Now," *Oregonian*, June 20, 1950; Minnesota Chippewa Tribal Executive Committee Resolution, November 6, 1950, CFPC; Fahnestock and Sorci, "Roe Cloud," CFPC, ch. 10, p. 13; Elizabeth's being honored as an Indian princess is interesting. The Indian princess stereotype includes Native women who are lighter, more assimilated, and helpers of whites, whereas the savage drudge stereotype pertains to Native women who are uncivilized, savage, and antagonistic to whites. This "Indian princess" honoring could allude to Elizabeth being viewed as closer to modern and a "good Indian" instead of a "bad Indian." See Green, "Pocahontas Perplex."

18. "Indian Woman Wins U.S. 'Mother Award," *Christian Science Monitor*, April 28, 1950, file: "Elizabeth Roe Cloud," box 68, NMAI.

19. "The American Mother of 1950" and "Mothers of the United Nations," *International Mothers' Digest* 1, no. 1 (1950), file: "Elizabeth Roe Cloud," box 68, NMAI.

20. "Script," *Northwest Neighbors* radio program, April 11, 1945, Portland OR, CFPC.

21. "Mother of Year Happy at "Fair Deal for Indians," May 20, 1950, no newspaper identified, file: "Elizabeth Roe Cloud," box 68, NMAI; Bomberry, "Indigenous Memory and Imagination."

22. Mrs. Henry Roe Cloud, "Acceptance Remarks," file: "Elizabeth Roe Cloud," box 68, NMAI.

23. Richard L. Neuberger, "Religion Is Dominant Influence in Life of Elizabeth Roe Cloud, American Mother of the Year—'Wonderful Woman, True Leader,'" *Post Dispatch*, n.d., CFPC; Fahnestock and Sorci, "Roe Cloud," CFPC, ch. 10, p. 9.

24. Kat Anderson, *Tending the Wild*.

25. Neuberger, "Religion Is Dominant Influence"; Fahnestock and Sorci, "Roe Cloud," CFPC, ch. 10, pp. 9–11.

26. Cloud North, memoir notes, n.d., CFPC.

27. Buffalohead, "Farmers, Warriors, Traders."

28. Cloud North, memoir notes, n.d., CFPC.

29. "Mother of Year Title Awarded to Half-Indian," *New York Herald Tribune*, April 28, 1950, CFPC.

30. Ramirez, *Native Hubs*.

31. Washington Merry-Go-Round, *Newport News*, June 4, 1950, CFPC.

32. "Mothers as Good or Better Than Ever, Says 'Champion,'" *Wichita Eagle*, June 4, 1950, CFPC.

33. Kinser, *Motherhood and Feminism*, 52–53.

34. "Indian Hope Gets Support," *Oregonian*, October 1, 1950, CFPC.

35. "American Mother of the Year Enjoyed Audience with Queen," *Wichita Eagle*, October 30, 1950, CFPC; Fahnestock and Sorci, "Roe Cloud," ch. 10, pp. 17–18, CFPC.

36. Thrush, *Indigenous London*.

37. E. Cloud, "Parents Declared to Hold Key to Democratic World," *Oregonian*, n.d., PHSA; L. Tetzloff, "Elizabeth Bender Cloud."

38. Proceedings of the Sixtieth Annual Convention of the General Federation of Women's Clubs, May 1951, Houston, GFWCH, 40; L. Tetzloff, "Elizabeth Bender Cloud."

39. Indian Council Fire, information sheet, n.d., CFPC; Fahnestock and Sorci, "Roe Cloud," CFPC, ch. 10, p. 17.

40. Indian Achievement Award winners, information book, n.d., CFPC; Fahnestock and Sorci, "Roe Cloud," CFPC, ch. 10, p. 17.

41. Cowger, *National Congress*, 123.

42. E. Bender, "New Frontiers for the American Indian," 1950–52, file: "Program Records," box 3, GFWCH.

43. Cowger, *National Congress*, 123.

44. "Antagonism Rife over Indian Policy," *New York Times*, November 2, 1951, CFPC; Fahnestock and Sorci, "Roe Cloud," CFPC, ch. 10, p. 22.

45. E. Bender, "New Frontiers for the American Indian," 1950–52, file: "Program Records," box 3, GFWCH.

46. E. Bender, "Charter of Indian Rights," 1950–52, file: "Program Records," box 4, GFWCH.

47. Elizabeth Roe Cloud, "Statement by Participants," guest editorial, *Amerindian*, September–October 1953, CFPC.

48. Elizabeth Roe Cloud, "Statement by Participants"; Fahnestock and Sorci, "Roe Cloud," CFPC, ch. 10, pp. 32–33.

49. E. Bender to Marion, Ed, Buzz, and Mark Hughes, June 22, 1953, CFPC.

50. E. Bender to Sophie Van S. Thies, May 18, 1954, file: "Elizabeth Bender Cloud," box 68, NMAI.

51. E. Bender to Helen Peterson, May 26, 1954, file: "Elizabeth Bender Cloud," box 68, NMAI.

52. E. Bender, "Six Weeks: Field Visits to Indian Communities in California and Arizona," file: "Elizabeth Bender Cloud," box 68, NMAI.

53. Some Native feminist texts include Ramirez, "Tribal Nation"; A. Smith, "Native American Feminism"; Suzack et al., *Indigenous Women and Feminism*; Goeman and Denetdale, "Native Feminisms"; A. Smith, *Conquest*; and Shanley, "Thoughts on Indian Feminism."

54. E. Bender to Douglas McKay, November 21, 1952, CFPC; Fahnestock and Sorci, "Roe Cloud," CFPC, ch. 10, pp. 23–24.

55. E. Bender to McKay, November 21, 1952, CFPC; Fahnestock and Sorci, "Roe Cloud," CFPC, ch. 10, p. 24.

56. Cowger, *National Congress*.

57. E. Bender to McKay, November 21, 1952, CFPC; Fahnestock and Sorci, "Roe Cloud," CFPC, ch. 10, p. 24.

58. Woody Crumbo to McKay, January 5, 1953, CFPC; Fahnestock and Sorci, "Roe Cloud," CFPC, ch. 10, p. 25.

59. "Indian Leader Gives Support to Emmons," *Gallup Independent*, June 13, 1953, CFPC; Fahnestock and Sorci, "Roe Cloud," CFPC, ch. 10, pp. 26–27.

60. Cowger, *National Congress*, 110.

61. Swift, *Chief Bender's Burden*.

62. Cowger, *National Congress*, 111.

63. Cowger, *National Congress*, 110–12.

64. E. Bender, "Policy Statement on American Indian Legislation," February 27, 1954, file: "Committees and Special Issues," box 257, NMAI.

65. E. Bender to Helen Peterson, March 30, 1954, file: "Elizabeth Bender Cloud," box 68, NMAI.

66. E. Bender to Louis Bruce, January 5, 1956, CFPC; Fahnestock and Sorci, "Roe Cloud," CFPC, ch. 10, p. 43.

67. Zelma Zimmerman to E. Bender, September 26, 1954, CFPC; Fahnestock and Sorci, "Roe Cloud," CFPC, ch. 10, p. 43.

68. "Parade Scenario," unknown newspaper, 115, file: "1965 Inaugural Committee Records," box 38, LBJL, 115, located by librarian Katherine Frankum; Fahnestock and Sorci, "Roe Cloud," CFPC, ch. 10, p. 49.

69. "Honored Indian Woman Dies at 77 in Portland," *Oregonian*, September 19, 1965, CFPC.

CONCLUSION

1. See Ramirez, *Native Hubs*, for a discussion of Roberts's notion of the hub.

2. Ramirez, *Native Hubs*.

3. W. North, interview, August 15, 1987, CFPC. When Natives called him a "white bull with a red face," my mother, Woesha, said, it "crushed" her dad.

4. J. Tetzloff, "To Do Some Good."

5. "Script," *Northwest Neighbors* radio program, April 11, 1945, Portland OR, CFPC.

6. Washington Merry-Go-Round, *Newport News*, June 4, 1950, CFPC.

BIBLIOGRAPHY

UNPUBLISHED SOURCES

American Indian Institute. Papers. Presbyterian Historical Society Archives (PHSA), Philadelphia.

Bender, Elizabeth, and Anna Bender. Student files. Hampton University Archive (HUA), Hampton VA.

Cloud, Henry. Student file. Northfield Mount Herman School Archives (NMHSA), Mount Herman MA.

Cloud, Henry Roe. Personal Correspondence. Bureau of Indian Affairs (BIA-K). National Archives and Records Administration, Kansas City MO.

Cloud Family. Papers. Cloud family's private collection (CFPC).

Dale, Edward E., Papers. Western History Collections (WHC). University of Oklahoma, Norman.

General Federation of Women's Clubs. Papers. Indian Affairs Division. General Federation of Women's Clubs Headquarters (GFWCH), Washington DC.

Inaugural Committee. Records. Lyndon Baines Johnson Library (LBJL). University of Texas, Austin.

National Congress of American Indians. Papers. Cultural Resource Center. National Museum of the American Indian (NMAI), Washington DC.

Reel, Estelle. Papers. Wyoming State Archives (WSA), Cheyenne.

Roe Family. Papers. Sterling Library (SL). Yale University, New Haven CT.

Society of American Indians Archives (SAIA). Newberry Library, Chicago.

Tomah and Kiowa Agencies. Records. Bureau of Indian Affairs (BIA-W). National Archives and Records Administration, Washington DC.

Umatilla Agency. Portland Area Office Records. Bureau of Indian Affairs (BIA-S). National Archives and Records Administration, Seattle.

Ackley, Kristina, and Cristina Stanciu. *Laura Cornelius Kellogg: Our Democracy and the American Indian and Other Works*. Syracuse: Syracuse University Press, 2015.

Adams, David Wallace. *Education for Extinction: American Indians and the Boarding School Experience, 1875–1928*. Lawrence: University Press of Kansas, 1995.

Anderson, Kat. *Tending the Wild: Native American Knowledge and the Management of California's Natural Resources*. Berkeley: University of California Press, 2013.

Anderson, Kim. *Life Stages and Native Women: Memory, Teachings, and Story Medicine*. Winnipeg: University of Manitoba Press, 2011.

Anderson, Virginia. *Creatures of Empire: How Domestic Animals Transformed Early America*. New York. Oxford University Press, 2004.

Anthony, David, Tyeeme Clark, and Joane Nagle. "White Men, Red Masks: Appropriations of 'Indian' Manhood in Imagined Wests." In Basso, McCall, and Garceau, *Across the Great Divide*, 109–30.

Appadurai, Arjun. "Putting Hierarchy in Its Place." *Cultural Anthropology* 3, no. 1 (1988): 36–49.

Arndt, Grant. *Ho-Chunk Powwows and the Politics of Tradition*. Lincoln: University of Nebraska Press, 2016.

Arvin, Maile, Eve Tuck, and Angie Morrill. "Decolonizing Feminism: Challenging Connections between Settler Colonialism and Hetereopatriarchy." *Feminist Formations* 25, no. 1 (2013): 8–34.

Avalos, Natalie, Sandy Grande, Jason Mancini, Rijuta Mehta, Michelle Neely, and Christopher Newell. "Standing with Standing Rock." *Cultural Anthropology*. December 22, 2016. https://culanth.org/fieldsights/1024-standing-with-standingrock.

Bailey, Pat. "UC Davis Scholar Jack Forbes Advocated for Indigenous People." February 25, 2011. UC Davis. www.ucdavis.edu/news/uc-davis-scholar-jack-forbes-advocated-indigenous-peoples/.

Ballinger, Franchot. *Living Sideways: Tricksters in American Indian Oral Tradition*. Norman: University of Oklahoma Press, 2004.

Barker, Joanne. *Native Acts: Law, Recognition, and Cultural Authenticity*. Durham: Duke University Press, 2011.

Basso, Matthew, Laura McCall, and Dee Garceau, eds. *Across the Great Divide: Culture of Manhood in the American West*. New York: Routledge, 2001.

Batker, Carol. *Reforming Fictions: Native, African, and Jewish American Women's Literature and Journalism in the Progressive Era*. New York: Columbia University Press, 2000.

Beaulieu, David. "A Place Among Nations: Experiences Among Indian People." In *Minnesota in a Century of Change: The State and Its People Since 1900*, edited by Clifford Clark Jr., 397–433. Saint Paul: Minnesota Historical Society, 1989.

Bender, Elizabeth. "A Hampton Graduate's Experience." *Southern Workman*, June 1916, 109–12.

———. "Training Indian Girls for Efficient Home Makers." *Red Man* 8, no. 5 (1916): 154–55.

Berkhofer, Robert. *The White Man's Indian: Images of the American Indian from Columbus to Press.* New York: Knopf, 1978.

Bhabha, Homi. "Foreword to the 1986 Edition." In Fanon, *Black Skin, White Masks,* xxi–xxxvii.

———. *The Location of Culture.* New York: Routledge, 2004.

Blaeser, Kimberly. *Gerald Vizenor: Writing in the Oral Tradition.* Norman: University of Oklahoma Press, 1996.

———. *Stories Migrating Home: A Collection of Anishinaabe Prose,* edited by Kimberly Blaeser. Bemidjii, MN: Loonfeather, 1999.

Bobroff, Kenneth. "Retelling Allotment: Indian Property and the Myth of Common Ownership." *Vanderbilt Law Review* 54, no. 4 (2001): 1559–623.

Bomberry, Victoria. "Indigenous Memory and Imagination: Thinking beyond the Nation." PhD diss., Stanford University, 2001.

Bonnin, Gertrude, Charles Fabens, and Matthew Sniffen. *Oklahoma's Poor Rich Indians: An Orgy of Graft and Exploitation of the Five Civilized Tribes; Legalized Robbery.* Philadelphia: Office of the Indian Rights Association, 1924.

Briggs, Laura. *Reproducing Empire: Race, Sex, Science, and U.S. Imperialism in Puerto Rico.* Berkeley: University of California Press, 2002.

Bruyneel, Kevin. *The Third Space of Sovereignty: Postcolonial Politics of U.S.-Indigenous Relations.* Minneapolis: University of Minnesota Press, 2007.

Buffalohead, Patricia. "Farmers, Warriors, Traders: A Fresh Look at Ojibway Women." *Minnesota History* 48, no. 6 (1983): 236–44.

Burt, Larry. *Tribalism in Crisis: Federal Indian Policy, 1953–1961.* Albuquerque: University of New Mexico Press, 1982.

Burton, Antoinette. *At the Heart of Empire: Indians and the Colonial Encounter in Late-Victorian Britain.* Berkeley: University of California Press, 1998.

———. *Gender, Sexuality and Colonial Modernities.* London: Routledge, 1999.

Cahill, Cathleen. *Federal Fathers and Mothers: A Social History of the United States Indian Service, 1869–1933.* Chapel Hill: University of North Carolina Press, 2011.

Carlson, Leonard. *Indians, Bureaucrats, and Land: The Dawes Act and the Decline of Indian Farming.* Westport CT: Greenwood, 1981.

Carroll, Bret. E., ed. *American Masculinities: A Historical Encyclopedia.* Thousand Oaks CA: Sage, 2003.

Cattelino, Jessica. *High Stakes: Florida Seminole Gaming and Sovereignty.* Durham: Duke University Press, 2008.

Champagne, Duane. "Economic Culture, Institutional Order, Sustained Market Enterprise: Comparison of Historical and Contemporary American Indian Cases." In *Property Rights and Indian Economies*, edited by Terry Anderson, 195–213. Lanham MD: Rowman and Littlefield, 1992.

Champagne, Duane, and Jay Stauss, eds. *Native American Studies in Higher Education: Models for Collaboration between Universities and Indigenous Nations*. Lanham MD: AltaMira, 2002.

Chaudhuri, Nupur, and Margaret Strobel. *Western Women and Imperialism: Complicity and Resistance*. Bloomington: Indiana University Press, 1992.

Child, Brenda. *Boarding School Seasons: American Indian Families, 1900–1940*. Lincoln: University of Nebraska Press, 1998.

———. *Holding Our World Together: Ojibwe Women and the Survival of Community*. New York: Penguin Books, 2013.

———. *My Grandfather's Knocking Sticks: Ojibwe Family Life and Labor on the Reservation*. Minneapolis: Minnesota Historical Society Press, 2014.

Clancy-Smith, Julia, and Frances Gouda, eds. *Domesticating the Empire: Race, Gender, and Family Life in French and Dutch Colonialism*. Charlottesville: University Press of Virginia, 1998.

Cloud, Henry. "Education of the American Indian." *Southern Workman* 44, no. 1 (1915): 12–16.

———. "From Wigwam to Pulpit: A Red Man's Own Story of His Progress from Darkness to Light." *Missionary Review of the World* 27 (May 1915): 329–39.

———. "Haskell and Her New Frontiers." *Indian Leader* 37, no. 40 (1934): 14–17.

———. "Missions to the American Indians." *Yale Courant* 45 (May 1909): 520–23.

———. "Salutatory." *Hermonite* 19, no. 15 (1906): 286–87.

———. "Some Social and Economic Aspects of the Reservation." *Quarterly Journal of the Society of American Indians* 1, no. 2 (1913): 149–58.

———. "The Winnebago Medicine Lodge." *Christian Intelligencer*, December 22, 1909.

Clow, Richmond. "Indian Reorganization Act and the Loss of Tribal Sovereignty: Constitutions on the Rosebud and Pine Ridge Reservations." *Great Plains Quarterly* 7, no. 2 (1987): 127–34.

Coombes, Annie E. *Rethinking Settler Colonialism: History and Memory in Australia, Canada, Aoteraroa New Zealand, and South Africa*. New York: Manchester University Press, 2006.

Coppersmith, Clifford. "Cultural Survival and a Native American Community: Chiricahua and Warm Springs Apaches in Oklahoma, 1913–1996." PhD diss., Oklahoma State University, 1996.

Cornell, Stephen. *The Return of the Native: American Indian Political Resurgence*. New York: Oxford University Press, 1988.

Cowger, Thomas. *The National Congress of American Indians: The Founding Years.* Lincoln: University of Nebraska Press, 1999.

Critchlow, Donald. "Lewis Meriam, Expertise, and Indian Reform." *Historian* 43, no. 3 (1981): 325–44.

Crum, Steven. "Henry Roe Cloud, a Winnebago Indian Reformer: His Quest for American Indian Higher Education." *Kansas History* 11, no. 3 (1988): 171–84.

Cuban, Larry. *How Teachers Taught: Constancy and Change in American Classrooms, 1880–1990.* New York: Longman, 1984.

Culin, Stewart. *Games of the North American Indians.* Vol. 1–2. Lincoln: University of Nebraska Press, 1992.

DeCora, Angel. "Angel DeCora: An Autobiography." *Red Man* 3 (March 1911): 280–85.

DeCoteau, Jerilyn. *2017 Annual Report.* National Native Boarding School Healing Coalition. Accessed April 15, 2018. https://boardingschoolhealing.org/wp-content/uploads/2017/12/NABS-2017-Annual-Report.pdf.

Deloria, Philip. "Historiography." In *A Companion to American Indian History*, edited by Philip J. Deloria and Neal Salisbury, 6–24 Malden, MA: Blackwell, 2002.

———. "'I Am of the Body': My Grandfather, Culture, and Sports." In P. Deloria, *Indians in Unexpected Places*, 109–35.

———. *Indians in Unexpected Places.* Lawrence: University Press of Kansas, 2004.

———. *Playing Indian.* New Haven: Yale University Press, 1999.

Deloria, Vine, Jr. *Behind the Trail of Broken Treaties: An Indian Declaration of Independence.* Austin: University of Texas Press, 1985.

Deloria, Vine, Jr., and Clifford Lytle. *The Nations Within: The Past and Future of American Indian Sovereignty.* Austin: University of Texas Press, 1984.

Deloria, Vine, Jr., and David Wilkins. *Tribes, Treaties, and Constitutional Tribulations.* Austin: University of Texas Press, 2000.

Denetdale, Jennifer. *Reclaiming Diné History: The Legacies of Chief Manuelito and Juanita.* Tucson: University of Arizona Press, 2007.

Densmore, Ruth. *Chippewa Customs.* Saint Paul: Minnesota Historical Society Press, 1979.

Dhillon, Jaskiran, and Nick Estes. "Standing Rock, #NoDAPL, Mni Wiconi." *Cultural Anthropology.* December 22, 2016. https://culanth.org/fieldsights/1010-standing-rock-nodapl-and-mni-wiconi.

Driskill, Qwo-Li, Chris Finley, Brian Gilley, and Scott Morgensen, eds. *Queer Indigenous Studies: Critical Interventions in Theory, Politics, and Literature.* Tuscon: University of Arizona Press, 2011.

Dussias, Allison. "Squaw Drudges, Farm Wives, and the Dann Sisters' Last Stand: American Indian Women's Resistance to Domestication and the Denial of Their Property Rights." *North Carolina Law Review* 77 no. 2 (1999): 637–729.

Edmonds, Penelope. "Unpacking Settler Colonialism's Urban Strategies: Indigenous Peoples in Victoria, British Columbia, and the Transition to a Settler-Colonial City." *Urban History Review* 38, no 2 (2010): 4–20.

Ellinghaus, Katherine. *Taking Assimilation to Heart: Marriages of White Women and Indigenous Men in the United States and Australia, 1887–1937*. Lincoln: University of Nebraska Press, 2006.

Emery, Jacqueline. "Writing against Erasure: Native American Boarding School Students and the Periodical Press, 1880–1920." PhD diss., Temple University, 2011.

Erai, Michelle. "Responding." *Settler Colonial Studies* 2, no. 2 (2012): 191–93.

Fanon, Frantz. *Black Skin, White Masks*. Sidmouth, England: Pluto, 2008.

Fisher, Andrew. "Tangled Nets: Treaty Rights and Tribal Identities at Celilo Falls." *Oregon Historical Society* 105, no. 2 (2004): 178–211.

Fixico, Donald. *Termination and Relocation: Federal Indian Policy, 1945–1960*. Albuquerque: University of New Mexico Press, 1986.

——, ed. *Treaties with American Indians: An Encyclopedia of Rights, Conflicts, and Sovereignty*. Santa Barbara: ABC-CLIO/Greenwood, 2007.

Fletcher, Alice. *Indian Games and Dances with Native Songs*. Lincoln: University of Nebraska Press, 1994.

Forbes, Jack, Steven Crum, Inez Hernandez-Avila, George Longfish, Martha Macri, Victor Montejo, and Stephano Varese. "A Hemispheric Approach." In Champagne and Stauss, *Native American Studies*, 97–123.

Foucault, Michel. *Discipline and Punish: The Birth of the Prison*. New York: Pantheon Books, 1977.

——. *The Order of Discourse*. Paris: Galliman, 1970.

Freire, Paulo. *Pedagogy of the Oppressed*. New York: Continuum, 1993.

Furlong, Charles. *Let 'er Buck: A Story of Passing of the Old West*. New York: Putnam's Sons, 1921.

Furness, Elizabeth. "Challenging the Myth of Indigenous Peoples' 'Last Stand' in Canada and Australia: Public Discourse and the Conditions of Silence." In Coombes, *Rethinking Settler Colonialism*, 172–92.

Garland, Hamlin. "The Red Man's Present Needs." *North American Review* 174, no. 545 (1902): 476–88.

Gates, Henry Louis, Jr. *Signifying Monkey: A Theory of African-American Literary Criticism*. New York: Oxford University Press, 1988.

Gibbons, Rosemary, and Dax Thomas. *The Residential School Experience: A Century of Genocide in the Americas*. Seattle: Native Voices at the University of Washington, 2002.

Glenn, Evelyn Nakano. "Settler Colonialism as Structure: A Framework for Comparative Studies of U.S. Race and Gender Formation. *Sociology of Race and Ethnicity* 1, no. 1 (2014): 54–74.

Goeman, Mishauna. "Introduction to Indigenous Performances: Upsetting the Terrains of Settler Colonialism." *American Indian Culture and Research Journal* 35, no. 4 (2011): 1–18.

———. *Mark My Words: Native Women Mapping Our Nations.* Minneapolis: University of Minnesota Press, 2013.

Goeman, Mishauna, and Jennifer Denetdale. "Native Feminisms, Legacies, and Indigenous Sovereignties." *Wicazo SA Review* 24, no. 3 (2009): 9–13.

Goodwin, John. "'Without Destroying Ourselves': American Indian Intellectual Activism for Higher Education, 1915–1978." Phd diss., Arizona State University, 2017.

Green, Rayna. "Pocahontas Perplex." In *Native American Voices: A Reader,* edited by Susan Lobo and Steve Talbot, 203–11. Upper Saddle River, NJ: Prentice-Hall, 2001.

Guenther, Richard L. "The Santee Normal Training School." *Nebraska History* 51, no. 3 (1970): 359–78.

Hale, Frederick. "Acceptance and Rejection of Assimilation in the Works of Luther Standing Bear." *SAIL: Studies in American Indian Literatures* 5, no. 4 (1993): 25–42.

Hall, Stuart. "Introduction: Who Needs Identity." In *Questions of Cultural Identity,* edited by Stuart Hall and Paul du Gay, 1–17. London: Sage, 1996.

Harper, Mattie. "French Africans in Ojibwe Country: Negotiating Marriage, Identity and Race, 1780–1890." PhD diss., University of California, Berkeley, 2012.

Hernandez, Krisha. "Agents of Pollination: Indigenous Lives and Bodies and U.S. Agriculture Technosciences." PhD diss., University of California, Santa Cruz, forthcoming.

Hertzberg, Hazel. *The Search for an American Indian Identity.* Syracuse: Syracuse University Press, 1971.

Hillaire, Pauline, and Gregory Fields, eds. *Rights Remembered: A Salish Grandmother Speaks on American Indian History.* Lincoln: University of Nebraska Press, 2016.

Hinzo, Angel. "Dialoguing with Ho-Chunk Tricksters on AlterNative Masculinities." Lecture given at the University of California, Davis, April 27, 2013.

———. "Voicing across Space: Subverting Colonial Structures in Ho-Chunk/Winnebago Tribal History." PhD diss., University of California, Davis, 2016.

Hoelscher, Steven. *Picturing Indians: Photographic Encounters and Tourist Fantasies in H. H. Bennett's Wisconsin Dells.* Madison: University of Wisconsin Press, 2008.

Hokowhitu, Brendan. "Maori Masculinity, Post-Structuralism, and the Emerging Self." *New Zealand Sociology* 18, no. 2 (2003): 179–201.

Hoxie, Frederick. *Talking Back to Civilization: Indian Voices from the Progressive Era.* Boston: Bedford/St. Martin's Press, 2001.

Hurtado, Albert. *Intimate Frontiers: Sex, Gender, and Culture in Old California.* Albuquerque: University of New Mexico Press, 1999.

Iverson, Peter. *Carlos Montezuma and the Changing World of American Indians.* Albuquerque: University of New Mexico Press, 1982.

Jackson, Helen Hunt. *A Century of Dishonor: A Sketch of the United States Dealings with Some of the Indian Tribes.* New York: Harper and Brothers, 1881.

Jacobs, Margaret. "Maternal Colonialism, White Women, and Indigenous Child Removal in the American West and Australia, 1880–1940." *Western Historical Quarterly* 36 (Winter 2005): 453–76.

——. *White Mother to a Dark Race: Settler Colonialism, Maternalism, and the Removal of Indigenous Children from the American West and Australia, 1880–1940.* Lincoln: University of Nebraska Press, 2009.

Jones, Tom, Michael Schmudlach, Matthew Mason, Amy Lonetree, and George Greendeer. *People of the Big Voice: Photographs of Ho-Chunk Families by Charles Van Schaick, 1879–1942.* Madison: Wisconsin Historical Society, 2011.

Kalt, Joseph, and Joseph Singer. "Myths and Realities of Tribal Sovereignty: The Law and Economics of Indian Self-Rule." Faculty Research Working Papers, John F. Kennedy School of Government, 2004.

Kelly, Lawrence C. *The Assault on Assimilation: John Collier and the Origins of Indian Policy Reform.* Albuquerque: University of New Mexico Press, 1963.

Kinser, Amber. *Motherhood and Feminism.* Berkeley: Seal, 2010.

Larner, John, ed. *The Papers of the Society of American Indians.* Wilmington DE: Scholarly Resources, 1986.

Lomawaima, K. Tsianina. *They Called It Prairie Light: The Story of Chilocco Indian School.* Lincoln: University of Nebraska Press, 1995.

Lonetree, Amy. "Visualizing Native Survivance: Encounters with My Ho-Chunk Ancestors in the Family Photographs of Charles Van Schaick." In Jones et al., *People of the Big Voice,* 13–23. Madison: Wisconsin Historical Society, 2011.

Luce, Charles, and William Johnson. "The Beginning of Modern Tribal Governance and Enacting Sovereignty." In *As Days Go By: Our History, Our Land, and Our People; The Cayuse, Umatilla, and Walla Walla,* edited by Jennifer Karson, 151–71. Pendleton OR: Tamastslikt Cultural Institute, 2006.

Lyons, Scott. *X-marks: Native Signatures of Assent.* Minneapolis: University of Minnesota Press, 2010.

Maddox, Lucy. *Citizen Indians: Native American Intellectuals, Race, and Reform,* Ithaca: Cornell University Press, 2005.

Madigan, Jennifer. "The Education of Women and Girls in the United States: A Historical Perspective." *Advances in Gender and Education* 1 (2009): 11–13.

Madsen, Deborah. *Understanding Gerald Vizenor.* Columbia: University of South Carolina Press, 2009.

Maracle, Lee. *I Am Woman: A Native Perspective on Sociology and Feminism.* Vancouver: Press Gang, 1996.

Martin, Gretchen. *Dancing the Colorline: African-American Tricksters in Nineteenth-Century American Literature.* Jackson: University of Mississippi Press, 2015.

Martinez, David. *Dakota Philosopher: Charles Eastman and American Indian Thought.* Saint Paul: Minnesota Historical Society, 2009.

May, Theresa, Suzanne Burcell, Kathleen McCovey, and Jean O'Hara. *Salmon Is Everything: Community-Based Theatre in Klamath Watershed.* Corvallis: Oregon State University Press, 2014.

McCall, Dorothy. *Ranch under the Rimrock.* Portland OR: Binfords and Mort, 1968.

McCall, Laura. "Introduction" in Basso, McCall, and Garceau, *Across the Great Divide,* 1–25.

McDonnell, Janet A. *The Dispossession of the American Indian, 1887–1934.* Bloomington: Indiana University Press, 1991.

Meriam, Lewis. *The Problem of Indian Administration.* Baltimore: Institute for Government Research, 1928.

Messer, David. *Henry Roe Cloud: A Biography.* Lanham MD: Hamilton Books, 2010.

Mihesuah, Devon. *Native and Academics: Researching and Writing about Native Americans.* Lincoln: University of Nebraska Press, 1998.

Miles, Tiya. *Ties That Bind: The Story of an Afro-Cherokee Family in Slavery and Freedom.* Berkeley: University of California Press, 2015.

Miner, H. Craig. *The Corporation and the Indian: Tribal Sovereignty and Industrial Civilization in Indian Territory, 1865–1907.* Columbia: University of Missouri Press, 1976.

Miranda, Deborah. *Bad Indians: A Tribal Memoir.* Berkeley: Heyday, 2013.

Molin, Paulette. "'Training the Hand, the Head, and the Heart': Indian Education at Hampton Institute." *Minnesota History* 51, no. 2 (1988): 82–99.

Moon, Krystyn. "The Quest for Music's Origin at the St. Louis World's Fair: Frances Densmore and the Racialization of Music." *American Music* 28 (Summer 2010): 191–210.

Morgan, Lewis Henry. *Ancient Society.* 1877. Reprint, Tucson: University of Arizona Press, 1985.

Morgensen, Scott. *Spaces between Us: Queer Settler Colonialism and Indigenous Decolonization.* Minneapolis: University of Minnesota Press, 2011.

——. "Theorizing Gender, Sexuality and Settler Colonialism: An Introduction." *Settler Colonial Studies* 2, no. 2 (2012): 2–22.

Moses, L. G. *Wild West Shows and Images of Indians, 1883–1933.* Albuquerque: University of New Mexico Press, 1999.

Ness, Immanuel, ed. *Encyclopedia of American Social Movements.* Vol. 2. New York: Routledge, 2015.

North, Woesha Cloud. "Informal Education in Winnebago Tribal Society with Implications for Formal Education." PhD diss., University of Nebraska, 1978.

Oskison, John M. "Making an Individual of the Indian." *Everybody's Magazine* 16 (June 1907): 723–33.

Otis, Delos. *The Dawes Act and the Allotment of Indian Lands*. Norman: University of Oklahoma Press, 1973.

Palmer, Mark, and Robert Rundstrom. "GIS, Internal Colonialism, and the U.S. Bureau of Indian Affairs." *Annals of the Association of American Geographers* 103, no. 5 (2012): 1142–59.

Parman, Donald, and Lewis Meriam. "Lewis Meriam's Letters during the Survey of Indian Affairs, 1926–1927." Part 2. *Arizona and the West* 24, no. 4 (1982): 341–70.

Pfister, Joel. *The Yale Indian: The Education of Henry Roe Cloud*. Durham: Duke University Press, 2009.

Philp, Kenneth. *John Collier's Crusade for Indian Reform, 1920–1954*. Tucson: University of Arizona Press, 1977.

——. "Termination: A Legacy of the New Indian Deal." *Western Historical Quarterly* 14 (April 1983): 165–80.

Porter, Joy. *To Be an Indian: The Life of Iroquois-Seneca Arthur Caswell Parker*. Norman: University of Oklahoma Press, 2001.

Pratt, Mary Louise. "Arts of the Contact Zone." *Profession* (1991): 33–40.

——. *Imperial Eyes: Travel Writing and Transculturation*. New York: Routledge, 1992.

Pratt, Richard H. 1973. "The Advantages of Mingling Indians with Whites." In *Americanizing the American Indians: Writings by the "Friends of the Indian," 1880–1900*, edited by Frances Prucha, 260–71. Cambridge MA: Harvard University Press, 1973.

Prucha, Frances. *The Great Father: The United States Government and the American Indian*. Vols. 1–2. Lincoln, University of Nebraska Press, 1986.

Radin, Paul. *The Trickster: A Study in American Indian Mythology*. New York: Philosophical Library, 1956.

——. *The Winnebago Tribe*. Lincoln: University of Nebraska Press, 1970.

Ramirez, Renya. "From Henry Roe Cloud to Henry Cloud: Ho-Chunk Strategies and Colonialism." *Settler Colonial Studies* 2, no. 2 (2012): 117–37.

——. "Henry Roe Cloud: A Granddaughter's Native Feminist Biographical Approach." *Wicazo SA Review* 24, no. 2 (2009): 77–103.

——. "Ho-Chunk Warrior, Intellectual, and Activist: Henry Roe Cloud Fights for the Apaches." *American Indian Quarterly* 37, no. 3 (2013): 291–309.

——. *Native Hubs: Culture, Community, and Belonging in Silicon Valley and Beyond*. Durham: Duke University Press, 2007.

——. "Race, Tribal Nation, and Gender: A Native Feminist Approach to Belonging." *Meridians* 7, no. 2 (2007): 22–40.

Reder, Deanna, and Linda Morra. *Troubling Tricksters: Revisioning Critical Conversations*. Waterloo: Wilfrid Laurier University Press, 2010.

Report of the Sixteenth Annual Meeting of the Lake Mohonk Conference. Lake Mohonk Conference of the Friends of the Indian and Other Dependent Peoples, Mohonk Lake NY, May 18–20, 1910.

Robertson, Paul. *The Power of the Land: Identity, Ethnicity, and Class among the Lakota Sioux*. New York: Routledge, 2002.

Rosaldo, Renato. "Cultural Citizenship, Inequality, and Multiculturalism." In *Latino Cultural Citizenship: Claiming Identity, Space, and Rights*, edited by William Flores and Rina Benmayor, 27–38. Boston: Beacon, 1997.

——. *Culture and Truth: The Remaking of Social Analysis*. Boston: Beacon, 1989.

Salamanca, Omar, Mezna Qato, Kareem Rabie, and Sobhi Samour. "Past Is Present: Settler Colonialism in Palestine." Special issue, *Settler Colonial Studies* 2, no. 1 (2012): 1–8.

Scott, James. *Domination and the Arts of Resistance: Hidden Transcripts*. New Haven: Yale University Press, 1992.

Shanley, Kate. "Thoughts on Indian Feminism." In *A Gathering of Spirit: Writing and Art by North American Indian Women*, edited by Beth Brant, 213–14. New York: Firebrand Books, 1988.

Silko, Leslie Marmon. *Gardens in the Dunes*. New York: Simon and Schuster, 2000.

——. "Language and Literature from a Pueblo Indian Perspective." In *Yellow Woman and a Beauty of the Spirit: Essays on Native American Life Today*, edited by Leslie Marmon Silko, 48–60. New York: Simon and Shuster, 1996.

Simpson, Audra. *Mohawk Interruptus: Political Life across Borders of Settler States*. Durham: Duke University Press, 2014.

Sinclair, Niigonwedom James. "Trickster Reflections, Part I." In Reder and Morra, *Troubling Tricksters*, 21–59.

Sinnema, Peter. Introduction to Samuel Smiles's *Self-Help*, edited by Peter Sinnema, vii–xxix. Oxford: Oxford University Press, 2002.

Smith, Andrea. *Conquest: Sexual Violence and American Indian Genocide*. Durham: Duke University Press, 2015.

——. "Native American Feminism, Sovereignty, and Social Change." *Feminist Studies* 31, no. 1 (2005): 116–32.

Smith, David Lee. *Folklore of the Winnebago Tribe*. Norman: University of Oklahoma Press, 1997.

Smith, Linda Tuhiwai. *Decolonizing Methodologies: Research and Indigenous People*. New York: Zed Books, 1999.

Snelgrove, Corey, Rita Dhamoon, and Jeff Corntassel. "Unsettling Settler Colonialism: The Discourse and Politics of Settlers, and Solidarity with Indigenous Nations." *Decolonization: Indigeneity, Education and Society* 3, no. 2 (2014): 1–32.

Spack, Ruth. "English, Pedagogy, and Ideology: A Case Study of the Hampton Institute, 1878–1900," *American Indian Culture and Research Journal* 24, no. 1 (2000): 1–24.

Speed, Shannon, Maylei Blackwell, Rosalva Aida Hernandez-Castillo, Rachel Seider, Maria Teresa Sierra, Renya Ramirez, Morna Macleod, and Juan Hererra. "Remapping Gender, Justice, and Rights in the Indigenous Americas: Toward

Comparative Analysis and Collaborative Methodology." *Journal of Latin America and Caribbean Anthropology* 14, no. 2 (2009): 300–331.

Standing Bear, Luther. *My People the Sioux*. Edited by Earl A. Brininstool. Lincoln: University of Nebraska Press, 1975.

———. *The Tragedy of the Sioux*. New York: American Mercury, 1931.

Steinmetz, Paul. "The New Missiology and Black Elk's Individuation." In *The Black Elk Reader*, edited by Clyde Holler, 262–82. Syracuse: Syracuse University Press, 2000.

Stockel, Henrietta. *Women of the Apache Nation: Voices of Truth*. Reno: University of Nevada Press, 1993.

Stoler, Ann. *Carnal Knowledge and Imperial Power: Race and the Intimate in Colonial Rule*. Berkeley: University of California Press, 2010.

———. "Tense and Tender Ties: The Politics of Comparison in North American History and (Post)Colonial Studies. *Journal of American History* 88, no. 3 (2001): 829–65.

Stromberg, Ernest. "The Rhetoric of Irony in Indian Boarding School Narratives by Frances La Flesche and Zitkala-Sa." In *American Indian Rhetorics of Survivance: Word Medicine, Word Magic*, edited by Ernest Stromberg, 95–110. Pittsburgh: University of Pittsburgh Press, 2006.

Suzack, Cheryl, Shari Huhndorf, Jeanne Perreault, and Jean Barman. *Indigenous Women and Feminism: Politics, Activism, Culture*. Vancouver: University of British Columbia Press, 2010.

Swift, Tom. *Chief Bender's Burden: The Silent Struggle of a Baseball Star*. Lincoln: University of Nebraska Press, 2008.

Tallbear, Kim. "Badass (Indigenous) Women Caretake Relations: #NoDAPL, #IdelNo-More, #BlackLivesMatter." *Cultural Anthropology*. December 22, 2016. https://culanth.org/fieldsights/1019-badass-indigenous-women-caretake-relations-nodapl-idlenomore-blacklivesmatter.

Tengan, Ty Kawaka. *Native Men Remade: Gender and Nation in Contemporary Hawaii* Durham: Duke University Press, 2008.

Tetzloff, Jason. "To Do Some Good among the Indians: Henry Roe Cloud and Twentieth-Century Native American Advocacy." PhD diss., Purdue University, 1996.

Tetzloff, Lisa. "Elizabeth Bender Cloud: Working for and with Our Indian People." *Frontiers: A Journal of Women's Studies* 30, no. 3 (2009): 77–115.

———. "'Shall the Indian Remain Indian?' Native Americans and the Women's Club Movement, 1899–1954." PhD diss., Purdue University, 2008.

Thrush, Coll-Peter. *Indigenous London: Native Travelers at the Heart of Empire*. New Haven: Yale University Press, 2016.

Tuck, Eve, Maile Arvin, and Angie Morrill. "Decolonizing Feminism: Challenging Connections between Settler Colonialism and Heteropatriarchy." *Feminist Formations* 25, no. 1 (2013): 8–34.

Turcheneske, John. *The Chiricahua Apache Prisoners of War: Fort Sill, 1894–1914*. Boulder: University Press of Colorado, 1997.

Van Dyke, Henry. "Work." All Poetry. Accessed April 15, 2018. https://allpoetry.com/poem/8507939-Work-by-Henry-Van-Dyke.

Veracini, Lorenzo. *Settler Colonialism: A Theoretical Overview*. New York: Palgrave/Macmillan, 2010.

Vigil, Kiara. *Indigenous Intellectuals: Sovereignty, Citizenship, and the American Imagination, 1880–1930*. New York: Cambridge University Press, 2015.

Vizenor, Gerald. "Trickster Discourse: Comic Holotropes and Language Games." In *Narrative Chance: Postmodern Discourse on Native American Literatures*, edited by Gerald Vizenor, 187–213. Albuquerque: University of New Mexico Press, 1989.

Vizenor, Gerald, and Jill Doerfler. *The White Earth Nation: Ratification of a Native Democratic Institution*. Lincoln: University of Nebraska Press, 2012.

Waggoner, Rebeca. *Happy Canyon: A History of the World's Most Unique Indian Pageant and Wild West Show*. Charleston SC: History Press, 2016.

Walker, Allen. *Every Warrior Has His Song*. Bloomington: Universe, 2010.

Warren, Kim. *The Quest for Citizenship: African American and Native American Education in Kansas, 1880–1935*. Chapel Hill: University of North Carolina Press, 2010.

Warrior, Robert. *Tribal Secrets: Recovering American Indian Intellectual Traditions*. Minneapolis: University of Minnesota Press, 1995.

Watermulder, G. A. "Injustice to the Apaches: An Appeal from the Geronimo Band." *Southern Workman* 50 (March 1921): 130–33

Wilkins, David, and Tsianina Lomawaima. *Uneven Ground: American Indian Sovereignty and Federal Law*. Norman: University of Oklahoma Press, 2001.

Wishart, David. "Roe Cloud, Henry (1884–1950)." In *Encyclopedia of the Great Plains*, edited by David Wishart, 176. Lincoln: University of Nebraska Press, 2004.

Wolfe, Patrick. "Settler Colonialism and the Elimination of the Native." *Journal of Genocide Research* 8, no. 4 (2006): 387–409.

———. *Settler Colonialism and the Transformation of Anthropology: The Politics and Poetics of an Ethnographic Event*. New York: Cassell, 1999.

Young, Iris Marion. *Justice and the Politics of Difference*. Princeton: Princeton University Press, 1990.

INDEX

Page numbers in italic indicate illustrations.

assimilation: and cultural identity, 4, 64–65, 79; by education, 6, 9, 12–13, 32, 34, 88, 109, 135–36, 215; means of resisting, 7–8, 15, 69, 198, 209; and Native humanity, 14; Natives complicit in, 96–97; by religion, 7, 13, 15, 61–62; U.S. policies for, 9–12, 139, 146, 153, 199; and Wild West shows, 160; and women's organizations, 164, 198, 216. *See also* citizenship; settler colonialism
Assiniboine Indians, 93
Associated Press, 212
Association of Tribal Archives, Libraries, and Museums, 241n74
Auburn Seminary, 63
Australia, 10
Ayala, Felipe Huaman Poma de, 248n83

Babcock, Omar L., 19, 151, 187, 194
Bacone College, 147
Baldwin, Marie, 72
Band of Mercy, 35
Barnhart, Andrew, 189, 190, 191
Bear Clan, 240n73
Beaver, Curtis, 107
Bellinger, R. A., 78
Bender, Albertus, 81, 83, 85–87
Bender, Albertus (son), 81
Bender, Anna, 81, 86–89, 206
Bender, Charles Albert, 81, 86, 97, 224
Bender, Emma, 81, 93, *94*, 131
Bender, Frank, 81
Bender, Fred, 81
Bender, George, 81
Bender, James, 81
Bender, John, 81, 86
Bender, Marie, 97
Bennett, Henry Hamilton, 9
Berry Schools, 116

Blackfeet Reservation, 91–92
Blackfoot Indians, 213
Blackhawk, John, 154
Blackhawk, Ned, 236
Blowsnake, Sam, 5–6
Blue Eagle, Ace, 228
Blue Earth River, 24
Blue Ridge Mountains, 151
boarding schools: abuses at, 19, 84, 87, 90, 99, 121–26, 134–35, 144, 206, 234; assimilation through, 6, 7, 9, 12–13, 135–36; closing of, 146; curriculum at, 37, 64, 68, 88, 99, 122, 132–34, 136, 137; Elizabeth Cloud's visits to, 219; first established, 93; Henry Cloud at, 32–34; hubs through, 93; in Philadelphia, 86–87; settler colonialism in, 53, 88, 95–97, 104, 157, 163; sexism in, 99, 107, 111; women's clubs compared with, 198. *See also* education; Meriam Report; *specific schools*; U.S. government
Bomberry, Victoria, 206
Bonneville Dam, 175–78
Bonnin, Gertrude. *See* Zitkala-Sa
Boston, 93
Bounds, Doris, 189–90
Brennan, J. P., 168
Brigham City UT, 213
Brigham Young University, 221
Bronson, Ruth Muskrat, 213, 214, 223, 228
Brookings Institution Institute for Government Research, 121
Brosius, Samuel, 76
Brown, Anson, 26
Browning MT, 92
Bruce, H. E., 242n11
Buchannan, Harold, 97, 147, 148
Bureau of Indian Affairs (BIA): and Apache land rights, 75, 77;

assimilation efforts of, 7, 160; commissioners of, 19, 221–23, 227; educational authority of, 89; Elizabeth Cloud with, 90–93; Henry Cloud as commissioner of, 121–22, 126–31, 133–34; Henry Cloud's criticism of, 109, 146, 151, 152, 153; Henry Cloud's employment with, 19, 116, 133, 143, 150, 152–54, 187–91, 193; Henry Cloud's speech to, 34; holding of Umatilla land, 151; investigative survey of, 120, 121, 122–26; mission of, 13; and Native fishing rights, 175, 179, 181; Native leadership in, 220–23; and Paiutes' land dispute, 214; tribal lists of, 193–94; and tribal sovereignty, 146, 152, 213; and tribal termination, 199, 209; Winnebagoes' petitions to, 68, 139. *See also* U.S. government

Butterfield, Mark, 2, 236

Butterfield, Raleigh, 175

Butterfield, Ramona Cloud, 73, *117*, 166, 204

Butterfield, Robin, 2, 26, 236

Cahill, Cathleen, 4, 15, 130–31, 153

California, 219, 227

California State University, Fresno, 187

Cameron State of Agriculture, 78

Campbell, Roberta, 147

Canada, 82

capitalism: Henry Cloud's encouragement of, 142–44; and hunting and fishing rights, 177, 180, 183–85; and Indian performances, 158–60, 170–71; on land allotments, 74; and settler colonialism, 9, 10, 13–14, 169

Carlisle Indian School, 13, 32, 68–69, 88, 93, 96, 97, 99

Carmen (surname unknown), 92–93, *94*

Carpenter Hall, 90

Carter, C. D., 77

Casas, Bartolomé de Las, 14

Cassiman, Arthur, 55, 56

Cassiman, Francis, 26

Cayuse Indians, 151, 172

Celilo Falls, 156, 178–86

A Century of Dishonor (Jackson), 226

Chaat, Robert, 100

"Charter of Indian Rights," 215–16

Chayskagah. *See* White Buffalo

Chemawa Indian School, 193

Cherokee Indians, 221, 228

Chetco Indians, 193

Cheyenne Indians, 33, 223

Chicago IL, 101, 212

Chippewa Indians, 202, 224, 255n17

Chiricahua Apache Indians. *See* Apache Indians

Christianity: assimilation through, 7, 13, 15; compared with Ho-Chunk spirituality, 29–32, 55, 56, 60, 63, 67; of Elizabeth Cloud, 20, 92, 98, 197, 202, 206–7, 217; of Henry Cloud, 21, 26–27, 34–36, 54, 69, 98, 124, 242n27; and identity, 4; of Oklahoma Natives, 51; Roes' reinforcement of, 56, 57; in schools, 17, 38, 39, 46, 51–52, 65, 83, 89, 101, 102, 116, 234; and settler colonialism, 9, 61–62, 67, 95, 156–57

Christian Science Monitor, 202

citizenship: and "Charter of Indian Rights," 215–16; and Christianity, 157; and cultural pluralism, 66–67, 109, 120, 136–37; definition of Native cultural, 3–4; Friends of the Indian for, 72; Natives' right to, 47, 196–97, 199, 209, 210, 212, 217, 222, 228–29;

citizenship (*continued*)
Natives' work for, 14, 17, 20, 139; of
Native women, 164; in schools, 122;
and tribal termination, 214–15. *See
also* assimilation; settler colonialism

civilization hierarchy: at boarding
schools, 64, 68, 89–90; Natives'
place in, 9–10, 13, 14, 39–40, 46–47,
53–54, 72, 162–63

civil rights, 207–8. *See also* Native
Americans: activism of; Red Power
movement

Clapp, Moses E., 78

Clark, William, 160, 222, 223

Cloud, Elizabeth Bender, *94, 102*;
admiration of husband, 93, 148; at
AII, 109–13, 116, *119*; appearance of,
197, 228; archives of, 1–2, 236; as
commissioner of Indian Affairs, 222;
culture and identity of, 4, 5, 71–72,
84–85, 196–97, 207, 208, 210–11,
215, 217, 228, 233; European trip of,
211–12; family-tribal history of, 82–
83; at Hampton Institute, 89; and
husband's buffalo blanket, 175; and
husband's illness and death, 165–66,
194, 201; and husband's white family, 59, 111–12; illness and death of,
228; as Indian princess, 202, 255n17;
as intellectual, 14, 15, 90, 93, 96–97,
108, 172, 186–87, 211, 232; and land
allotments, 79–80; life's work of,
2–3, 18–20, 196–97, 228–29, 231–35;
marriage of, 54, 56, 71–73, 97, 120,
235, 244n78; as Mother of the Year,
19, 20, 165, 196, 200–209, *203*; as
nurse, 92; in Oregon, 151, 153, 170,
176, 193, 194, 195; personal characteristics of, 164–65, 201–4, 206, 229;
retirement of, 227, 228; as teacher,

91–95, 99; in Tomah WI, 147; tribal
affiliation of, 240n73

Cloud, Henry II, 73, 113, *114, 118*, 131–32

Cloud, Henry Roe, 22, *44, 94, 102, 118,
119, 148*; admiration of wife, 97, 172;
appearance of, 37, 47, *145*, 154, *155*;
archives of, 1–2; athleticism of, 43–46,
147, 150, 166; attitude toward work,
40–43, 106–7, 142–43; birth date of,
26, 242n11; criticism of, 111–12, 153–
54; culture and identity of, 4, 5, 21,
25–27, 30–32, 35, 38, 41, 45–51, 56–61,
64–65, 68–70, 73, 80–81, 96, 104–7,
112, 146, 147, 151, 157, 167, 170, 175, 185,
190, 233, 240n73, 242n27; as father,
115–16, *117, 205*; film about, 236; at
Hahnemann Hospital, 92–93; honor-
ing of, 147, *161*, 228; horses of, 148, *159*,
166; illness and death of, 165–68, 194,
195, 200, 201; as intellectual, 14, 15,
68–70, 78, 79, 105, 106, 156–57, 170,
174, 185–87, 194–95, 232; life's work
of, 2–3, 195, 231, 234, 235; marriage
of, 56, 71–73, 80, 97, 112, 120, 235,
244n78; name of, 17, 25–26, 112, 167,
235–36; as orphan, 36, 55, 167; political savvy of, 138–39; relationship
with mother-in-law, 81; resistance of,
18, 19, 233; self-support of, 38, 42–47,
50–51, 55, 57, 61, 65, 97–98; working
relationship with wife, 109–11, 202,
204–6; writing of, 166

Clow, Richmond, 146

"clown stories." *See* tricksters

Cody, Buffalo Bill, 158–60

Collier, John: as GFWC agent, 197;
Henry Cloud's complaint to, 157–58,
160–62; and IRA, 139, 146; and leadership of Indian Affairs, 129, 130,
133, 220; as medal nominee, 147

Kansas Federation of Women's Clubs, 138
Kash Kash, James, 189
Keeler, William, 221, 223
Kennedy, E. Jean, 38
Kensington MD, 131
Kickapoo Indians, 138
kinship systems: adoption in, 57–59,
113; and fishing rights, 178, 180; and
Ho-Chunk naming, 25; importance
to Henry Cloud, 167–68; and land
allotments, 74; and settler colonial-
ism, 11, 52–56, 157, 235. *See also*
family-tribal histories
Kiowa-Comanche-Apache reservation
lands, 75
Kiowa Indians, 76, 77
Kirkham, Art, 143
Klamath Indians, 224
Klickitat River, 185–86

Lac Courte Oreilles band, 208
LaFlesche, Rosa B., 72
La Follette Bennett, Robert, 227
LaFrances, Francis, 193–94
Lake Geneva, 98
Lake Mohonk, 72
Lake Winnebago, 24
Lakota Indians, 24, 97. *See also* Sioux
Indians
LaMere, Moses, 107
land: Apaches' rights to, 75–79, 207,
208; English dispossession of, 168–
69; Ho-Chunk ownership of, 24,
147; Indian culture tied to, 59–60,
74, 84–85, 177, 206–7, 232–33;
money from allotment of, 41, 140–
43; ownership in Umatilla River
Valley, 151–52, 177–78, 183–85, 188–
90; of Pawnees, 102–4; recovery
of stolen, 214; settler colonial view

of, 9–10, 12–14, 96, 125–26, 139–41,
157, 160, 161, 225, 226, 234, 250n45;
taxation of Indian, 63, 64, 67–68,
141, 142, 199; U.S. policy on Indian
ownership of, 130, 139–46, 199–
200, 209; women's rights to, 79–80,
82. *See also* Dawes Allotment Act
language: at AII, 108; of Elizabeth
Cloud, 56, 81, 85, 86, 208; at federal
boarding schools, 13, 32, 34, 37, 66,
89, 137; of Henry Cloud, 21, 33, 42,
68–69, 113–15; of Hunters, 113, 115;
preservation of Native, 157
LaRose family, 36, 232
Laslay, Walter, 100
Lavina (surname unknown), 92–93
Lawson, Roberta Campbell, 198
Lee-Smith, David, 170
LeFlore, Louie, 198
Lewis, Meriwether, 160, 222, 223
Lincoln, Helene, 107
Lincoln Institute, 86–87
Little, E. C., 137–38
Littlebear, Minnie, 29
Lonetree, Amy, 53, 170, 236
Lowe, Truman, 170
Luce, Charles, 189, 191
Lyon, Scott, 17
Lytle, Clifford, 105–6

Mack, Connie, 224
Macy NE, 34
Maddox, Lucy, 3–4, 14, 15, 63, 96,
245n3
Marshall Plan, 211
Martin, George, 100
Martinez, David, 4
Mashunpeewingah (Good Feather
Woman), 26
Ma-un-a, 26, 28

68, 69, 97–98, 111–13, 167, 235–36, 240n73, 244n78

Roe, Walter: adoption of, 58–59; on Apache situation, 73; on Henry Cloud's speech topic, 62; relationship with Henry Cloud, 17, 57, 69, 167, 235–36, 240n73; school named for, 98–99; school of, 51

Rogers, Will, 228

Roosevelt, Eleanor, 165

Roosevelt, Franklin D., 133, 201

Roosevelt, Theodore, 43

Rosaldo, Renato, 3

Rosebud Reservation, 121–23, 146

Ross, Elsie, 139

Sacajawea, 222, 223, 228

Sac and Fox Indians, 24, 138

Saint Augustine school (Winnebago NE), 202

San Carlos Reservation, 219

San Francisco State University, 120, 187

Santee Mission School, 32, 36–37, 40, 133. *See also* boarding schools

Sarett, Lew, 147

Sawmill AZ, 218

Scott, James, 239n37

The Search for an American Identity (Hertzberg), 211

Self-Help (Smiles), 37–38

Sells, Cato, 75

Seminole OK, 134

Sepúlveda, Juan Ginés de, 14

Sequoyah, 228

settler colonialism: at boarding schools, 53, 88, 95–97, 104, 124–26; and conservation, 172–74, 182, 185–86; description of, 8–11, 168–69, 240n51; effect on Ho-Chunks, 23; Elizabeth Cloud's resistance to, 71–72, 85, 197, 207–9, 216, 226, 228; and gender, 11, 52–54, 95–96, 200, 235; Henry Cloud's resistance to, 22, 23, 64, 68–69, 96, 104, 105, 156–57, 180, 185; of IRA, 144, 146; and land dispossession, 80, 139–41, 182, 214; of Mary Roe, 52, 55, 56, 63, 167; Natives complicit with, 10–11, 61–63, 134, 153, 164, 188, 189, 195, 198, 209–11, 215, 233, 258n3; Native students' resistance to, 36, 124, 134–35; and racism, 39, 40; and religion, 67; and storytelling, 5–6, 234; studies about, 16–17; in Umatilla River Valley, 152; of U.S. policies, 12–13, 19, 21, 33, 63, 225, 234, 235; and Wild West shows, 160–63, 170–72; and women's organizations, 163, 165; zones of, 6–7. *See also* assimilation; citizenship

Seufert Brothers Company, 180

Shakespeare, William, 108

shape-shifting, 7, 18, 20, 23, 49, 197, 216–17, 233

Sherman Institute, 219

Siletz OR, 192–94. *See also* Grand Ronde–Siletz Agency

Silko, Leslie Marmon, 58, 84–85

Simpson, Alvin, 221–22

Sinclair, Niigonwedom James, 5

Sioux Indians, 33, 36, 37, 213, 221, 223. *See also* Dakota Indians; Lakota Indians

Sisters School of Saint Joseph, 83

Smiles, Samuel, 37–38

Snake, George, 107

Snake, Walter, 107

Sniffen, Matthew, 76

In the New Visions in Native American and Indigenous Studies series

To order or obtain more information on these or other University of Nebraska Press titles, visit nebraskapress.unl.edu.